Handbook to the Textual Criticism of the New Testament

Sir Frederic George Kenyon

HANDBOOK TO THE TEXTUAL CRITICISM

OF

THE NEW TESTAMENT

HANDBOOK

TO THE

TEXTUAL CRITICISM

OF THE

NEW TESTAMENT

BY

FREDERIC G. KENYON
ASSISTANT KEEPER OF MANUSCRIPTS, BRITISH MUSEUM

WITH SIXTEEN FACSIMILES

London
MACMILLAN AND CO., LIMITED
NEW YORK: THE MACMILLAN COMPANY
1901

Georgio Ridding

EPISCOPO SOUTHWELLENSI

COLLEGII B.V.M. WINTON PROPE WINTON

OLIM INFORMATORI

HUNC LIBRUM GRATO ANIMO

DEDICAT DISCIPULUS

PREFACE

THE object of this volume is to provide a serviceable handbook to the textual criticism of the New Testament for the use of students who are comparatively new to the subject. It lays no claim to rival the standard works of Gregory and Scrivener as a storehouse of statistics and bibliographical information, though in certain details it has been possible to supplement them and bring them up to date ; on the other hand, the discussion of textual theories is somewhat fuller than the plans of those works admitted of. It seemed advisable to indicate to the student the present state of the principal controversies with regard to textual theory ; and I have tried to represent all the more important views fully and fairly, whether I agree with them or not.

The lists of authorities prefixed to the several chapters are not intended to be exhaustive, but to indicate either those works which I have chiefly consulted, or those which will be most useful to the student (especially the English student), who wishes to push his inquiries further. Such a work as this is in great measure dependent on the labours of others, to whom my indebtedness is, I hope, fully acknowledged throughout. I have also to thank Cavaliere F. Carta, Chief Librarian of the National Library at Turin, for his courtesy in enabling me to obtain a photograph of a page of the Codex Bobiensis ;

Mr. W. E. Crum for much information with regard to the Coptic Versions ; and especially Mr. C. H. Turner, Fellow of Magdalen College, Oxford, and the Rev. H. E. Salter, vicar of Shirburn, for their kindness in reading the proofs and making many valuable suggestions and corrections.

F. G. K.

October 21, 1901.

CONTENTS

PLATES

[Most of the facsimiles are reduced in scale, in order to show complete pages ; the scale of reduction is stated in each case on the plate.]

CHAPTER I

THE FUNCTION OF TEXTUAL CRITICISM

THE province of Textual Criticism is the ascertainment of the true form of a literary work, as originally composed and written down by its author. The science owes its existence to the conditions under which, until comparatively modern days, literary works have been preserved. If the author's autograph of every book were still in existence, there could be no dispute as to what he had written ; or if printing had been practised from the earliest days of literary composition, we could be sure that every book had been handed down to us in practically unaltered form. For authors of the last four centuries, with few exceptions, we are in the happy condition of being certain that we possess their works, to all intents and purposes, precisely as they wrote them. In several instances the author's autograph is still extant ; in the rest we have early printed editions, issued under the author's eye. But when once we go back into the ages before the invention of printing, the conditions are wholly different. Only in the rarest possible cases (the great English chronicler of the thirteenth century, Matthew Paris, is perhaps an example) do we possess the author's own copy of his work ; in all other instances we have only copies made by hand at varying distances of time after the composition of the book in question. It is to this copying by hand that the problems of textual criticism are due. Unfortunately for our knowledge of ancient literature, the frailty of the

B

human hand and eye and mind is such that no copy, except of short passages, can be trusted to be wholly accurate ; and since different copyists will make different mistakes, it results that no two copies of an ancient book are quite the same. This would be immaterial, so long as the original autograph was in existence ; but when once that has disappeared, the student who would know exactly what an author wrote has to discover it by an examination of later copies, of which the only fact certain *a priori* is that all will be different and all will be incorrect.

The function of textual criticism, then, is to recover the true form of an author's text from the various divergent copies that may be in existence. The problems presented to it are of all kinds of complexity. If evidence is forthcoming from a period shortly after the writer's date, there will have been little time for the text to have been corrupted, and common sense should be able to detect most of the errors that have crept in. If the interval between the composition of the work and the earliest extant specimens be longer, much will depend on the amount of evidence available ; for among many copies there is more chance that the truth will have survived in some, especially if the extant copies have no common ancestor much later than the author's autograph. The line of textual tradition for any given literary work is like a genealogical tree, starting from a single point and spreading out as it descends to the living members of the family. If the distance of time be great, but the extant copies many, then the textual problem will be one of considerable difficulty, and requiring nice taste and discernment, but it will be hopeful, because the materials are plentiful ; whereas if the extant copies be few, there is a great likelihood that the truth will, in some places, have been wholly lost, and is only to be recovered by guessing ——a process precarious in the extreme, and seldom allowing any one but the guesser to feel confident in the truth of its results.

Now the textual criticism of the New Testament, as it is the most important branch of the science, so also is it the most complicated. It is the most important branch, because it has to do with a book, the importance of which is quite incommensurable with that of any other book in the history of the world ; and it is the most complicated, because the extant materials are incomparably more plentiful in number, and more varied in kind, than in any other instance. The difference in this respect between it and any other ancient book can be made plain by a few examples. The plays of Aeschylus are preserved in perhaps fifty [1] manuscripts, none of which is complete. Sophocles is represented by about a hundred manuscripts, of which only seven have any appreciable independent value. The Greek Anthology has survived in one solitary copy. The same is the case with a considerable part of Tacitus' Annals. Of the poems of Catullus there are only three independent manuscripts, all of which were derived from an archetype which was itself written no earlier than the beginning of the fourteenth century. Some of the classical authors, such as Euripides, Cicero, Ovid, and especially Virgil, are, no doubt, in a far more favourable position than those who have just been named. In their cases the extant copies of their works, or of portions of them, may be numbered by hundreds. Yet even these do not approach the number of witnesses for the text of the New Testament. The number of manuscripts of it, or of parts of it, in the original Greek, is over three thousand ; and to these have to be added a yet greater number of witnesses of a kind to which the classical authors offer no parallel. It is seldom that ancient translations of the classical authors into other languages exist, and still more seldom that they are of any value for textual purposes ; but in the case of the New Testament translations are both numerous and

---

[1] Forty appears to be the number of those that have been collated ; but there are probably several that have not been collated. Very few, however, contain more than the three plays which were habitually read by the Byzantine public.

important. It is estimated that there are at least eight thousand copies extant of the Latin Vulgate translation alone ; and a thousand would be a moderate estimate for the extant manuscripts of the other early versions, in Syriac, Coptic, Armenian, Ethiopic, Gothic, and the rest. It is therefore probably within the mark to say that there are now in existence twelve thousand manuscript copies of the New Testament, of which no two are precisely alike.

The contrast in this respect between the New Testament and classical authors may be regarded from two points of view. On the one hand, this enormous mass of witnesses gives good ground for supposing that the true text cannot be wholly lost ; on the other hand, the task of selecting the true text out of all these many and multifarious authorities is one of extreme difficulty. Merely to examine and record the available evidence is an enormous labour ; to estimate its value, to distinguish between manuscript and manuscript, and between version and version, is the hardest problem that has ever been set to textual criticism. In another respect, however, besides number, the manuscripts of the New Testament differ from those of the classical authors, and this time the difference is clear gain. In no other case is the interval of time between the composition of the book and the date of the earliest extant manuscripts so short as in that of the New Testament. The books of the New Testament were written in the latter part of the first century ; the earliest extant manuscripts (trifling scraps excepted) are of the fourth century—say, from 250 to 300 years later. This may sound a considerable interval, but it is nothing to that which parts most of the great classical authors from their earliest manuscripts. We believe that we have substantially an accurate text of the seven extant plays of Sophocles ; yet the earliest manuscript upon which it is based was written more than 1400 years after the poet's death. Aeschylus, Aristophanes, and Thucydides are in the same state ; while with Euripides the interval is increased to 1600 years. For Plato it may be put at 1300 years, for Demosthenes as low as 1200. The great Latin authors are somewhat better off. Horace is represented by several manuscripts written within 900 years of his death. There is an excellent copy of Terence after an interval of about 700 years, and portions of Livy only about 500 years after his date. For Lucretius, however, we have an interval of nearly 1000 years, for Catullus about 1600. Only Virgil approaches the New Testament in earliness of attestation. He died eight years before the Christian era ; and there is at least one nearly complete manuscript which is attributed to the fourth century, besides several small fragments, and two more of the fifth century. Yet even so his text is not in so favourable a position as that of the New Testament by nearly 100 years.

The task of textual criticism, then, in relation to the New Testament, is to try to extract the actual words written by the apostles and evangelists from the great mass of divergent manuscripts in which their works have been preserved. It is a task at once hopeful and hopeless. Hopeful, because in so great · a crowd of manuscripts, reaching back to so early a date as many of them do, the truth must, it would seem, somewhere be on record ; hopeless, because the discernment of it requires a super-human degree of knowledge and judgment, and because means do not exist for conclusively demonstrating it. The actual extent to which the text of the New Testament is open to doubt cannot be precisely stated, but the estimate of Dr. Hort, whose lifetime was devoted to this subject, is commonly accepted as an approximate guide. He says[1] : " The proportion of words virtually accepted on all hands as raised above doubt is very great, not less, on a rough computation, than seven-eighths of the whole. The remaining eighth, therefore, formed in great part by changes of order and other comparative trivialities, constitutes the whole area of criticism. If the principles followed

---

[1] *Introduction to the New Testament in the Original Greek*, p. 2 (1882).

in this edition are sound, this area may be very greatly reduced. Recognising to the full the duty of abstinence from peremptory decision in cases where the evidence leaves the judgment in suspense between two or more readings, we find that, setting aside differences of orthography, the words in our opinion still subject to doubt only make up about one-sixtieth of the whole New Testament. In this second estimate the proportion of comparatively trivial variations is beyond measure larger than in the former; so that the amount of what can in any sense be called substantial variation is but a small fraction of the whole residuary variation, and can hardly form more than a thousandth part of the entire text." It is further to be remembered that, although some doubt attaches to the record of certain incidents and sayings of great interest and value, yet no doctrine of Christianity rests solely upon a disputed text. The Christian student can approach the subject without misgiving, and may follow whithersoever honest inquiry seems to lead him, without thought of doctrinal consequences. His researches should unquestionably be conducted in a reverent spirit, but he may avail himself, without hesitation or mistrust, of all the resources of secular science.

The methods of textual criticism may be broadly described as two in number—the comparison of documentary evidence, and conjecture. The two methods are mutually complementary. Where documentary evidence is plentiful, conjecture will be scarce; but where the former is wanting, the latter will have to try to take its place to the best of its ability. In the case of the New Testament the documentary evidence is so full that conjecture is almost excluded, and it is with the principles of the interpretation of documentary evidence that we are most concerned here. Some statement of these is necessary, as an introduction to a summary of the evidence itself.

The task of the textual critic is, in brief, to counteract the errors of the copyist; and these errors are many,— some capable of being classified under heads, while some resist classification. In the first place the critic has to correct simple slips of the pen, obvious blunders which have no meaning, and which occasion no more difficulty than similar mistakes in the letters of a contemporary correspondent. If the scribe of the Codex Sinaiticus writes ποισαι for ποιῆσαι, or εκ του καλουντας for ἐκ τοῦ καλοῦντος, there is no difficulty in either seeing or correcting the error. A somewhat less elementary form of blunder arises when the scribe, in place of the word which he should write, writes one which resembles it either in sound or in appearance. Thus in Sophocles' *Ajax* 61 some manuscripts have φόνου, others πόνου, and the context is such as to make the decision between them not absolutely certain ; but whichever is wrong, the error was no doubt due to the similarity of sound. On the other hand in Bacchylides v. 23 the scribe of the only extant manuscript has written φοιβωι for φόβῳ, an error of eye, not of ear ; and here the metre and the sense alike make the error obvious and easy to correct. Another common form of error is due to the fact that in ancient manuscripts accents and breathings were rare, and separation of words almost unknown ;[1] which led to trouble when the time came for these aids to intelligence to be introduced. Thus in Sophocles' *Ajax* 1056 the earliest MSS. had, at the end of the line, the letters ΕΛΟΙΔΟΡΙ. Now ει and ι are constantly interchanged in manuscripts, and hence ΕΛΟΙΔΟΡΕΙ was probably written as often as ΕΛΟΙΔΟΡΙ. The result is that, in the margin of the best extant MS. of Sophocles, the reading ἐλοιδόρει is given, in place of the correct ἕλοι δορί.

Another form of error, very common in all manuscripts, is that of omission. This may be due to mere unaccountable accident, and then the lost word or words can only be recovered either by comparison with other manuscripts or by sheer guessing. Oftener, however, it

---

[1] Early vellum MSS., from the fourth to the ninth centuries, are almost wholly without accents, breathings, and divisions. Papyrus MSS., which are still earlier, not infrequently have occasional accents, and, in rare instances, the separation of words is indicated by a dot in cases of doubt.

arises from the similarity of adjoining words, which led the scribe's eye to slip from one to the other, and so omit the intervening words. For instance, in John xvii. 15 the correct text runs οὐκ ἐρωτῶ ἵνα ἄρῃς αὐτοὺς ἐκ τοῦ κόσμου ἀλλ' ἵνα τηρήσῃς αὐτοὺς ἐκ τοῦ πονηροῦ, but the scribe of the Codex Vaticanus let his eye slip from the first ἐκ τοῦ to the second, and so gives the passage as οὐκ ἐρωτῶ ἵνα ἄρῃς αὐτοὺς ἐκ τοῦ πονηροῦ. Similarly in John iii. 20, 21, where the true text runs πᾶς γὰρ ὁ φαῦλα πράσσων μισεῖ τὸ φῶς καὶ οὐκ ἔρχεται πρὸς τὸ φῶς ἵνα μὴ ἐλεγχθῇ τὰ ἔργα αὐτοῦ, ὁ δὲ ποιῶν ἀλήθειαν ἔρχεται πρὸς τὸ φῶς ἵνα φανερωθῇ τὰ ἔργα αὐτοῦ ὅτι ἐν θεῷ ἐστὶν εἰργασμένα, the scribe of the Codex Sinaiticus has made two mistakes from this same cause (technically known as homoioteleuton), omitting καὶ οὐκ ἔρχεται πρὸς τὸ φῶς and ὁ δὲ ποιῶν . . . αὐτοῦ, the former owing to the double occurrence of τὸ φῶς, the latter owing to the double occurrence of τὰ ἔργα αὐτοῦ. Often the omissions are smaller than these, and cause less trouble, as when a scribe writes ΚΑΤΗΝ for ΚΑΤΑΤΗΝ (κατὰ τὴν) or ἔπεμψε for ἐπέπεμψε. But in one form or another the error is a very common one, and has to be borne in mind constantly in the criticism of manuscripts.

Various other classes of error exist and may be briefly mentioned. One that is frequently invoked in the criticism of classical authors is the intrusion into the text of words which were originally explanatory notes written in the margin. Sometimes the paraphrase has extruded the original phrase, sometimes the true and the false remain side by side. This, however, is a form of corruption which occurs less often in the Biblical writings than in profane authors, and even in the latter the instances where it is proved to have taken place are much fewer than those in which it is assumed by some critics. Then there is the class of deliberate alterations, such as are known to have been made in the texts of the Greek dramatists by the actors, and such as are suspected to have been made by the scholars of Alexandria in the texts of the Attic authors generally, in deference to certain supposed laws of style and euphony. In regard to the Old Testament we know that the text of the Septuagint was extensively altered by Origen in order to bring it into closer conformity with the Hebrew text current in his day; in the case of the New Testament there is good reason to suppose that many of the divergences which now exist were due to deliberate editing, intended, no doubt, to secure the best possible text according to the materials available for the scribe or his director, but often resulting in departures from the true and original reading. In the case of religious books there is also always the danger of deliberate alteration for doctrinal reasons, and we know that various heretical sects had their own recensions of certain books of the Bible; but this danger is discounted by the enormous mass and variety of evidence in existence for the New Testament. There is no possibility that all the sources should be tainted; one or other of them would be sure to have escaped, and when once the alternatives are presented to the critic, there is generally little difficulty in detecting a doctrinal perversion.

A special form of deliberate alteration, for which the student of the New Testament has to be on his guard, occurs in the case of the Synoptic Gospels. When the same event is recorded by two or more writers, there was a natural temptation to scribes to amplify one by the insertion of details mentioned in another, or to use the phrases of the more familiar version in transcribing that which was less familiar. This is a form of corruption which is constantly found in the later MSS. of the Gospels; and any one who will take the trouble to compare the Authorised and Revised Versions of the English Bible will find many instances in which the Revisers have removed such "harmonistic" corruptions from the text. The identification of them, however, involves the whole question of the origin of the Synoptic tradition; for if, as is now universally held in one form or another, a common document forms the substratum of the three Gospels, it may be questioned whether the verbal variations which now appear in the narratives are due to modifications of the original document by the evangelists themselves, or to the errors of early scribes. Even, however, if the latter be the true explanation (which is hardly probable), the divergences certainly established themselves at a very early date, and the removal of them in later manuscripts may in most, if not in all, cases be assigned with confidence to the editorial initiative of scribes and not to the following of primitive authorities ; and this class of deliberate alteration must be kept constantly in mind by the textual critic of the Gospels.

Finally there are errors of which nothing can be said save that they are unaccountable. Every one who has done much writing must know that now and again he puts down words which have no meaning in the context in which he uses them, or (if he is copying) are wholly unlike the words which he should have copied. His mind has strayed, and he has written down words which some obscure train of association has put into his head. Errors such as these are sometimes made by the copyists of manuscripts, and since they have no traceable connexion with the true text, they do not, as some kinds of error do, provide the means for their own correction. The same may be said of errors due to the defectiveness of the manuscript from which the copy has been made. A word may be defaced or obliterated, and the copyist must either omit it or guess at it ; and since a copyist often has but a hazy idea of the sense of what he is copying, his guesses are often very wide of the mark. Errors from mutilation would arise with especial ease during the period when papyrus was the material in use for literary purposes. The surface was more delicate than that of vellum, and therefore more liable to small and local injuries, which will obscure, or wholly obliterate, a word or a sentence. Here again the true reading is often irrecoverable except by guessing, and even if a

guess be right, it can rarely be proved to be right ; and
an unverified guess can carry but little weight for practical
purposes.   A good example of this has recently come to
light in the sphere of classical literature.   In a quotation
from a poem by Solon, preserved to us by the rhetorician
Aristides, where the lawgiver is depicting the miseries
of his country, a certain section of the population was
described as

$$\text{τοὺς δ' ἀναγκαίης ὑπο}$$
$$\text{χρησμὸν λέγοντας, γλῶσσαν οὐκέτ' Ἀττικὴν}$$
$$\text{ἱέντας.}$$

Here the words χρησμὸν λέγοντας were practically un-
intelligible, in spite of the bravest efforts of conscientious
commentators.   Various emendations were suggested, but
none was generally accepted as satisfactory ; till at last
the discovery of Aristotle's Ἀθηναίων πολιτεία, where the
passage is quoted, revealed the fact that the true reading
is χρειοῦς φυγόντας.   The change is not great, only seven
letters being affected ; but there is no palaeographical
similarity between the false letters and the true, to account
for the corruption.   It is probable, therefore, that the two
words were injured in an early manuscript of Aristides'
treatise, and that the scribe of the copy from which all
the extant manuscripts of it are derived, wrote down two
familiar words similar in general appearance.   It is
instructive to observe that one modern scholar had, in
fact, guessed approximately the right reading ; but the
guess, wanting confirmation and not supplying in itself
any explanation of the origin of the corruption, remained
wholly without authority or acceptance.   The same has
doubtless happened in many of the corrupt passages of
the classical writers, but in the New Testament the
number and diversity of the witnesses renders it almost
certain that, even if such an error has vitiated one group
of manuscripts, the true reading will be preserved elsewhere.

These, then, are the main forms of error with which
the textual critic has to contend ; and to meet them he

has, as has been said above, the two weapons of comparison of documents and conjecture. He has before him a number of manuscripts, and in the first instance he may (or in the case of the New Testament it may almost be said that he must) assume that the truth lies somewhere among them. In many cases the choice is obvious. Errors of spelling or grammar, when confronted with the true readings, must give way at once. Where conviction does not lie quite on the surface, the critic who bears in mind the common causes of error enumerated above can often see how the divergence has arisen, and which of the conflicting readings is original. In some cases he will see that homoioteleuton will account for an omission; in others, that the intrusion of a marginal comment accounts for an addition; in others, that two or three letters have been mistaken by the scribe for others which resemble them. Sometimes he may suspect deliberate alteration, whether with the object of bringing out a doctrine more clearly, or to improve the literary form of the passage, or to reconcile two divergent readings which the scribe had before him. By these methods considerable progress may be made in weeding out errors, and at the same time the critic will be accumulating materials for the second stage of his work, namely, the discernment of the comparative merits of his various authorities. He will learn which manuscripts are most often right, which are closely akin to one another, which groups are nearest in the line of descent to the original autograph. Hence he will have some clue to guide him when the choice between divergent readings is not evident at first sight. In such cases it is clearly safest to follow, as a rule, the authority which has shown itself to be most trustworthy. The more the parentage of the several manuscripts can be traced, the more they can be classified into groups, and the history and origin of the groups made clear, the better is the chance of arriving at a sound text of the author under examination. Examples of the use of such methods will be found in the succeeding pages of this handbook ; for the present it must be sufficient to describe them merely in outline.

One proposition is so often stated as a leading principle in textual criticism as to deserve a brief separate mention. It is that which is formulated by Bengel in the words, *Proclivi scriptioni praestat ardua*, or, as it is sometimes expressed, *Difficilior lectio potior*; the harder reading is to be preferred to the easier. Stated so absolutely, this proposition is misleading. Many forms of mistake produce a reading harder than the true one. Thus χρησμὸν λέγοντας, in the instance quoted above, is manifestly a more difficult reading than χρειοῦς φυγόντας, but it is none the less wrong. Similarly, errors due to homoioteleuton often produce nonsense, as in the case quoted on p. 8 from the Codex Vaticanus. In fact, it may be said generally that in the case of *accidental* errors the principle is not sound ; but in the case of errors due to deliberate alteration it is generally true. A scribe or commentator fails to understand a passage, and puts in some word which he thinks makes it easier ; an odd word is replaced by a commoner one ; a marginal paraphrase extrudes the phrase which it was intended to explain ; an expression which may give offence is omitted or toned down. In all such cases the more difficult reading is likely to be the true one. A hard reading will not be deliberately inserted instead of an easy one ; but the reverse may, and not infrequently does, take place. The difficulty, of course, is to determine whether a discrepancy between two or more manuscripts is due to accidental or deliberate alteration ; and where this cannot be discerned with certainty, Bengel's canon must be applied with great caution.

Of wider application and less qualified truth is another canon, in which this of Bengel's is included, namely, that of two or more alternative readings, that one is most likely to be right which most easily accounts for the origin of the others. The "difficilior lectio" is preferable just because a hard reading is likely to be altered into an easy one, not an easy reading into a hard one. So too a scribe, writing without any clear comprehension of the sense of the text which he is copying, not infrequently substitutes a familiar phrase for a strange one, even though in reality it reduces the passage to nonsense. Even where both alternatives make sense, one can easily be seen to have suggested the other, while the reverse process is impossible or improbable. Thus in another part of the poem of Solon mentioned above, the MS. of the ᾿Αθηναίων πολιτεία, in which it is quoted, has πρὶν ἀνταράξας πῦαρ ἐξεῖλεν γάλα, while the MSS. of Plutarch, who also quotes it, have πρὶν ἂν ταράξας πῖαρ ἐξέλῃ γάλα. Here it is easy to understand how the scribe of some ancestor of the Plutarch MSS. (copying, of course, from a MS. in which the words were not separated) took αν to be the familiar particle ἄν, not the syncopated form of the preposition ἀνά in composition, and so altered ἐξεῖλεν into ἐξέλῃ because πρὶν ἄν requires a subjunctive; but it is highly improbable that any one, with a *correct* reading πρὶν ἂν ταράξας . . . ἐξέλῃ before him, would be dissatisfied with it and alter it to πρὶν ἀνταράξας . . . ἐξεῖλεν. On the other hand, considerations of sense make the πῖαρ of the Plutarch MSS. preferable to the πῦαρ of the Aristotle MS.

It remains to ask what place is left for the second weapon of textual criticism, conjecture; and it has been usual to answer that in the criticism of the New Testament it has no place at all. Where manuscript evidence is scanty, as it is for many of the classical authors, it happens at times that a passage is obviously and certainly corrupt in all the extant copies; and then the defect must be healed by conjecture, if it is to be healed at all. But where the evidence is so plentiful and varied as it is for the New Testament, the chances that the true reading should have been lost by all are plainly very much smaller. Whether, however, conjecture is to be absolutely excluded depends in a large measure on the view which the critic takes of the character of the existing manuscript evidence. As will be shown in a later chapter, one school of critics regards the large majority of extant manuscripts as representing a relatively late recension of the sacred text, and therefore considers its evidence as of little value.   The number of authorities which remain is thus comparatively small, and they differ considerably among themselves ; and hence critics of this school are prepared to admit that, here and there, the original readings may have been wholly lost.   Thus in Col. ii. 18 Westcott and Hort (in substantial agreement with Lightfoot) are inclined to believe that the apostle wrote, not ΑΕΟΡΑΚΕΝΕΜΒΑΤΕΥΩΝ (ἃ ἑόρακεν ἐμβατεύων), but ΑΕΡΑΚΕΝΕΜΒΑΤΕΥΩΝ (ἀέρα κενεμβατεύων), the mistake being palaeographically very easy, and the improvement in sense through the conjecture considerable.[1]   It is universally agreed, however, that the sphere of conjecture in the case of the New Testament is infinitesimal ; and it may further be added that for practical purposes it must be treated as non-existent.   No authority could be attached to words which rested only upon conjecture ; and a critic who should devote himself to editing the Scriptures on conjectural lines would be merely wasting his time.   Where nothing but questions of literary style are involved, we may be willing to accept a reading upon conjecture, if no better evidence is to be had ; but where it is a question of the Word of Life, some surer foundation is required.

Putting conjecture aside, therefore, the function of the textual critic is, first, to collect documentary evidence, and, secondly, to examine it and estimate its value.   The object of the present volume is to show what has been done in both these directions.   In Chapters II.–VI. an account will be given of the available textual material— the copies of the New Testament in the original Greek, the ancient translations of it into other languages, and the quotations from it which are found in the early writers of the Christian Church.   The materials having been thus

---

[1] For other examples of conjectural emendations proposed in the N.T. text, see Nestle, *Introd. to the Textual Criticism of the N.T.*, Eng. Tr. pp. 167-170.

passed in review, an attempt will be made in Chapters VII. and VIII. to summarise what has hitherto been done in the way of using these materials, to discuss the principal theories now current with regard to the early history of the New Testament text, and to estimate the general position of the textual problem at the present day.   It is all well-trodden ground, and each newcomer is infinitely indebted to the labours of his predecessors ; but it is ground which each generation must tread afresh for itself, if it is to keep its interest alive in a subject of such importance, and if it is to add ever so little to the knowledge which past generations have handed down to it.   It is but a humble part that textual criticism has to play.   It is but the temple-sweeper in the courts of the Lord ; but honest labour, even in that humble field, is not lost.

CHAPTER II

THE AUTOGRAPHS OF THE NEW TESTAMENT

[**Authorities**: Sir E. Maunde Thompson, *Handbook of Greek and Latin Palaeography* (London, 1893); Kenyon, *Palaeography of Greek Papyri* (Oxford, 1899); K. Dziatzko, *Untersuchungen über ausgewählte Kapitel des antiken Buchwesens* (Leipzig, 1900).]

THE manuscript history of the New Testament covers a space of fourteen hundred years, from the original composition of the several books in the latter part of the first century to the invention of printing in the latter part of the fifteenth. It falls into three periods, distinguished by well-marked differences in the style of the writing employed. The first, from the middle of the first century to the beginning of the fourth, may be called the Papyrus period, during which copies of the Scriptures (as of all other books) were normally written upon papyrus, and in the style of writing suitable to that material. The second, from the fourth century to the ninth, is the Uncial period, when the material was vellum and the writing in large characters, each formed separately; while the third, from the ninth century to the fifteenth, is the Minuscule or Cursive period, in which the material is sometimes vellum and sometimes (from the fourteenth century onwards [1]) paper, and the writing is in small characters, often linked

[1] Paper was made and used in Europe in the thirteenth, and even in the twelfth, century; but it only comes into anything like common use in the fourteenth century, and never entirely superseded vellum before the invention of printing.

C

together into a running hand.   Each of these periods will
have to be described in detail in this and the following
chapters.

From the papyrus period, covering the first three
centuries of the history of Christianity, no complete copy
of any book of the Bible is extant.   Of all the copies
which must have been written during that period, only a
handful of small scraps is at present known to exist, and
all but two of these belong to the Old Testament, not to
the New.   There is a fragment of a Psalter (Ps. xii. 7–
xv. 4) in the British Museum ; of Isaiah (xxxviii. 3–5,
13–16) in the Rainer collection at Vienna ; of Ezekiel
(v. 12–vi. 3) in the Bodleian Library ; of St. Matthew
(i. 1–9, 12, 14–20) and St. John (i. 23–31, 33–41, xx. 11–
17, 19–25) among the Egypt Exploration Fund papyri
recently discovered at Oxyrhynchus.[1]   All these are
assigned with much plausibility to the third century, the
earliest being probably the fragment of St. Matthew.   To
these may be added, not as being manuscripts of the
Bible but as more or less connected with them, the page
of *logia* or sayings of our Lord,[2] discovered at Oxyrhynchus together with the fragment of St. Matthew, and the
still more tiny scrap in the Rainer collection which appears
to contain an uncanonical version of St. Peter's denial.[3]
But these fragments, interesting as they are as examples
of what the soil of Egypt may yet be holding for us, are
so slight in themselves as barely to deserve mention ; and
if the papyrus period possessed no importance beyond
what they could give it, it might be passed over very
lightly and briefly indeed.   Its real importance lies in the
fact that it is the period to which the autographs of
the New Testament belong, and that by indirect means
we can learn something as to the appearance of these

---

[1] There are also some papyrus fragments of later dates, belonging to the
period after the introduction of vellum, but before the use of papyrus had been
entirely abandoned.   For a complete list of these (so far as the N.T. is concerned), see p. 36 ff.

[2] *Logia Christi*, ed. Grenfell and Hunt (1897).

[3] See Bickell, *Mittheilungen aus der Sammlung der Papyrus Erzherzog
Rainer*, i. 52.

autographs and of the conditions under which the Christian Scriptures circulated during the first three centuries of their existence.

It is only within the last few years that this knowledge has been made accessible. Before the present century, manuscripts upon papyrus were practically unknown, and it is only within the last ten years or less that they have been known in sufficient quantities to provide a continuous record of palaeography during the ages which preceded the rise of vellum. Now, however, thanks to a succession of discoveries in Egypt (the only country of which the air and soil are dry enough to preserve the brittle material), literary manuscripts upon papyrus can be counted by the hundred, and non-literary documents by the thousand, and we are in a position to realise with fair accuracy the appearance of a Greek book during the three centuries which lie on each side of the beginning of the Christian era.

A papyrus book was very unlike a vellum book, or such volumes as we are accustomed to at the present day. The material of which it was made was much more fragile than vellum, but perhaps not more so originally than paper, though by lapse of time it has in almost all cases become so brittle as to require the most careful handling. It was composed of the pith of the stem of the papyrus plant, which grew plentifully in antiquity in the Nile and its adjacent marshes. The pith was cut longitudinally into thin strips, which were laid side by side to form a layer, while a second layer was composed of similar strips at right angles to those of the first layer. The two layers were then fastened together, probably by glue, to form a sheet, the height of which might vary approximately from 6 to over 15 inches, and its width from 3 to 9 inches. Several of these sheets were then fastened together so as to form a roll, the length of which (in the case of Greek books) rarely, if ever, exceeded 30 feet, while it might be very much less. On one side of the roll, as will be seen from the above description, the fibres of papyrus lay horizontally or in the direction of the length of the roll, while on the other they lay perpendicularly or in the direction of its height ; and it was the former (technically known as the *recto*) that was primarily intended to receive the writing. The back (or *verso*) would normally be left blank, though an author whose matter outran his available stock of papyrus might occasionally be reduced to writing upon it,[1] or some one who desired a copy of a literary work for his own private use might sometimes inscribe it on the back of a roll which already had other writing on its *recto*.[2]

The writing on a papyrus roll was arranged in columns, the width of which varies considerably in different manuscripts. In the case of poetry it would naturally be determined by the length of the lines, and a hexameter verse, written in good sized characters, occupies from 5 to 6 inches. In prose works the columns are almost always much narrower, generally measuring from 2 to 3 inches, though there are examples of columns as narrow as $1\frac{3}{4}$ inches, and as wide as $3\frac{1}{2}$ inches. The only prose manuscripts at present known in which the columns are wider than this are a few which are not written in a formal literary hand, but in the running hands of everyday life, and evidently were intended solely for private use. The columns not infrequently lean a little to the right. Corrections are written between the lines, or, if too long for this method, in the margins at the top and bottom of the columns. Only very sumptuously written MSS. have sufficient space between the columns to allow corrections or notes to be inserted there.

Greek writing upon papyrus falls into two main classes :

[1] Thus the description of the book seen by Ezekiel in his vision (Ezek. ii. 10), "written within and without, and there was written therein lamentations, and mourning, and woe," implies a great superabundance of matter (cf. Rev. v. 1).

[2] The unique MSS. of Aristotle's Ἀθηναίων πολιτεία and the Funeral Oration of Hyperides are so written. The use of such volumes is mentioned as a sign of poverty by Lucian (*Vit. auct.* c. 9), where Diogenes promises his disciple, ἡ πήρα δέ σοι θέρμων ἔσται μεστή, καὶ ὀπισθογράφων βιβλίων. Copies so written may have been articles of commerce in a small way, but hardly as part of the regular book-trade.

the literary hand, for use in the transcription of books, and the non-literary hand, for use in business documents and private letters. In the former, ligatures between the letters are rare, the characters being for the most part formed separately. They are smaller and less formal than the writing of the best vellum uncials, but are carefully and gracefully written. Dated or approximately datable examples of the literary hand are rare, but the general sequence of development can be made out, from the small and angular hands of the Ptolemaic period to the larger, squarer, and more rounded forms which characterise the period of Roman rule in Egypt. Side by side with this goes the non-literary hand of everyday life, the stages of which can be fully traced by the aid of large numbers of dated documents from the beginning of the third century B.C. onwards. From the first (that is, as far back as our knowledge at present extends) it is written with the utmost freedom, showing that even persons of quite moderate stations in life were fully able to write a running hand with ease. For the purposes of textual criticism the non-literary hand only requires notice owing to the fact that literary works were sometimes copied in it by private individuals for their own use, and that copies of this kind may have entered into the textual tradition of the New Testament during the early days of Christianity. The distinction between the literary and non-literary hands of any given period is, roughly speaking, the same as that between print and writing nowadays —the one carefully formed, with separate letters of fair size, the other cursive and irregular, sometimes large and coarse, sometimes small and ill-formed, sometimes neat and flowing ; but the distinction, though obvious enough between average specimens of each type, is partially obscured by approximations in each to the style of the other, the literary hand admitting of ligatures between the letters to some extent, while non-literary documents sometimes approach the care and formality of the literary type.

Aids to the reader, such as accents, breathings, and punctuation, are not so wholly wanting in papyri as they are in the vellum manuscripts of the uncial period. It is true that non-literary documents are almost entirely without them, and that they are nowhere supplied so fully as they are in a modern printed text; but several literary papyri are partially equipped with accents, and have a rudimentary system of punctuation. So far as can be gathered from the extant specimens (and it must be remembered that these generally come from the personal possessions of private individuals in country towns and villages, not from the great libraries of a capital), the more carefully a manuscript is written, the more fully is it supplied with these aids to the understanding. The words are not separated in any case, but accents are placed upon the longer and more deceptive words, as to which mistakes were most likely to be made, and the more important pauses are marked either by small blank spaces in the text, or by a dot above or in the line of writing, or by a short line (*paragraphus*) drawn below the beginning of the line in which the pause occurs, or by some combination of these devices. Capital letters, which are occasionally used in business documents to mark the beginning of a clause, do not occur in literary papyri; nor are lines left unfinished at the ends of paragraphs.[1]

This description may serve to give some idea of the appearance and character of the original autographs of the New Testament. That they were written on papyrus hardly admits of doubt. It is true that skins had been used for the reception of writing in Palestine and elsewhere at an earlier date, and from the tradition recorded in the Talmud, which required all synagogue rolls to be so written, it is fair to conclude that the Old Testament books were habitually written on skins in the first century; but this proves nothing as to the material commonly used

---

[1] Fuller details as to papyrus manuscripts, with facsimiles, may be found in Sir E. Maunde Thompson's *Handbook to Greek and Latin Palaeography* (1893), or in the present writer's *Palaeography of Greek Papyri* (1899).

for ordinary writing, and the first point to be remembered in trying to reconstruct the early history of the New Testament books is that originally they would be regarded as ordinary books, and not as sacred. Skins, which might be employed for the purposes of public service in the synagogue, would be too cumbrous for books intended for free circulation, and especially for letters ; vellum did not come into general use anywhere until two or three centuries later ; and there is thus every reason to suppose that papyrus, which we know from the statements and allusions of contemporary writers to have been the material universally employed in the neighbouring country of Egypt, in Greece, and in Rome, was also commonly used in Palestine. Even if there were any doubt upon this point, it would only affect the books which were written in that country ; and these can, at most, be only the Gospel of St. Matthew and the Epistle of St. James. For the remaining books of the New Testament, which were written in Greece, in Asia Minor, or in Rome, we may say with confidence that they were originally written on papyrus.

This being so, it has been shown above that we now have adequate material for ascertaining their general character and appearance, by an examination of extant manuscripts of the same date. Among the papyri already publicly known, there are about 100 precisely dated documents belonging to the first century, and some fifteen or twenty literary works (some of them, however, small fragments), which, though not possessing exact dates, may be assigned to this period. It is true that all these were written in Egypt, while the autographs of the New Testament were all written outside that country ; but there is not much force in this consideration. No doubt, if we had as many extant examples of writing from each of these other countries as we have from Egypt, it is probable that an expert would be able to detect local types of calligraphy, and assign manuscripts to their respective countries on their handwritings alone, just as he is able

to do with mediaeval Latin manuscripts.   But the instance
of these very manuscripts shows the extent to which alone
these local variations affect the general development.   It
is not necessary to write a separate history of palaeography
for each nation.   The local differences may be discerned
by long experience, but the general development of writing is the same throughout.   It is easier to tell the date
of a MS. from its handwriting than its country.   So,
there is every reason to suppose, it would be with papyri,
and with this further reason for expecting uniformity,
that all Greek manuscripts, in whatever country, would be
written either by Greeks or by those who had learnt
their writing from Greeks.   Nor are we without means of
verifying this belief.   The papyri from Herculaneum,
though they are not exactly like any of the Egyptian
papyri, yet do not differ from some of them more than
they differ among themselves.   The two most recently discovered papyri of Hyperides, those of the speeches against
Philippides and Athenogenes, find the nearest analogies
to their handwritings in some of the Herculanean manuscripts.   Similarly, to take an example of a non-literary
hand, a Latin papyrus containing a deed of sale of a slave
boy, executed at Seleucia in Syria in the year 166, has a
Greek subscription in a hand essentially the same as those
current in Egypt at the same time.   There is thus every
reason, both *a priori* and *a posteriori*, to hold that what
we know of writing in Egypt during the first century may
be applied with confidence to writing in other parts of
the Graeco-Roman world.

We may refer, then, to the extant papyrus manuscripts of the first century as fairly representing the general
appearance of the New Testament autographs.   Chief
among these are (1) a beautiful copy of the third book of
the *Odyssey*,[1] in a rather large and graceful hand, without
ligatures, in columns about 6 inches broad, with wide
margins, written about the beginning of the first century ;

---

[1] Brit. Mus. Pap. 271; facsimile in Palaeographical Society's publications,
ii. 182.

(2) a large papyrus containing three orations of Hyperides,[1] less handsome than the *Odyssey*, but still neatly written in a well-rounded hand with a few ligatures, in columns about 2 inches wide and slightly leaning to the right, written about the last quarter of the first century; (3) a copy of the oration of Isocrates, *De pace*,[2] written about the same date, in columns of about the same size, but in a much less regular and ornamental style, more approaching the cursive type; and (4) the well-known papyrus of the Ἀθηναίων πολιτεία of Aristotle,[3] written between A.D. 90 and 100 in four different hands, of which two are very small and cursive, belonging wholly to the non-literary style of writing, while one is a larger and less well-formed cursive, and one a fairly regular but ugly uncial, evidently the work of an illiterate scribe. These four manuscripts are representatives of four classes of workmanship, to one or the other of which all the New Testament autographs must belong. The first is the work of a thoroughly good professional scribe of the best type; the second is a good ordinary professional hand; the third is the work of an educated man, not a professional scribe, writing a careful copy of a literary work; while the fourth is the running hand of common everyday writing.

To which class the original autograph of each of the New Testament books belonged depends upon the circumstances under which they were severally written; and these must remain in large measure a matter of conjecture. To take first the Pauline Epistles, as the earliest group among them, with the possible exception of the Epistle of St. James. These, we know, were not generally written by St. Paul with his own hand, but by one of

---

[1] Brit. Mus. Papp. 108 and 115; complete facsimile in editions by Babington; specimen facsimiles in *Pal. Soc.* i. 126, and *Catalogue of Ancient MSS. in the British Museum* (*Greek*). Plate I in the present volume shows the last four columns on a reduced scale.

[2] Brit. Mus. Pap. 132; specimen facsimiles in *Classical Texts from Papyri in the British Museum*

[3] Brit. Mus. Pap. 131; complete facsimile published by the Trustees of the British Museum; specimen in *Pal. Soc.* ii. 122. Plate II shows a portion of the eighth column of the MS., written by the first (and principal) hand.

his companions, Tertius, Sosthenes, Timothy, Silvanus, or some other, an autograph sentence or two by the apostle being invariably added at the end. Now, while it may be taken for certain that these were educated men, there is no reason to suppose that they were trained professional scribes ; and what we have to expect from them, therefore, is the careful writing of the educated amateur. The epistles would be written carefully, because they were weighty compositions, intended to be read more than once, and perhaps circulated among the neighbouring churches ; on the other hand, they would not be written by professional scribes, because they were not books, but letters. One is thus led to think of the two last of the types mentioned above, the Isocrates and the Aristotle. The Aristotle hands, however, are hardly suitable, some of them being too rapid and cursive, with small letters and contractions, while one is the work of a hireling, and a rather uneducated one. The Isocrates, which is neither uneducated nor professional, seems to come nearest to the general type of the Pauline autographs. One little circumstance may be taken as confirming this conclusion. In a well-known passage at the end of the Epistle to the Galatians, St. Paul refers to his own writing as a large hand : "See with how large letters I have written unto you with my own hand." It may be remarked in passing that exact analogies to this may be found in many Egyptian papyri, where the body of a document is written by a friend or a clerk, and the principal appends his ratification in a large hand at the end ; but the point specially noticeable here is that the phrase implies that the body of the epistle was written in a hand of small or medium size. It cannot have been an uncial such as those of the great vellum MSS. which we all know, neither can it have been such a hand as that of the Odyssey, or even the Hyperides, described above, which are themselves large and bold : it must have more nearly resembled the hand of the Isocrates. Of course this is merely suggested as the generic type. The individual hands, no doubt,

PLATE II.

ARISTOTLE, ΑΘΗΝΑΙΩΝ ΠΟΛΙΤΕΙΑ. Late First Century.

differed in different epistles, and none would be precisely similar to this.

Of the circumstances of the Catholic epistles we know less, and can therefore say less. The second and third epistles of St. John are private communications, and would almost certainly be written in a private hand, and on small sheets of papyrus. The first epistle is a more formal document, and, if it accompanied the Gospel, may very probably have been written in the same manner. The epistles of James, of Peter, and of Jude are formal and deliberate writings, intended for circulation among many churches, and must be treated as literary works, not as private and personal correspondence. They may, therefore, have been formally written by professional scribes, the author's autograph never coming into circulation at all. One may, therefore, think of the hand of the Hyperides or an improved form of the second Aristotle.

There remain the narrative books, namely, the four Gospels, the Acts, and the Apocalypse. Of the publication of the latter, and of the extent to which it circulated, we know too little to be able to judge of the character of its manuscripts; but it cannot be doubted that it must have originally existed in the personal autograph of the author. The author speaks of himself as writing and as being told to write; and one can hardly conceive of experiences so intimate and personal being dictated in the first instance to a professional scribe. With the Gospel of St. John the case is different. Composed at the end of a very long life, it may well have been taken down from the apostle's lips rather than written by his hand. One may compare the circumstances of its first composition with those of the first translation of it into English, taken down by the disciples of Bede from the lips of their dying master. The Gospel thus dictated seems to have been finally issued by a committee of the heads of the Church of Ephesus; and a book thus composed, and issued in the midst of a flourishing church during a time of tolera- tion, can hardly have been written except by a professional scribe, under the revision of the committee of elders. Here, if anywhere, one may think of an original copy of a New Testament book as written in the best style of contemporary calligraphy.   It is only unfortunate that we have so few specimens definitely assignable to the end of the first century to enable us to judge what that was like.   Some Homer papyri, probably written about this period (Brit. Mus. Papp. 107, 114, 732), in a clear, square, but somewhat unornamental hand, may furnish a clue, or we may think of an improved specimen of the Hyperides type.

The Gospel of St. Matthew was probably written in Judaea, and the same resources of penmanship would perhaps hardly be found there; moreover the Jews, for whom it was intended, were a less literary and aesthetic people than the Greeks.   Whether, if the Gospel were originally in Aramaic, its Greek form was also written in Judaea is a question which it would be rash to discuss and impossible to solve; but in any case the second of the considerations just mentioned, the Jewish character of the public for whom it was intended, remains unaffected, so that one would not look for any very ornamental form of writing as representing its original appearance.   The Gospel of St. Mark was probably written in Rome, where scribes were plentiful and good; on the other hand, the supporters of the Church were not relatively so important or so numerous as in Asia Minor, and it would not command so public a circulation.   Further, it may be doubted whether the Gospel was ever finished, and if it were not, the author could have been responsible for nothing except his own autograph; and this, as the writing of an educated man but not a professional scribe, would be on the same footing as the autographs of the epistles of St. Paul, some of which may even have been written by Mark himself. It may, therefore, be referred to the Isocrates type, or, if it were only the author's private draft, to that of the principal Aristotle hand.

The Gospel of St. Luke and the Acts go together, as

the works of the same author, and issued in the same
manner. Here a special feature is introduced by the fact
that both books were dedicated to a definite person,
Theophilus, and one who, as appears from the title
κράτιστος attached to his name, held high rank in the
official world.[1] It is evident that one copy, and that a
carefully and even elaborately written copy, would be
prepared for presentation to this dignitary (though Dr.
Salmon is probably wrong in saying that it would be on
vellum), and that another copy would be the archetype
from which the transcripts for general circulation would
be made. It is possible, if Luke himself were a good
calligraphist, that the presentation copy would be in his
own hand ; but it is more probable that it was written by
a professional scribe from the author's autograph draft,
and that the same scribe or another made from the same
draft the first copies for circulation. Professor Blass'
theory (of which more will have to be said in a later
chapter) that the divergences between the two editions
of the Acts are due to Luke having prepared two originals,
one for Theophilus and one for the public, making various
small alterations in the second, implies that Luke acted
as his own scribe ; and this can hardly be assumed. On
the other hand, Professor Ramsay's theory that the Acts
was never finished would make it doubtful whether the
presentation copy for Theophilus was ever written out
at all.

Another characteristic of the New Testament autographs to which the extant papyrus MSS. give us a clue
is the length of the rolls in which they were contained.
The shortest epistles, namely the second and third of St.
John, might be written in a single rather broad column
on a sheet of papyrus about 11 inches high by 6 inches
broad,—a size of which there are many extant examples
among the recently discovered papyri of the first and

[1] In Egypt the epithet is applied only to the Prefect, the δικαιοδότης, and the
ἰδιολόγος, whose jurisdiction extended over the whole province, and to the
three epistrategi, or governors of the three great districts into which it was
divided.

second centuries. The epistle of St. Jude and that to Philemon could be written in two moderate columns on a slightly broader sheet. 2 Thessalonians would be a roll of about 15 inches in length, arranged in some five columns. The other epistles of St. Paul would range in length upwards from this to about 11 feet 6 inches in the case of the epistle to the Romans. The Apocalypse may be estimated at 15 feet. Of the longer books, the Gospel of St. Mark would occupy about 19 feet, that of St. John 23 feet 6 inches, St. Matthew 30 feet, the Acts and St. Luke's Gospel about 31 or 32 feet. In all these cases a copy written with especial elegance would require a somewhat greater length.[1]

[1] For the purpose of comparison, the dimensions of some of the extant papyrus MSS. may be stated. The Hyperides MS. mentioned above (containing the oration against Demosthenes and those for Lycophron and Euxenippus), must have measured, when perfect, about 28 feet; a MS. of the last two books of the *Iliad*, about 25 feet; the Mimes of Herodas, about the same; the Isocrates mentioned above, 14 feet; and the longest of the rolls of the Aristotle, over 7 feet. In height the Hyperides measures 11¾ inches, the Isocrates and Aristotle 11 inches, the Homer 9¾ inches, and the Herodas (which is in the nature of a pocket volume of poetry), only 5 inches. The fine Odyssey papyrus measures 13 inches in height, and, supposing it to have contained the first three books of the poem, would have measured about 24 feet.

An ingenious theory with regard to the New Testament autographs was formerly proposed by Mr. Rendel Harris ("New Testament Autographs," in the American *Journal of Philology*, No. 12, supplement). Observing that the columns of the Codex Vaticanus consist of 42 lines, and that the ends of the several books very frequently fall in or about the 14th, 28th, or 42nd line, he argued that the columns of the archetype from which it was derived probably consisted of 14 lines of similar length. On like grounds he concluded that the columns of the Codex Sinaiticus, which consist of 48 lines, represent four original columns of 12 lines each. Thus, since each page of the Vaticanus contains three columns, and each page of the Sinaiticus four columns, it appears that they respectively contain three times three, and four times four, of the supposed original columns; and this he supposed to be the meaning of the well-known passage in Eusebius, where it is said that the copies of the Greek Bible, made at Constantine's order for the churches in his new capital, were sent ἐν πολυτελῶς ἠσκημένοις τεύχεσι τρισσὰ καὶ τετρασσά. The theory is very ingenious, but unfortunately it is inconsistent with the evidence derived from the extant papyri, as stated above. (1) Columns of the size supposed by Mr. Harris imply rolls of papyrus only 5 or 6 inches in height; and these are never found except in the case of the Herodas MS., which, as just remarked, is evidently intended for a pocket volume. Such a *format* would be as unsuitable for a Gospel as that of the Temple Shakespeare for a Bampton Lecture. (2) Mr. Harris argues that the early Christians, being poor, would use papyrus of very moderate height, because it was cheaper; but this argument rests on a misapprehension. Pliny gives the dimensions of various kinds of papyrus, stating that the largest was the most expensive, while the smallest was the cheapest; but it is now certain that his dimensions apply, not to the height of the papyrus roll, but to the width of the sheets out of which a roll was

One important deduction from the figures which have just been given is that no complete copy of the New Testament in a single volume could exist during the papyrus period. Such a copy, even when written in a small hand and with narrow margins, would occupy a roll more than 200 feet in length, which is far in excess of even the largest Egyptian papyri (which, being intended less for reading than for show, are often of great length), and is seven or eight times the length of an average Greek papyrus. It would not even be possible to include all the Gospels in a single roll. Each book must have existed and circulated separately, and if any given individual possessed one of them, he would not necessarily possess the rest also. Further, it will be understood (and this is a point which applies also to vellum MSS.) that it was not very easy to verify references, when divisions of the text were few and a numeration by chapters and verses unknown. The earliest known division of the sacred text into sections does not reach back into the papyrus period. Hence ignorance of any particular book on the part of an early Christian writer does not necessarily imply the non-existence of that book at that time ; and inexactness of quotation is to be expected rather than wondered at.

It is to its fortunes during the papyrus period that the New Testament owes its peculiar textual history. All other works of ancient literature which have come down to us were written avowedly as literary works, and were formally copied by professional copyists from the very earliest times of their existence. The texts which we now possess of Sophocles or of Virgil are linked to the authors' original autographs by a continuous chain of formal transcripts, each of which was intended for public use—in

composed. The papyri discovered in Egypt show that even the poorest people used papyrus measuring 9 or 10 inches in height, and upwards. (3) Mr. Harris' theory would require rolls of excessive length to contain the principal books of the New Testament. The longer epistles, such as Romans and 1 Corinthians, would become portly rolls of 25 feet in length, while the Gospel of St. Luke and the Acts would reach the impossible dimensions of 70 feet or thereabouts.

most cases, it is probable, for preservation in a public library. We cannot say the same of the text of the New Testament. The several books were not composed in the first instance as literary works, nor by men whose profession was that of letters. They were not copied for their literary skill, but for the substance contained in them, the record of facts of intense importance or the admonitions of a revered and authoritative teacher. Many of the early copies were no doubt made by private individuals for their own use, few or none as ordinary items in the book-trade. From time to time the owners of them were the objects of persecution, and the sacred writings themselves were condemned to be destroyed; and in such cases the official copies preserved by the churches would be the most likely to suffer, while the private copies would escape more easily and would be the sources from which, when the storm of persecution was past, the stream of tradition would be re-established.

Under these circumstances it was only natural that great divergences should spring up in the text. Even the classical texts, which have been handed down from library to library, have suffered much in the process—how much, we cannot always tell, for want of a sufficient variety of authorities; and with the Christian Scriptures it was inevitable, humanly speaking, that they should be much corrupted during these early centuries, when in some cases verbal accuracy was little thought of, in others it was unattainable by reason of the position of the Church, and when the copies made by private individuals for their own use played an important part in the textual tradition. What such copies might be like we learn from some of the papyrus MSS. of classical authors which have been discovered of late years. Many of these MSS. were evidently private copies, or, at least, did not come from any of the great museums, but from the little libraries of ordinary provincials; and it is a recognised fact that the texts of these papyri are less pure than those of the best vellum MSS., although they are often a thousand years older.

Of all the papyri of Homer which have been discovered (and they are many), none is so good as the great vellum Venetian MS. of the 10th century. It is a representative of the purer channel of tradition, which ran through the great libraries ; while the papyri (some of which are excessively corrupt) show what might happen in the case of copies made at a distance from these centres of scholarship and accuracy. Hence if we find great divergences among the copies of the New Testament as far back as the extant evidence takes us, we need not be surprised ; nor need we be discouraged, since it will be found that the divergences do not seriously affect the substance of the record which these books enshrine.

After describing, as has been done above, the character and appearance of papyrus manuscripts at the time when the autographs of the New Testament were written, little need be said of the rest of the papyrus period. During the second century, the general characteristics of the writing in current use remained the same. With the assistance of a very large number of dated documents (several to each year) it is possible to trace the development of the non-literary hand with some minuteness ; but for the literary hand the extant specimens are too few to enable nice distinctions to be drawn, and the first two centuries of our era must be grouped together as a single palaeographical period, within which a precise accuracy of arrangement is not to be expected until further evidence is available. In the third century two changes are observable. The writing, which hitherto has been upright, now frequently develops a sloping formation ; and experiments are made in the use of the codex or modern book-form of volume, instead of the roll. The former is a point of merely palaeographical interest, useful chiefly as a means of determining the dates of manuscripts ; but the latter paves the way for the revolution of the fourth century, when papyrus was superseded by vellum, and when complete copies of the New Testament for the first time became possible.

D

The history of the codex or book-form goes back to the wax tablets which were commonly employed as note-books by the Greeks and Romans from the earliest days of their habitual use of writing.   These tablets consisted of thin rectangular plates of wood, with raised rims to retain and protect the wax, in general appearance much like a school-boy's slate ; and a number of them could be joined together by passing strings or thongs through holes bored in the rims on one side.   Several sets of tablets with such holes in their rims exist to this day ; and these were the earliest *codices*.   Next, from about the first century B.C., vellum was used in the same way, but as yet only for notes and rough drafts, not as a rival to papyrus for books intended for circulation.   Then, the advantages of this method of book-formation becoming evident, an attempt was made to use papyrus in the same manner ; and from the third and following centuries several examples of papyrus codices have come down to us.   In some cases (and these may be supposed to be the earliest) the writing is only on one side of the leaf,[1] as though the scribe was too much accustomed to the older manner of writing upon papyrus to think of using both sides of it ; but oftener it is on both sides, as in an ordinary vellum codex.   Usually the leaves are narrow in proportion to their height,[2] which indicates that the papyrus of which they are composed is not of the best quality, so that they were probably cheap and inferior copies.[3]   But as Christians in the early days of the Church were rarely rich, it is likely that many copies of the Scriptures existed in this form ; and the extant evidence points in this direction. Nearly all the Christian papyri of the third century are codices, while for non-Christian writings the roll form is still predominant.   Examples may be seen in the earliest portions of the New Testament now extant in manuscript,

[1] E.g. Brit. Mus. Pap. 126 (containing part of Homer, *Il.* ii.–iv.).

[2] E.g. the Homer papyrus mentioned in the preceding note, Brit. Mus. Pap. 46 (a papyrus containing magical formulae), and a similar magical papyrus in the Bibliothèque Nationale at Paris.

[3] Thus the above-mentioned Homer is the worst of all the papyri.

the Oxyrhynchus fragments of St. Matthew and St. John
(Pap.[1] and Pap.[6] in the list at the end of this chapter).
These, like the fragment of a collection of sayings of our
Lord which was found with them, are probably parts of
pocket volumes, written for private use rather than general
circulation ; and no doubt many such existed among the
humble circles in which Christianity at this time chiefly
flourished.   Valuable as such copies may be, on account
of their age, we cannot look to them with any confidence
for purity of text.

The papyrus period, then, may be summarily characterised as the period in which the textual problems came into
being, which we have to try to solve with the help of
the evidence afforded by the later periods.   During that
period the Christian Scriptures were scattered over the
face of the accessible world, wherever the Roman Empire
spread, or wherever, beyond the boundaries of that
empire, Christian missionaries were able to make their
way.   But as yet they spread and were reproduced without the aid, without the sanction, and often in defiance of
the express mandates, of the civil power.   At certain times
and in certain places Christianity was allowed to do its
work unchecked, and was able to command the services of
competent scribes to multiply its sacred books ; but oftener
it was discouraged, or was followed only by the humble
and poor, while from time to time it was the object of
direct persecution, in which its books were sought out and
destroyed by order of the Government.   The full history
of the New Testament text during this confused period can
never be known ; but it is the function of textual criticism
to trace it as far as possible.   Up to the present time, no
evidence worth mentioning is extant which comes from
within this period itself.   We can only see the results at
the end of the period, and try to work back to the causes.
It is far from impossible, or even improbable, that Egypt,
which has given us so many precious manuscripts of early
date, may yet bring to light a Gospel or an Epistle written
in the second or third century.   Such a discovery would

be full of interest, and might possibly go far towards settling some outstanding controversies; but it would have to be received with caution, and its character would need careful examination. As has been shown above, it might contain a text inferior in quality to that of some existing manuscripts. It would be in the broad characteristics of its text, rather than in its precise details, that its value would be most likely to consist; and it might raise as many problems as it laid. In any case, the best preparation for dealing judiciously with such new testimony is a sound knowledge of the evidence already in existence; and it is with the statement and examination of this evidence that the following chapters will be concerned.

By way of conclusion, however, to the present chapter, it may be useful to give a list of the extant fragments of the New Testament on papyrus. Hitherto most of them have not found a place in the standard lists of New Testament manuscripts, so that they have no generally accepted notation. Such a notation will be increasingly necessary as the number of such fragments is increased by successive discoveries; and seeing that they form a department somewhat apart by themselves it may be suggested that they should have a notation distinct from that of the vellum MSS. The simplest would be to indicate them as Pap.[1], Pap.[2], Pap.[3], etc., as in the list which now follows; and this system may be offered to the consideration of future editors of Scrivener's and Gregory's lists. It is becoming increasingly difficult to find distinctive letters for all the extant MSS. of the New Testament, and it is wasteful to appropriate separate letters to small fragments, as has sometimes been done. The system here suggested would obviate these difficulties.

Pap.[1] Matthew i. 1-9, 12, 14-20. One leaf of a book. Third century. Found at Oxyrhynchus in Egypt in 1896, and published by Messrs. Grenfell and Hunt in *Oxyrhynchus Papyri*, Part I. (1898). The variants of this fragment are of small importance in themselves, but so far as they go they tend to support the oldest vellum uncials, the Codex Vaticanus and the Codex Sinaiticus. It was the property of the Egypt Exploration Fund, but has now been presented to the University of Pennsylvania.

Pap.[2] Matthew xviii. (the exact verses not stated), in the Rainer collection at Vienna. Fourth or fifth century, probably in book-form. Cf. Gregory (Tischendorf's *Novum Testamentum Graece*, iii. 450).

Pap.[3] Mark xv. 29-38, also in the Rainer collection. Fourth century, probably in book-form. Cf. Gregory, *loc. cit.*

Pap.[4] Luke i. 74-80, v. 3-8 (both these portions very fragmentary), and v. 30-vi. 4, discovered in Egypt, attached to a papyrus MS. of Philo; now in the Bibliothèque Nationale at Paris. Fourth century, in book-form. Edited by Scheil (*Mémoires de la Mission archéologique française au Caire*, tom. 9, 1893). Evl. 943 in Gregory (*op. cit.*).

Pap.[5] Luke vii. 36-43, x. 38-42; in the Rainer collection. Sixth century, in book-form. Described by Wessely (*Führer durch die Ausstellung der Papyrus Erzherzog Rainer*, no. 539).

Pap.[6] John i. 23-31, 33-41, xx. 11-17, 19-25; nearly the outermost sheet of a single quire of some twenty-five sheets, containing the whole Gospel of St. John; a quite unparalleled form of book. Third century. In the Egypt Exploration Fund collection of papyri from Oxyrhynchus; published by Grenfell and Hunt in *Oxyrhynchus Papyri*, Part II. (1899), no. ccviii.; now in British Museum (Pap. 782). Its text agrees generally with that of the Codex Sinaiticus.

Pap.[7] John i. 29; in the Rainer collection. Seventh century, probably in book-form. Cf. Gregory, *ubi supra.*

Pap.[8] Romans i. 1-7; in the Egypt Exploration Fund collection from Oxyrhynchus. Early fourth century; written in a rough uncial hand, apparently as a schoolboy's exercise. Published by Grenfell and Hunt, *op. cit.* no. ccix.; now in the library of Harvard University.

Pap.[9] 1 Cor. i. 17-20, vi. 13-18, vii. 3, 4, 10-14; in the Uspensky collection at Kiew. Fifth century. The first papyrus fragment of the New Testament to be brought to light, having been brought by Bishop Porphyry Uspensky from the East, and read by Tischendorf in 1862. Cf. Gregory, *op. cit.* iii. 434, where it has the letter Q assigned to it.

Pap.[10] 1 Cor. i. 25-27, ii. 6-8, iii. 8-10, 20 ; in the monastery of St. Catherine on Mt. Sinai. Fifth century, in book-form. Discovered and edited by Rendel Harris, *Biblical Fragments from Mt. Sinai* (1896), no. 14. Included in the *addenda* to Scrivener and Gregory, as ‎ק[9] and ‎ק[14] respectively.

Pap.[11] 2 Thess. i. 1-ii. 2 ; in the Berlin Museum. A single leaf, with two columns on each page. Fourth or fifth century. Mentioned (but not described) by H. Landwehr in *Philologus*, xliii. p. 108 (1883) ; described here from personal examination. Included in Scrivener and Gregory as Paul. 487.

Pap.[12] Heb. i. 1 ; in Lord Amherst's collection of papyri. Third or early fourth century ; written in the margin of a letter from a Roman Christian. Published by Grenfell and Hunt, *Amherst Papyri*, Part I. no. 3 *b* (1900).

CHAPTER III

THE UNCIAL MANUSCRIPTS

[**Authorities**: Gregory, Prolegomena to Tischendorf's *Novum Testamentum Graece* (Leipzig, 1884-1894), and *Textkritik des Neuen Testamentes* (vol. i. Leipzig, 1900); Scrivener, *A Plain Introduction to the Criticism of the New Testament* (4th ed., by E. Miller, London, 1894); Thompson, *op. cit.*; Tischendorf, *Notitia editionis codicis Bibliorum Sinaitici* (1860), and other works; Westcott and Hort, *The New Testament in Greek*, 1881; Nestle, *Introduction to the Textual Criticism of the Greek N.T.*, Eng. Tr. from 2nd ed. (London, 1901); and special works on the individual MSS., mentioned in the course of the chapter.]

IN the early years of the fourth century we reach an epoch of the greatest importance in the history of the New Testament Scriptures. Several causes combined to alter completely the circumstances under which they were copied and transmitted; and it so happens that it is from this very period that the earliest concrete evidence, in the shape of actual substantial copies of the Scriptures, has come down to our times. In the first place, the conversion of the Emperor Constantine, and the consequent recognition of Christianity as the state religion of the Roman Empire, led to a great multiplication of copies of the Scriptures, and also enabled them to be made with due care and with all the resources of ordinary literary production available at that date. Next, the adoption of vellum instead of papyrus as the material employed for the best copies of books rendered possible the combination of all the sacred writings within the compass of a single volume; while at the same time the increased publicity given to Christianity and the growth of doctrinal controversies led to the precise definition and demarcation of the canonical books which such a volume should contain. It is true that this definition did not take place once for all at any given moment or by any authoritative decision, but was a gradual process spread over a considerable time, as our earliest extant manuscripts testify by their inclusion of sundry other books in addition to those which we now recognise as canonical. The process was not wholly completed before the end of the century; but a practical unanimity had been reached in most quarters by that time, and the process is a prominent feature in the history of the New Testament during this period.

These causes acted and reacted on one another in a manner which makes it difficult to say precisely which is cause and which effect. Thus the adoption of vellum, and therewith of the codex form in place of the roll form, made it possible to unite all the Scriptures in a single volume; while the needs of the churchmen and of the lawyers alike demanded some form of book in which their sacred writings or their authorised codes could be kept together without danger of loss or separation. The formation of a canon of authoritative Scripture was both necessitated by the development of controversy, and itself in turn facilitated and promoted such controversy. But whatever the exact play and counter-play of cause and effect may have been, the concrete phenomenon which marks the fourth century in the textual history of the New Testament is the appearance of complete copies, either of the New Testament or of the whole Greek Bible, written upon vellum and arranged in the form of a codex.

The use of vellum, as has been briefly mentioned in the last chapter, was not a new thing at this date.[1] For some centuries it had been used for note-books or for cheap copies of literary works; but it is only in the fourth century that it ousts papyrus from the post of honour as the recognised material for the best copies in general circulation. For a

---

[1] See *Palaeography of Greek Papyri*, ch. v. ; Thompson's *Handbook of Greek and Latin Palaeography*, 35-37.

time, no doubt, the two materials overlapped, and there are examples of papyrus books (but in codex form, not as rolls) as late as the seventh century, or, in the case of Coptic works, still later.[1] But on the whole the victory of vellum was won early in the fourth century ; and the proof of it is found, not only in the decline of literary papyri, both in number and in quality, at this point (though non-literary papyri exists in immense numbers up to the seventh or eighth century), and in the appearance of vellum codices, but in two definite pieces of external evidence. On the one hand there is the statement of Eusebius (*Vit. Constant.* iv. 36) that the Emperor Constantine about the year 331 ordered fifty copies of the Scriptures *on vellum* for the churches in his new capital ; on the other, there is the statement of Jerome that the (papyrus) volumes in the library of Pamphilus at Caesarea were replaced by copies on vellum through the efforts of Acacius and Euzoius (*circ.* 350).[2]

The change of material was accompanied by a change in the style of writing. Vellum is, of course, a far stronger substance than papyrus, and therefore admitted a firmer style of writing, with thicker and heavier strokes. Moreover, economy of space being less necessary, now that the roll form had been abandoned, larger letters could be employed ; and the general result is that early writing upon vellum is on a larger and more handsome scale than most writing upon papyrus. Further, the scribes who wrote it seem to have cast back for their models to the best ages of the papyrus hand. The papyrus manuscripts of the

[1] There are (besides many smaller fragments) two collections of magical formulae, one in the British Museum and one in the Bibliothèque Nationale, apparently of the fourth century ; a Psalter (containing Ps. xi. 2-xix. 6, xxi. 14-xxxv. 6) in the British Museum, of the seventh century ; part of Zechariah and Malachi at Heidelberg, of the seventh century ; part of Cyril of Alexandria *De Adoratione* at Dublin, of the sixth or seventh century ; a large Coptic codex of the Psalms of the seventh century, and an equally large one of homilies, perhaps rather later, both in the British Museum. There are also said to be many late literary papyri in the Oxyrhynchus collection ; and some fragments, principally of the Psalms, from the fifth to the seventh centuries, are in Lord Amherst's collection.

[2] It may be added that the records of the persecution of A.D. 303 in Africa mention both rolls (*libri*) and codices among the books sought out and destroyed (Routh, *Rell. Sacr.* iv. 289 ff. and 322 ff.).

third century are mostly written in a sloping hand which is not very graceful in appearance; but the vellum manuscripts of the fourth century recall rather the best hands of the first century, which have a strong claim to be regarded as the finest specimens of calligraphy in the whole papyrus period. At the same time we are able wholly to put out of consideration the non-literary styles of writing. During the papyrus period we have abundant examples of the non-literary hand of everyday use, side by side with the literary hand which was reserved mainly for book-production; and in the case of the New Testament we have seen reason to believe that the non-literary hand played a considerable part in the preservation and transmission of the sacred books. But with the rise of vellum, and the simultaneous emergence of Christianity into the position of an authorised and established religion, the spheres of book-production and ordinary writing became more sharply separated. No doubt a non-literary hand continued to exist, since it was required for the common affairs of daily life; indeed up to the close of the seventh century, or even later, we have plentiful evidence of its existence upon papyrus; but it ceased to affect the channels by which the text of the New Testament was handed down. Thenceforward, through all the centuries until the invention of printing, we have only to do with the formal book-hand in the various modifications which it assumed in the course of successive generations.

Writing upon vellum, as has been briefly indicated above (p. 17), falls into two main periods. In the first of these the book-hand consists of capital or *uncial*[1] letters,

---

[1] The term is derived from a passage in Jerome's preface to his Latin translation of the book of Job, where he inveighs against the extravagant style in which many books were written in his day, "uncialibus, ut vulgo aiunt, litteris." The word apparently means "inch-long" letters, but it occurs nowhere else, and it has sometimes been supposed to be merely a misreading of *initialibus*, which closely resembles it and is actually found in many copies of the passage in question. But no one would be likely to use the term "initial" to describe a particular type of writing, nor is the word itself so unfamiliar as to need the apologetic "ut vulgo aiunt," which, on the other hand, is quite in place as a qualification of the exaggerated phrase "inch-long." The characters of some early MSS. are quite large enough to justify the phrase as a

formed singly and separately, without ligatures, and usually of a considerable size. Examples may be seen in plates III.-VIII. of the present volume. The earliest of them, in the fourth century, show evident traces of their descent from papyri. The writing is little, if at all, larger than that of the best papyri ; it is arranged in narrow columns, three or four to the page ; and it is wholly devoid of ornamentation. There are no accents or capital letters. The most that is done in the way of making a new paragraph is to begin a new line and slightly draw back the first letter into the margin, but without enlarging it. In the fifth century the writing grows rather larger and the columns broader, so that there are not more than two to a page, and sometimes only one. Enlarged initials mark the beginnings of paragraphs ; or if, as often happens, the new paragraph does not begin a new line, but follows on in the same line as the end of the previous paragraph, with only a short blank space to mark the break, the enlarged letter is the first in the first full line of the new paragraph. In the sixth century the writing is generally heavier and thicker, and often larger ; while in the seventh century, instead of being upright, as hitherto, it shows a tendency to slope to the right, the letters being at the same time compressed into more oval and pointed shapes. This tendency increases through the eighth and ninth centuries, culminating in the heavy and angular forms of what is known as the Slavonic hand, which (with certain exceptions and modifications, and occasional reactionary attempts to revive the earlier upright and rounded style) predominates throughout that period ; until in the tenth century a new form of writing, which had arisen in the previous century, finally prevailed over this large and cumbrous style, and the uncial period of Greek palaeography comes to an end.[1]

pardonable exaggeration ; e.g. in the New Testament MS. known as N (see below) the letters measure about five-eighths of an inch, with capitals nearly twice that size.

[1] For a fuller sketch of the development of Greek uncial writing, see Thompson, *Greek and Latin Palaeography*, 149-158.

The uncial period, then, covers a space of some six centuries ; and it is to this period that the most valuable of the extant manuscripts of the New Testament belong. We come now to the consideration and description of these in detail ; but before commencing this task, it will be convenient to explain the system which regulates the numeration and nomenclature of New Testament manuscripts. Very few of them contain the whole New Testament, and it has therefore been found convenient to classify the books in four groups, each of which has its own numeration of manuscripts. These groups are (1) the four Gospels, (2) the Acts and Catholic Epistles (which generally go together), (3) the Pauline Epistles, (4) the Apocalypse. Uncial manuscripts are indicated by the capital letters, first of the Latin alphabet from A to Z, next of the Greek alphabet (so far as that differs from the Latin) from Γ to Ω, and finally of the Hebrew alphabet, the resources of which have not yet been exhausted. Since, however, each group has its own numeration, a letter which denotes a certain manuscript in one group will often denote a different manuscript in another group. Thus, the great Codex Vaticanus, which is known as B in the Gospels, Acts, and Pauline Epistles, does not contain the Apocalypse ; hence in the case of that book B denotes a different MS. Similarly D of the Gospels and Acts (Codex Bezae) does not contain the Pauline Epistles, and the letter is consequently given there to another MS (Codex Claromontanus). In order to avoid confusion, it is usual to distinguish these second holders of a title by a subsidiary mark, either B_2, D_2, or $B^{apoc.}$, $D^{paul.}$, and the like. Minuscule manuscripts (i.e. manuscripts written in the smaller kind of hand which succeeded the uncial type) are indicated by numbers, each group of books having, as before, a separate numeration, the complications of which will be explained in the next chapter.

According to the catalogue of New Testament manuscripts which follows, the total number of uncials at present known to exist stands thus :—

Gospels   101
Acts and Catholic Epistles   .   .   22
Pauline Epistles   27
Apocalypse   6
                                        ——
                          Total   156 [1]

This total, however, requires explanation; for several manuscripts, which contain more than one of the four sections into which the numeration is divided, are reckoned twice or oftener in the total. Allowing for these duplications, the total of distinct manuscripts is reduced to 129. Further, it is to be remembered that the large majority of these manuscripts consists of fragments, sometimes extremely small. Of the 129 manuscripts above mentioned, forty-seven may be reckoned as containing some substantial part of the New Testament, while the remainder are mere fragments. Only one uncial manuscript (ℵ, the Codex Sinaiticus) contains the New Testament complete.[2] Four more (ABCΨ) originally contained the whole New Testament, and still contain most of it, but have suffered some mutilation. Seven (ℵBKMSUΩ) have complete copies of the four Gospels; five (ℵABP₂S₂) of the Acts; seven (ℵABK₂L₂P₂S₂) of the Catholic Epistles; five (ℵAD₂G₃P₂) of the Pauline Epistles; and four (ℵAB₂P₂) of the Apocalypse.[3]

With regard to the dates of these manuscripts, it is only very rarely that the exact year in which they were written is known; and the few to which precise dates can be affixed are among the latest. For the rest, their dates must, as a rule, be fixed on palaeographical evidence alone, with slight assistance in a few cases from collateral testimony of various kinds. Hence there is inevitably some

---

[1] In Scrivener's *Introduction to the Criticism of the New Testament*, 4th ed. (by Miller), the total appears as 127. The difference is due mainly to an increase in the small fragments, enumerated below under the letters T and W.

[2] The tenth century MS. at Kosinitsa, known as Ɔ, should perhaps be added.

[3] Small mutilations, affecting only a few verses, have been ignored in this computation.

divergence in the dates assigned to these manuscripts, especially in the case of the small fragments. The following estimate may, however, be taken as approximately correct. Two great manuscripts, the Codex Sinaiticus and the Codex Vaticanus, the one complete and the other nearly so, may be assigned with considerable confidence to the fourth century. Two more, the Codex Alexandrinus and the Codex Ephraemi, both originally complete Bibles, though the latter is now much mutilated, belong to the fifth century, together with about twelve small fragments. Thirty-four manuscripts (mostly small fragments) may be assigned to the sixth century, fifteen to the seventh, nineteen to the eighth, thirty-eight to the ninth, and seven to the tenth. These figures, though not to be relied on as absolutely accurate in detail, will at least serve to show approximately the chronological distribution of the uncial evidence.

The examination and classification of the textual evidence must be reserved until the several witnesses have been individually described ; but a provisional distinction may be drawn which will be useful for the purpose of this description. Speaking very generally, it may be said that the manuscripts of the New Testament fall into two great classes,—those which support what is known as the Textus Receptus, and those which depart from it. The Textus Receptus is that type of text which, having been adopted in the earliest printed editions of the New Testament, has continued, with only slight modifications, to hold its own as the standard text in ordinary use. It is found in our ordinary editions of the Greek Testament, and in an English dress it is familiar to us in the Authorised Version; and it is supported by a vast numerical majority of manuscripts. On the other hand, there is a type of text which (especially in the Gospels) often departs very markedly from the Textus Receptus. The evidence for it is very various, being collected from a few manuscripts, some of the versions, and some of the Fathers ; but the remarkable feature about it is, that it includes the earliest testimony in each of these branches, and consequently its weight is far greater than its merely numerical following would show. The result is that this type of text has been adopted in most of the modern critical editions of the Greek Testament, and a form of it appears in the Revised Version of the English Bible. It is a main purpose of the present volume to estimate the value of these two great types of text ; but it would be premature to discuss the question now. For the present, it will be best simply to call the Textus Receptus type the *a*-text, and its opponent the *β*-text ; though it must be remembered that within each of these classes (and especially in the second) there are considerable divergences of detail. The classification is of the broadest, and is merely adopted as a rough basis for inquiry. In the nomenclature here adopted there is the advantage that the chief representative of the *a*-text is the manuscript known as A, while the great champion of the *β*-text is the manuscript known as B ; and we avoid begging the question as to the relative merits of the rival types. A subdivision of the *β*-type, of which the principal Greek representative is the manuscript known as D, may be entitled the *δ*-text. Its most obvious characteristic is a very wide departure from the *a*-text, with apparently arbitrary modifications and not infrequent additions to it ; the character of these variants will form an important subject of inquiry later on.

It now remains to consider the several uncial manuscripts in detail. The more important ones will need examination at some length, while for the less important reference may be made to the standard catalogues of manuscripts in Scrivener and Gregory.[1]

ℵ, Codex Sinaiticus (Plate III.).—First in the list (not strictly in alphabetical precedence, since the Hebrew alphabet properly follows the English and Greek, but in practical usage) stands this well-known manuscript, notable alike for its intrinsic value and for the circumstances

---

[1] Scrivener, i. 90-188, Gregory (Prolegomena to Tischendorf's *Novum Testamentum Graece*, 8th ed.), 345-450.

attending its discovery. The story is familiar, but cannot be passed over in any history of the New Testament text.[1] In 1844 the well-known German Biblical scholar, Constantin Tischendorf, was travelling in the East under the patronage of King Frederick Augustus of Saxony, in search of manuscripts; and in the course of his travels he visited the monastery of St. Catherine on Mt. Sinai. There, in a waste-paper basket containing a number of leaves of various manuscripts, destined to light the monastery fires, he chanced to notice several leaves of vellum bearing Greek writing of an extremely early type, which on examination proved to be part of a copy of the Septuagint version of the Old Testament. No objection was offered to the visitor's appropriating the supposed waste paper, and he was informed that much similar material had already met with the fate for which these sheets were intended. He was also shown further portions of the same manuscript, containing the books of Isaiah and the Maccabees; but these he was not allowed to appropriate, and he was obliged to content himself with warning the monks that such things were too valuable to be used as fuel. Returning to Europe with his spoil, which consisted of forty-three leaves from the books of 1 Chronicles, Jeremiah, Nehemiah, and Esther, he deposited it in the University library at Leipzig, where, under the name of the Codex Friderico-Augustanus (from King Frederick Augustus, the discoverer's sovereign and patron) it still remains; and in 1846 he published its contents. In 1853 he returned to the East, and revisited the monastery of St. Catherine, hoping to acquire the rest of the manuscript; but this time he could neither see nor hear anything of it, though

---

[1] It is told several times by Tischendorf in the various publications to which his discovery gave rise, viz. *Notitia editionis codicis Bibliorum Sinaitici* (1860), *Bibliorum Codex Sinaiticus Petropolitanus*, 4 vols. (1862), *Novum Testamentum Sinaiticum* (1863), *Novum Testamentum Graecum ex Sinaitico codice* (1865), *Die Sinaibibel* (1871); besides a few controversial articles. I do not see that any sufficient cause has been shown to question the truth of Tischendorf's story or the good faith of his dealings in the matter, as has sometimes been done (cf. Gregory, *Textkritik*, pp. 23-29).

(as subsequently appeared) it had meanwhile been shown
to the learned Russian bishop, Porphyry Uspensky, and to
an English officer, Major Macdonald. Believing that the
treasure must have already found its way into Europe,
Tischendorf resigned his search and abandoned his hopes ;
but in 1859 his work took him back to Mount Sinai, this
time under the patronage of the Tsar Alexander II. His
stay was only of a few days' duration, but shortly before
its end he happened to be conversing with the steward of
the monastery on the subject of the Septuagint, copies of
his recent edition of which he had brought with him to
present to the monastery. The steward observed that he
too had a copy of the Septuagint, and presently produced
it, wrapped in a napkin, the only protection of its loose
and often mutilated leaves; and there the astonished
visitor beheld the very manuscript which for the last
fifteen years had been so much in his thoughts. The
prize was even greater than he had hoped ; for not only
was much of the Old Testament there, but also the New
Testament intact and in excellent condition, with the
addition of the Epistle of Barnabas and much of the
Shepherd of Hermas—two early Christian works which
hovered for a time on the edge of the Canon before being
ultimately excluded from it. Tischendorf's delight may
be imagined, and could not be concealed. He obtained
leave to take the precious manuscript to his room ; and
that night, thinking it sacrilege to sleep, he spent in
transcribing the Epistle of Barnabas, of which no copy in
Greek was previously known to exist.

After discovery, diplomacy. Without much difficulty,
apparently, Tischendorf persuaded the monks to let him
have the manuscript sent to Cairo, where a first transcript
was made ; but some time elapsed before he could
induce them to part altogether with their property.
Ultimately, however, he prevailed upon them to present it
to the Tsar, the great protector of the Greek Church and
his own immediate patron ; and in October 1859 he had
the satisfaction of carrying his treasure to St. Petersburg,

where, in the Imperial Library, it has since found its
permanent home. As an acknowledgment of the gift, the
Imperial Government made a present of 7000 roubles to
the convent of Mount Sinai and 2000 to that of Mount
Tabor. A preliminary account of the MS. was issued by
Tischendorf in 1860, and at the end of 1862 the
complete MS. was published in facsimile type.[1] A critical
edition of the New Testament for general use followed in
May 1863.

The Codex Sinaiticus, when complete, evidently contained the whole of the Greek Bible ; but much of the
Old Testament had disappeared before Tischendorf's discovery of it. Part may have perished only shortly before
his first visit to Sinai, through the fate from which he
rescued the leaves which now form the Codex Friderico-
Augustanus at Leipzig ; but the original mutilation was
of much earlier date, since fragments were found to have
been used in the bindings of other MSS.[2] The details of
the Old Testament portion of the MS., however, do not
concern us here ; they may be found in the Prolegomena
to the Cambridge edition of the Septuagint by Professor
Swete. The New Testament is intact, and includes in
addition the non-canonical books known as the Epistle of
Barnabas and the Shepherd of Hermas, the latter being
incomplete. It is written on very thin vellum of excellent
quality, prepared from the skins of antelopes or asses,
arranged (as a rule) in quaternions of four sheets (= eight
leaves or sixteen pages). Each page measures 15 inches
by $13\frac{1}{2}$, and there are signs that they were originally
larger, but have suffered from the binders' shears. Each
page contains four narrow columns of writing,[3] about $2\frac{1}{2}$
inches in width, and consisting of 48 lines. There are no
enlarged initials, but the first letter of a paragraph pro-
jects slightly into the left-hand margin. There are no

---

[1] Some specimens of the edition were sent to the Exhibition of 1862 in
London, several months before the appearance of the complete work.

[2] These were discovered by Bishop Porphyry on his visit to Sinai in 1845.

[3] Except in the poetical books of the Old Testament, where there are only
two columns to the page.

accents, and punctuation by the first hand is rare, but the text is divided into short paragraphs, and the remainder of a line in which a paragraph ends is left blank. The writing is a rather large uncial, larger than is found in any but a very few papyri, but not so large as uncials subsequently became on vellum. In width of column and in shape of writing the Codex Sinaiticus recalls the best literary papyri of the first and second centuries; and the resemblance is increased when, instead of a single page, the open codex itself is seen, since the two pages shown side by side, with their eight narrow columns, present very much the appearance of a papyrus roll.

According to Tischendorf, the original text of the MS. was written by four different scribes, one of whom (in addition to part of the Old Testament) wrote the whole of the New Testament except seven leaves [1] and the "Shepherd." The writer to whom these latter portions were due, besides writing the books of Tobit and Judith in the Old Testament, also corrected the New Testament throughout; and it may reasonably be presumed that the appearance of his hand in the seven leaves named is due to the corrections needed in the original pages being of such a kind or extent that he found it advisable to rewrite them. The corrections by this hand, together with some others which appear to be about coeval with the MS., are indicated in critical editions by the sign $\aleph^a$. Tischendorf (and on such a point no one can have an opinion who has not minutely examined the original MS.) distinguishes five other correctors of some importance: $\aleph^b$, whose labours have been directed to orthographical matters, such as accents and stops, and who appears to have tired of his work before he reached the end of the first Gospel; $\aleph^{ca}$ and $\aleph^{cb}$, correctors nearly contemporary with one another, and probably of the seventh century,

---

[1] Two leaves in Matthew, the last leaf of Mark and the first of Luke, a leaf from 1 Thess., and a leaf from Hebrews, and the beginning of the Apocalypse. The six first-named leaves form three sheets, or attached pairs of leaves. As stated below, Tischendorf believed the scribe of these leaves to be identical with the scribe of the Codex Vaticanus (B).

both active in the Gospels (where, however, they clearly used different texts), but only ℵ[ca] appearing subsequently,[1] except in the Epistle of Barnabas, which is touched only by ℵ[cb]; ℵ[cc], a slightly later corrector, who apparently used the MS. for purposes of study, and indicates his admiration of various passages; and ℵ[d], who restored faded portions of the text, with occasional notes of various readings, about the eighth century. Later notes are few, and unimportant.

In connexion with the different hands of this MS. an important remark is made by Tischendorf, to the effect that the scribe who wrote the seven leaves above mentioned (together with Tobit, Judith, and Hermas) is identical with the scribe of the New Testament in the Codex Vaticanus (B). The importance of this fact, if it be true, lies in the identity of time and place which it establishes beyond reasonable doubt for these two great codices. *Prima facie*, the identification does not seem probable. The hand of the seven leaves is not strikingly like that of B; indeed, so far as can be judged from facsimiles,[2] it resembles it less than it does the remaining hands of ℵ. Tischendorf's conclusion, however, rested upon subtler arguments than this.[3] He pointed out that in ℵ ι is constantly written for ει, while in B ει is as constantly written for ι: B regularly has Ιωανης, ℵ Ιωαννης: B writes υἱός, ἄνθρωπος, οὐρανός at full length, while ℵ

---

[1] ℵ[ca] is a corrector of considerable importance. At the end of Esther is a note in his hand stating that the MS. had been collated with a very early copy, which itself had been corrected by the hand of the holy martyr Pamphilus. Pamphilus was the disciple of Origen, co-editor with Eusebius of a text of the Septuagint embodying the results of Origen's labours, and founder of a library at Caesarea which was the centre of textual study of the Scriptures, initiated and inspired by Origen. Copies of Origen's works were the special objects of Pamphilus' zeal as a librarian (Jerome, *Ep.* cxli.). Bousset (*Textkritische Studien zum N.T.*, in Harnack and Gebhardt's *Texte und Untersuchungen*, xi. 4) has examined the statement in question, and found it confirmed by the fact that the variants introduced by ℵ[ca] agree with what we know from other sources of the text of Pamphilus' codex.

[2] Dean Burgon procured photographs of four pages of ℵ, one of which (containing the end of St. Mark, cf. Plate III.) belongs to the seven leaves in question; and a few other photographs are also available (e.g. *Pal. Soc.* i. 105). It is greatly to be desired, however, that a complete photographic facsimile may be made of this MS., as has been done in the case of A, B, and D.

[3] See his *Novum Testamentum Vaticanum* (1867), p. xxi.

PLATE III.

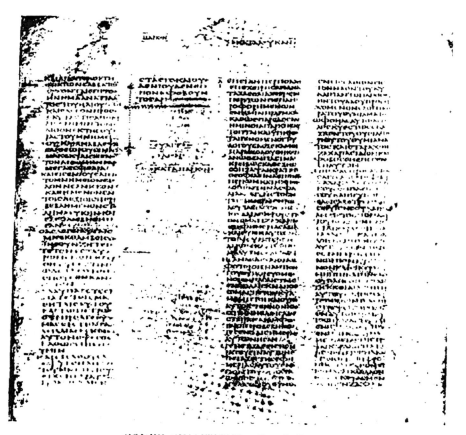

CODEX SINAITICUS. Fourth Century.

(Scale 3 : 8. The page shown contains Mark xvi. 2-Luke i. 18, the last twelve verses
of St. Mark being omitted. This is one of the pages written by the corrector,
whom Tischendorf believes to be identical with the scribe of the Codex Vaticanus.)

abbreviates them ; and in all these points the scribe of the seven leaves in א follows the usage of B. The method of punctuation in the seven leaves is the same as in B, while in the rest of א it is different. Tischendorf likewise points to the two dots which indicate the end of St. Mark in א, and which are also found at the ends of books in B ; but as they occur also at the end of St. John in א the argument is not conclusive. Taken altogether, these similarities are certainly striking, and have proved sufficient to satisfy such critics as Hort and Scrivener. Without an examination of א itself, or at least of a complete photographic facsimile, it is impossible to express a decided opinion, and much weight must be allowed to Tischendorf's judgment, since he alone has minutely examined the original MS. At the same time it is difficult to accept it as certain. It seems unlikely that the scribe of B, when he came to correct א, should have so modified and enlarged his hand as to make it resemble the general appearance of א ; and there are minute differences in the formation of certain letters (e.g. ϵ, ζ, χ) which tell against the identity. A curious habit of B, of writing M near the end of a line (when space had to be economised) in the Egyptian form (ᴎ), recurs in the seven leaves of א, and might seem to be a decisive confirmation of Tischendorf's theory, were it not that it also appears in the other leaves of א ; so that it rather leads one to mistrust the cogency of other similarities in small details, which may represent the usage of a school or locality rather than that of an individual. It must be admitted that, until a fresh examination of א is undertaken by a competent palaeographer, the opinion of Tischendorf holds the field ; but it is much to be desired that such a re-examination should be made.

Palaeographers are generally agreed in assigning the original writing of the manuscript to the fourth century ; but as the matter is not one upon which demonstrative evidence exists, it may be as well to indicate the considerations by which the dates of this and other early

vellum uncials are fixed.   It is only in a few of the latest
uncial manuscripts that the date of production is expressly
stated ; the earliest is the Uspensky Psalter of the year
862.   For earlier manuscripts it is necessary to rely upon
circumstantial evidence, and to reason back from points
which may be regarded as fairly certain to those which
are less so.   A trained palaeographer will learn to distinguish the *relative* antiquity of different writings ; and thus,
by allowing a reasonable space of time for each stage of
development, it is possible to arrive at approximate dates
in cases in which there is nothing but palaeographical
evidence to go upon.   A copy of Dioscorides, at Vienna,
is known to have been written for Juliana, daughter of
Flavius Anicius Olybrius, Emperor of the West in 472, and
this supplies us with an approximately dated example of
writing about the beginning of the sixth century.   Again,
the Codex Laudianus of the Acts must have been written
(as will be shown below) somewhere about the beginning
of the seventh century.   But it is clear that these manuscripts are not as early as several others which are known
to us.   They are less simple, more ornamented, showing
evidence of progress and development ; and therefore the
other MSS. must be assigned to earlier dates in proportion
to their degree of relative priority.   Thus, to take the
four oldest copies of the New Testament—the Sinaiticus,
Vaticanus, Alexandrinus, and Ephraemi—it is clear that all
of them are earlier than the above-mentioned Dioscorides ;
and it is likewise highly probable that the two first-named,
which are the simplest and least adorned of all, and
show a greater resemblance to papyrus MSS., are earlier
than the other two.   If, then, the Codex Alexandrinus
and the Codex Ephraemi be placed a generation or two
before the Dioscorides, about the middle of the fifth
century or even earlier, the Codex Sinaiticus and Vaticanus must be thrown back into the fourth century.
Collateral considerations, derived from the non-canonical
additions found in them, the evidence of early systems of
division of the sacred text, the comparison of early Latin

manuscripts of which the dates can be approximately ascertained, and so on, all tend to confirm this conclusion ; so that, though demonstrative evidence may not be forthcoming, there is very good reason to accept the general belief that these manuscripts are not later than the fourth century.

It may be asked, however, whether they may not be earlier ; and it may be pointed out that we now know uncial hands of a type bearing some resemblance to those of these manuscripts to have been in use on papyrus before the end of the first century.   There are, however, various considerations which forbid us to push back the great vellum uncials to anything like so early a date.   As has been shown in the first chapter, there is good reason to believe that for the first three centuries of our era papyrus held its own as the chief literary material ; and the circumstances of the Church make it highly improbable that such manuscripts as the Codex Sinaiticus or Vaticanus would be produced before the recognition of Christianity by Constantine.   Further, it is certain that the Codex Alexandrinus cannot have been written before the latter part of the fourth century, at earliest, since it contains (attached to the Psalter) compositions of Eusebius and Athanasius, who died in 340 and 373 respectively ; and the Sinaiticus and Vaticanus cannot be separated from the Alexandrinus by any very great gap.   In the case of the Sinaiticus evidence to the same effect is furnished by the fact that it bears in its margins the section numbers compiled for the Gospels by Eusebius, who, as just stated, died in 340.[1]   It is true that they are not inserted by the first hand ; but it is clear that they are not of much

---

[1] Eusebius divided each of the Gospels into sections, which he numbered, St. Matthew containing 355, St. Mark 236, St. Luke 342, and St. John 232. He then compiled canons, or tables, placing in parallel columns the numbers of those sections in each Gospel which contain descriptions of the same event. These tables consequently serve the purpose of a harmony of the Gospels, without the labour of transcribing all the passages at full length.   Thus one table gives, in four parallel columns, references to incidents described in all four Gospels ; three, of three columns, give those common to three Gospels (the combination Mark, Luke, John does not occur); five, of two columns, give those common to two Gospels (the combination Mark, John does not

later date, since they are omitted from two of the leaves
supplied by the corrector אᵃ (see above, p. 51), who was
contemporary with the original scribe.   The section numbers must therefore have been inserted throughout the
Gospels before these two leaves were re-written by the
corrector ; and consequently the MS. as a whole must, at
the very least, be later than the date at which Eusebius
devised his system of section numeration.[1]   All the indications, therefore, point the same way ; and though
precise accuracy is not obtainable with the existing
evidence, it is clear that the Codex Sinaiticus cannot be
much earlier than the second half of the fourth century,
while it can hardly be materially later.

A problem of considerable interest, if only it could be
plausibly solved, is that of the place of origin of this MS. ;
but it will be convenient to defer the consideration of it
until we come to speak of the Codex Vaticanus.   If
Tischendorf's opinion as to the identity of the corrector
of א and the scribe of B be true, it is more than probable
that the two MSS. were written in the same place ; and
in any case the similarity of text suggests at least the
possibility of a community of origin.   For the present,
then, it will be sufficient to state that, while Hort is
inclined to assign it to Rome, Ceriani to southern Italy,
and others to Egypt, the opinion most generally held
now would associate it with Caesarea and the library of
Pamphilus in that place.

The character of the text contained in the Codex
Sinaiticus cannot be fully investigated here ; but it may

occur) ; while one, of one column, gives the passages peculiar to each evangelist.
These tables are very commonly prefixed to manuscripts of the Gospels, while
the section numbers, with a reference to the number of the table to which each
section belongs, are given in the margins of the text (often with the numbers of
the corresponding sections in the other Gospels, which really dispenses with the
necessity of a reference to the tables).   Eusebius' section-division was based
on a harmony of the Gospels (now lost) by Ammonius of Alexandria, in which,
the Gospel of St. Matthew being taken as a standard, the corresponding sections
in the other Gospels were written down in parallel columns ; and hence, through
a misunderstanding of the words in which Eusebius expresses his indebtedness,
the sections are commonly spoken of as the *Ammonian sections*, while the tables
are called the *Eusebian canons*.

[1] See note by Dean Gwynn in Scrivener, i. 94.

be said broadly that it is one of the principal representatives of what has been called above the β-text, though with not infrequent traces of the influence of the δ-text. Tischendorf's seventh edition of the Greek Testament was issued in 1859, a few months before his discovery of the Codex Sinaiticus, and while the Codex Vaticanus was still practically unknown to scholars. This edition was consequently based mainly upon authorities of the a-type, agreeing substantially with the Textus Receptus ; but his eighth edition, published ten years later, was prepared under the influence of these two great fourth-century codices, and it has been computed that it differs from its predecessor in more than 3000 places.[1] The Sinaitic and Vatican manuscripts are, in fact, the two great champions of the β-text, and it is primarily (though not by any means entirely) to their influence that the textual differences between our Authorised and Revised Versions are due. It may be useful to indicate a few of the more important passages in which the Codex Sinaiticus departs from the Textus Receptus. In Matt. i. 25 it omits τὸν πρωτότοκον (with B and Z) ; in Matt. v. 44 it omits εὐλογεῖτε τοὺς καταρωμένους ὑμᾶς, καλῶς ποιεῖτε τοὺς μισοῦντας ὑμᾶς (with B) ; in Matt. vi. 13 it omits the doxology of the Lord's Prayer (with BDZ) ; it omits Matt. xii. 47 (with BLΓ ; ℵᵃ inserts the verse) ; it omits Matt. xvi. 2, 3 (ὀψίας ... δύνασθε), with B and a few other uncials ; it omits Matt. xvii. 21 (with B) ; it omits Matt. xviii. 11 (with BL) ; it has the Revised Version reading in Matt. xix. 17 (with BDL) ; in Matt. xxiv. 36 it adds οὐδὲ ὁ υἱός (with BD ; ℵᶜᵃ has cancelled the words) ; in Matt. xxvii. 49 it adds the incident of the piercing of our Lord's side (with BCLΓ). In St. Mark it omits υἱοῦ τοῦ Θεοῦ at i. 1 (here departing from B and being corrected by ℵᵃ) ; at vi. 20 it reads πολλὰ ἠπόρει for πολλὰ ἐποίει (with BL) ; it omits ix. 44, 46 (with BCLΔ), and the end of 49 with BLΔ ; it omits the last twelve verses of the Gospel (with B). In St. Luke it

---

[1] Scrivener, ii. 283.

reads εὐδοκίας for εὐδοκία in ii. 14 (with ABD); it omits δευτεροπρώτῳ in vi. 1 (with BL); in x. 42 it reads ὀλίγων δέ ἐστι χρεία ἢ ἑνός (with BC²L); in xi. 2-4 it has the shortened version of the Lord's Prayer which appears in the Revised Version (with BL); in xxii. 43, 44 it has the incident of the Bloody Sweat (with most uncials, but against ABRT; another hand, which Tischendorf takes to be אª, has enclosed the passage with marks of omission); in xxiii. 34 it has the word from the Cross, "Father, forgive them" (with most uncials, but against BD); in xxiii. 45 it has τοῦ ἡλίου ἐκλείποντος instead of καὶ ἐσκοτίσθη ὁ ἥλιος (with BCL); in xxiv. 51 it omits καὶ ἀνεφέρετο εἰς τὸν οὐρανόν (with D). In John i. 18 it has μονογενὴς Θεός for ὁ μονογενὴς υἱός (with BCL); in ii. 3 it reads οἶνον οὐκ εἶχον, ὅτι συνετελέσθη ὁ οἶνος τοῦ γάμου (without support from any Greek MS.); in iii. 13 it omits ὁ ὢν ἐν τῷ οὐρανῷ (with BL); in v. 3, 4 it omits ἐκδεχομένων τὴν τοῦ ὕδατος κίνησιν (with ABCL), and the whole mention of the angel (ἄγγελος . . . νοσήματι) with BCD; in vi. 69 it reads ὁ ἅγιος τοῦ Θεοῦ instead of ὁ χριστὸς ὁ υἱὸς τοῦ Θεοῦ τοῦ ζῶντος (with BCDL); it omits the incident of the woman taken in adultery (with all the principal uncials); and (alone of all manuscripts) it omits the last verse of the Gospel. These examples from the four Gospels may suffice to show something of the character of this manuscript; the bearing and value of its testimony must be considered later, in connexion with that of the other witnesses, who now remain to be examined.

A. **Codex Alexandrinus** (Plate IV.).—In contradistinction to א, this has been the longest and best known of the early uncial copies of the Greek Bible. Its original home appears to have been in Alexandria, and thence it was brought to Constantinople by Cyril Lucar in 1621, on his transference from the patriarchate of Alexandria to that of Constantinople. By Lucar it was offered as a gift to James I. of England, through the intermediary of Sir Thomas Roe, the English ambassador to the court of the Sultan ; but James having died before the gift took effect, it was actually received by Charles I. in 1627, and deposited by him in the Royal Library, whereby, when George II. in 1757 presented that Library to the nation, it ultimately passed into the possession of the British Museum. The Epistles of Clement, which are attached to the New Testament (and of which at that time no other copy was known), were promptly published in 1633 by Patrick Young, the Royal Librarian; the Old Testament was edited by Grabe in 1707-20, and the New Testament by Woide in 1786. Previously to this date the text had been repeatedly collated by various editors of the New Testament (first for Walton's Polyglot in 1657, then for Mill's great edition in 1707), so that its contents were already well known. Woide's edition was reproduced in a handier form by B. H. Cowper in 1860, and in 1879 a definitive publication was reached by the issue of a photographic facsimile under the editorship of Mr. (now Sir) E. Maunde Thompson, the present Director of the British Museum.[1]

In its present binding, bearing the royal arms of Charles I., the Codex Alexandrinus consists of four volumes of moderate quarto size ; but originally it formed a single volume of considerable thickness. It consists of 773 leaves[2] of thin vellum (so thin that in many places the ink has worn completely through it), measuring $12\frac{3}{4}$ inches by 10 inches, and written in a firm and fairly large square uncial hand, with two columns to the page. New paragraphs are marked by enlarged capital letters ; but if the end of a paragraph falls near the beginning of a line,

---

[1] The Old Testament was published in facsimile type, with elaborate prolegomena, in 1816-28 by the Rev. H. H. Baber, Keeper of Manuscripts in the British Museum ; and a photographic facsimile, edited by Mr. Maunde Thompson, followed that of the New Testament in 1881-83. It has also been collated throughout for the Cambridge Septuagint. Specimen facsimiles in *Pal. Soc.* i. 106, and in *Facsimiles of Biblical MSS. in the British Museum*, Pl. II. The fullest description of the MS. is contained in Thompson's introduction to the facsimile publication.

[2] Originally 822, allowing two leaves for the lost conclusion of the Second Epistle of Clement, and six for the Psalms of Solomon, in addition to the forty-one which are missing from parts of the Old and New Testament and 1 Clement, as described below.

the succeeding paragraph is commenced in the same line, the enlarged capital being reserved for the first letter of the line that follows (see p. 43). Three different hands may be discerned in the original text of the New Testament, one having written Matthew, Mark, and most of the Pauline Epistles, the second Luke, John, Acts, the Catholic Epistles, and the first part of the Pauline Epistles (to 1 Cor. x. 8), and the third the Apocalypse and Clementine Epistles. Several correctors' hands have been employed upon the MS., but the only alterations that are of much importance are (1) those made by the original scribe (A^1), and especially (2) those made by the first corrector (A^a), who would appear to have been nearly or quite contemporary with the MS. Other corrections are very much fewer and less important.

When complete, the manuscript contained the whole of the Old and New Testaments, with the addition of the two Epistles of Clement of Rome and the Psalms of Solomon. The latter work has now completely disappeared from the MS., but its former presence is proved by the table of contents at the beginning, in which, however, its title is distinctly separated by a space from those of the canonical books. The Epistles of Clement, on the other hand, are included with the canonical books, following the Apocalypse in the list of contents without break or distinction. The latter part of the (so-called) Second Epistle of Clement has disappeared along with the Psalms of Solomon; and one leaf of the First Epistle is also missing. In the New Testament nearly the whole of St. Matthew is lost (as far as chap. xxv. 6); also John vi. 50-viii. 52 (where it should be noted that a calculation of the extent of space missing shows that the section on the woman taken in adultery, vii. 53-viii. 11, can never have formed part of the MS.); and 2 Cor. iv. 13-xii. 6.

In point of age, the date usually assigned to the Codex Alexandrinus is the fifth century; and unless more precise evidence should come to light, it is not likely that this estimate will be disturbed. A superior limit is given

PLATE IV.

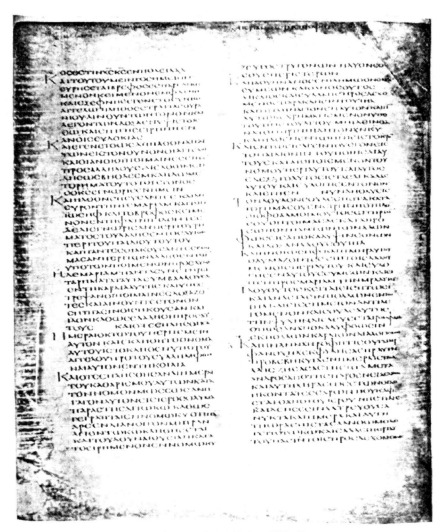

CODEX ALEXANDRINUS.   Fifth Century.

(Scale 2 : 5.   The page shown contains Luke ii. 11-38, showing the reading ἐν ἀνθρώποις εὐδοκίας in verse 14, which is found also in ℵBD, the Old Latin and Vulgate versions, and in Origen and Irenaeus.)

To face p. 60.

by the fact (mentioned above) that it contains, prefixed to the Psalter, treatises by Eusebius, who died in 340, and Athanasius, who died in 373. It also contains the Eusebian canons and sections. The manuscript cannot, therefore, at the very earliest, have been written before the second half of the fourth century; but this is the date which has already been assigned on fairly good grounds to the Codex Sinaiticus, and although it is not necessary to separate the two manuscripts by any wide interval, there are indications that the Alexandrinus is the later of the two. The handwriting is firmer and heavier, less reminiscent of the papyrus type; the use of enlarged capital letters marks an advance; and the arrangement of the text in two columns to the page is also a later stage than the three columns of the Vaticanus (B) and the four of the Sinaiticus. If, therefore, we place the Alexandrinus in the first half of the fifth century, it is not likely that we shall be far wrong.

Its early history is partially revealed by inscriptions on its fly-leaves. A note by Cyril Lucar states that, according to tradition, it was written by Thecla, a noble lady of Egypt, shortly after the Council of Nicaea (A.D. 325), and that originally her name was inscribed at the end of the volume, but that the page had been lost through the mutilation of this part of the manuscript. The date is evidently too early, for reasons given above, but the rest of the tradition is plausible enough, save that the whole MS. was certainly not written by one hand. An Arabic note, of the thirteenth or fourteenth century, so far confirms it as to say that the MS. was written by "Thecla the martyr." Another Arabic note, signed by "Athanasius the humble" (probably the patriarch Athanasius III., who died about 1308), states that it was presented to the patriarchal cell of Alexandria; and a somewhat later Latin note assigns the gift to the year 1098, but without giving reasons for this assertion. In Alexandria, and in the possession of the patriarch, it certainly was at a later date, since Cyril Lucar brought it

thence to Europe; and all the evidence points to
its having been produced in or about that town. The
titles of some of the books, which have been inserted by
a writer slightly later than the original scribe, contain
forms of the letters a and μ which are characteristically
Coptic, and almost demonstrate a very early residence of
the MS. in Egypt. Further, in the Old Testament this
manuscript has a type of text which is by some scholars[1]
identified with that of the edition of the Septuagint by
Hesychius, which was prepared and circulated in Egypt;
while others,[2] who doubt the actual identification, at least
admit a close kinship. Thus, though demonstrative proof
is wanting, such indications as there are point to Alexandria as the place of production, while there is no
evidence in a contrary direction.

In character the text of the Codex Alexandrinus in
the New Testament presents a curious phenomenon; for
whereas in the Gospels it belongs emphatically to the a-
type, and indeed is the best representative of that family,
having the text in a purer form than that which appears
in our Textus Receptus, in the Acts and Epistles, and
still more in the Apocalypse, it belongs rather to the β-
type. The phenomenon is, of course, quite easy of explanation. When codices first superseded papyrus rolls,
and it became possible to unite all the books of the New
Testament in a single volume, the texts of different parts
of such volumes would necessarily be taken from different
rolls; and it might easily happen, as has been the case
here, that different books, or groups of books, would be
copied from rolls containing different types of text.
Thus in the MS. described below as Δ, the Gospel of St.
Mark has evidently been copied from an original of a
different family from that of the other three Gospels. It
must consequently be remembered that A in the
Gospels represents a different type of text from that
which it has in the rest of the New Testament.

[1] E.g. Ceriani (*De Codice Marchaliano*, 105, 106).
[2] E.g. Cornill (*Ezechiel*, 67 ff.).

B. **Codex Vaticanus** (Plate V.).—This is generally held to be both the oldest and the most valuable of all the manuscripts of the Greek Bible. Its modern home is, as its name implies, in the Vatican Library at Rome, and here it has been at least from 1481, since it appears (as a " Biblia in tribus columnis ex memb.") in a catalogue of that date.[1] It was thus in Europe a century and a half before the Alexandrinus, and nearly four centuries before the Sinaiticus, and yet it was later than either of these in becoming fully accessible to modern scholarship. During the greater part of that period scholars did not care to investigate it scientifically, and when at last they wished to do so, permission could not be obtained. A few readings from it were supplied to Erasmus by his correspondent Sepulveda, but too late for use in his editions of the New Testament. In 1669 a collation was made by Bartolocci, librarian of the Vatican ; but this was not published, and was never used until Scholz in 1819 found a copy of it in the Royal Library at Paris. Another was made in 1720 for Bentley by Mico, and revised by Rulotta ; but the former, which was imperfect, was not published until 1799, and the revision not until 1862, while a further collation by Birch in 1780 was quite incomplete. When the manuscript was carried to Paris by Napoleon, along with other treasures of the Vatican, it was examined by Hug, who first proclaimed its extreme age and great importance; but nothing more was done in the way of a complete publication of its contents before it returned to Italy, and then it was withdrawn from the use of foreign scholars. First-rate textual critics, such as Tischendorf and Tregelles, were barely allowed a sight of it, and only a few of its readings were grudgingly

---

[1] It is stated by Vercellone (*Dell' antichissimo codice Vaticano della Bibbia greca*, 1860) and repeated by Gregory (*Textkritik*, i. 35) that this entry occurs in the catalogue of 1475 ; but this catalogue has been printed in full by E. Müntz and P. Fabre (*La Bibliothèque du Vatican au xve Siècle*, 1887, 159-250), and it contains no Bible answering to this description. Vercellone's reference relates really to the catalogue of 1481 (Bibl. Vat. MS. Lat. 3952, f. 50), mentioned, but not printed, by Müntz and Fabre (p. 250). It would appear, therefore, that the MS. entered the Vatican between 1475 and 1481. I have to thank Dr. F. Spiro for verifying the above reference to the Vatican catalogue.

conceded to the world from time to time. The fact was that the Vatican had itself taken the publication of it in hand, and had had the text in type since 1838; but though the work was committed to a scholar of European reputation, Cardinal Mai, he executed it in so slovenly a way that it was held back from publication during his lifetime, while the two editions (large and small) which were issued after his death, in 1857 and 1859, were so inaccurate and so much at variance with one another as only to prove conclusively the necessity of having the work done over again. In 1866 Tischendorf obtained leave to examine it in passages as to which special doubt existed, and was able to work at it for forty-two hours in all—a time which would have been longer but for his own breach of contract in copying twenty pages in full instead of confining himself to an examination of isolated passages. Out of all the material then available, supplemented and corrected by his own labours, Tischendorf in 1867 produced an edition of the Vatican New Testament, which represented a great advance on all previous knowledge of the MS.; but in 1868 the Papal authorities themselves issued an edition of the New Testament, prepared by Vercellone and Cozza, which was followed in successive years by volumes containing the Old Testament. Finally, in 1889-90 all previous publications were superseded by a photographic facsimile of the whole MS., which renders its evidence available to all scholars, except so far as certain questions as to the distinction between the hands of correctors and the original scribe must always necessitate a reference to the original.[1]

The manuscript on which so much labour and so many searchings of heart have been spent is written on very fine vellum, said to be made from antelopes' skins. In shape it is square, the leaves measuring $10\frac{1}{2}$ inches by 10 inches, and ten leaves (or five sheets) making a quire.

---

[1] A specimen facsimile of a page may also be seen in *Pal. Soc.* i. 104, and partial or reduced facsimiles in many handbooks to the Bible.

PLATE V.

CODEX VATICANUS. Fourth Century.

(Scale 3 : 7. The page shown contains 2 Cor. iii. 1-iv. 6. Col. 2, ll. 33-36, show the untouched writing of the original scribe.)

To face p. 65

The writing is a small, neat uncial, distinctly recalling the papyrus hands of the first and second centuries, on which it appears to be modelled ; it has little of the heaviness which soon came to mark the style of writing upon vellum.   Unfortunately its appearance has been spoilt by a corrector, who thought it necessary to trace over every letter afresh, only sparing those which he regarded as incorrect and therefore better allowed to fade away.[1] There are three narrow columns to each page, a survival from the usage on papyrus, though not so marked as in the Sinaiticus.   There appear to be no accents, breathings, or stops by the first hand.   Corrections have been made by two hands—one a contemporary or nearly contemporary reviser (B²), while the other (B³), who retraced the whole, is placed by Tischendorf in the tenth or eleventh century.   The original scribe of the New Testament, as has been stated above (p. 52), is declared by Tischendorf to be identical with the corrector (ℵ^a) of the Sinaiticus.   He is different from the scribes of the Old Testament, of whom, according to the same scholar, there are two.

The Codex Vaticanus originally contained the whole of the Greek Bible, but has now lost Gen. i. 1-xlvi. 28, Psalms cv. 27-cxxxvii. 6 in the Old Testament, while the books of the Maccabees were never included in it ; in the New Testament the conclusion of the Epistle to the Hebrews (ch. ix. 14 to the end), the Pastoral Epistles of St. Paul, and the Apocalypse, are absent.   The Catholic Epistles follow the Acts, according to the common order in Greek MSS., and so have escaped destruction.

With regard to the date of the Vatican MS., there has been substantial agreement among palaeographers since Hug originally assigned it to the fourth century.   In simplicity of writing and the absence of ornament or of enlarged capitals, it presents features earlier in type than any of the other great vellum manuscripts ; and to this must be added the fact that its divisions of the text seem

---

[1] Four untouched lines may be seen on p. 1479 of the MS. (Plate V.).

F

to be earlier than any other. The Eusebian sections do not appear in it, but in place of them there is a different division of the Gospels, found only in one other MS. (Ξ); of these sections there are 170 in St. Matthew, 62 in St. Mark, 152 in St. Luke, and 80 in St. John. In the Acts there are two independent sets of sections, the earlier consisting of 36 sections, the later of 69; the second of these is also found in part in א. Similarly in the Catholic and Pauline Epistles there are two sets of sections. Since the Eusebian sections, when once they were introduced, rapidly spread into general acceptance, the divisions in B appear to be of earlier origin, and tend to show at least that the manuscript represents an old tradition. If Tischendorf is right in his identification of the scribe of the New Testament in the Vatican MS. with the corrector of the Sinaiticus, the two MSS. must be practically contemporaneous; and the reasons given above for assigning א to the fourth century are valid also for B. Unless future discoveries should seriously disturb the basis of our palaeographical knowledge, the position of the Vaticanus may be regarded as substantially fixed.[1]

It is far from being the same with respect to its place of origin, about which the most distinguished critics have disagreed. The Roman editors suggest Egypt—a suggestion also made by some of the earliest critics; Ceriani is in favour of southern Italy; Hort inclines to Rome;

---

[1] An attempt has been made by A. Rahlfs (*Nachrichten der königl. Gesellschaft der Wissenschaften zu Göttingen*, 1899, pp. 72 ff.) to fix the date of B more closely. He argues that it must have been written later than A.D. 367, because its contents correspond with the list of canonical books prescribed by Athanasius in his thirty-ninth Festal Letter, written in that year. Von Gebhardt, however (*Theologische Literaturzeitung*, 1899, col. 556), while admitting the probability of Athanasian influence to be shown by the coincidence, argues that B must have been written *before* 367, because the sharp distinction drawn by Athanasius between canonical books (κανονιζόμενα) and books recommended by the Fathers of the Church to be read (ἀναγιγνωσκόμενα) is not observed, the ἀναγιγνωσκόμενα (Wisdom, Ecclus., Esther, Judith, Tobit, in the Old Testament) being inserted among the canonical books in B without distinction. The New Testament ἀναγιγνωσκόμενα mentioned by Athanasius (the Didaché and Hermas) do not of course appear in B, since the end of the MS. is lost. The *data* are consequently too uncertain for any conclusion to be drawn with confidence. The most that can be said is that the contents of B rather tend to support a belief in its Egyptian origin.

Mr. Rendel Harris has pleaded hard for Caesarea, and for a close connexion, at least, with the library founded there by Pamphilus and Eusebius, and this view (which had already been propounded by Canon Cook and Scrivener) has found considerable favour of late years.

Some such connexion appears to be suggested by the following facts. The later chapter-division of the Acts in B (into sixty-nine chapters, made by a hand only slightly later than the first), which is also inserted in the margin of ℵ by a very early hand, appears to be based on the division adopted by Euthalius in his edition of the book,[1] made about the middle of the fourth century. Now the earliest extant MS. of this edition (Cod. H_3) contains a colophon stating that it was collated with a volume in the library of Caesarea written by Pamphilus himself. This colophon was very possibly copied from an earlier MS. (as is not unusual with such notes) ; and in that case we should have evidence that a very early copy (if not the archetype) of the Euthalian edition of the Acts was at Caesarea, whence its system of chapter-division may have been inserted into B and ℵ. Another MS. of this edition contains, in addition to the ordinary chapter-division of Euthalius, another division into thirty-six chapters which is identical with the *earlier* chapter-division in B. These coincidences do not *prove* a common residence at Caesarea for ℵ, B, and the Euthalian archetype, still less that ℵ and B were actually written there, but they point in that direction. Moreover, as already shown, excellent authorities believe that there are proofs of a community of origin between B and ℵ, and the

---

[1] Euthalius, bishop of an unknown place called Sulca, was the author of an edition of the Acts and Epistles in which the text was arranged colometrically (i.e. in short clauses, corresponding to pauses in the sense), and provided with prologues and chapter-summaries. Until recently he was supposed to have lived in the middle of the fifth century ; but Canon Armitage Robinson (*Euthaliana* in the Cambridge *Texts and Studies*, iii. 3, 1895) has shown good grounds for placing him a century earlier. Euthalius' chapter-division in the Acts was into forty chapters and forty-eight sub-sections, making a total of eighty-eight ; but Canon Robinson points out that some of the sub-section marks, being only asterisks or letters, might easily be dropped out or overlooked, and argues that the coincidence of the sixty-nine divisions in B with those of Euthalius is so general (though not universal), even in some rather unlikely divisions, as to point to a common origin.

note of the corrector of ℵ at the end of Esther (see p. 52 above) shows that in the seventh century at least that MS. was at Caesarea.   Further, the text of B in the Old Testament is held by competent critics, such as Hort and Cornill, to be substantially that which under- lies Origen's Hexapla edition, completed by him at Caesarea and issued as an independent work (apart from the other versions with which Origen associated it) by Eusebius and Pamphilus.   Dr. Gregory, the author of the Prolegomena to Tischendorf's last edition of the New Testament, is even disposed to regard B and ℵ as having been among the fifty MSS. prepared by Eusebius about 331 at Constantine's command for the churches of his new capital (and so also von Gebhardt); but there is not the least sign of either of them ever having been at Constantinople.   That there was some connexion between the MSS. and Caesarea seems fairly certain; but the arguments which prove it do not go so far as to show that this was actually their place of origin.   The fact that ℵ was collated with the MS. of Pamphilus so late as the seventh century seems to show that it was not originally written at Caesarea; otherwise it would surely have been collated earlier with so excellent an authority.   Origen's textual information was collected in Egypt, where he began the preparation of the Hexapla, rather than in Caesarea (the home only of his later life), and if B is in harmony with the text used by him it would be accounted for by the hypothesis that B was written in Egypt.   Indeed, if B and ℵ had been written at Caesarea, it is probable that in the Old Testament they would have contained the Eusebian edition of the Septuagint, which is not the case.   Further, it is noteworthy that the section numeration of the Pauline Epistles in B shows that it was copied from a manuscript in which the Epistle to the Hebrews was placed between Galatians and Ephesians; an arrangement which elsewhere occurs only in the Sahidic version, current in Upper Egypt.[1]

[1] Cf. Scrivener, i. 57.

A connexion with Egypt is also indicated by the fact that, as in the Codex Alexandrinus, the titles of some of the books contain letters of a distinctively Coptic character, especially the Coptic ϻ, which is used not only in titles, but also very frequently at the ends of lines, when space is to be economised.[1] The resemblance of the writing of both B and א to hands found in Egyptian papyri cannot be pressed, since we do not know enough about the contemporary hands outside Egypt to say if this resemblance is worth anything ; nor is there any force in the argument derived from the fact that two damaged leaves have been patched with papyrus, since papyrus was still used out of Egypt in and after the fourth century. On the whole, it can only be said that the evidence does not admit of a decisive verdict. There is fair evidence of a connexion with the textual school of Caesarea, which does not exclude an actual origin in Egypt, from which the school of Caesarea took its rise ; and other evidence is rather in favour of such an origin. The evidence in favour of Rome, on which Hort relied, has only been summarily stated, but it does not appear to be very weighty.[2]

Of the character of the text of B much will have to be said in a later chapter. Here it must be sufficient to say that it is the foremost champion of what we have called the β-text, and to refer to some examples of its readings, generally in common with א, which have been given above (p. 57). It differs from the α-text especially

---

[1] It must be remembered, however, that, although this form of μ was undoubtedly used in Egypt, we cannot affirm, for want of evidence, that its use was confined to that country. Still, its frequent occurrence in B is *prima facie* more favourable to an eastern than a western origin for that MS., and consequently for א too (in which it likewise occurs, though less frequently).

[2] Hort (*Introduction*, pp. 264–7) rests his argument mainly on (1) certain spellings of proper names, such as Ἰσάκ and Ἰστραήλ, which show Western or Latin influence ; (2) the fact that the chapter-division in the Acts common to א and B (see above, p. 66) occurs in no other Greek MSS., but is found in several MSS. of the Latin Vulgate, including the Codex Amiatinus. But this argument is placed in quite a different light by Canon Armitage Robinson (*Euthaliana*, pp. 42, 101), who connects this system with the divisions of Euthalius, and suggests that it was introduced into the Vulgate by Jerome himself, as a result of his studies at Caesarea. If one basis of Hort's belief be thus removed, the other is too slight by itself to give it much support.

in the Gospels, and most notably in the way of omissions. When it was first examined, the witnesses that supported it to any great extent were few. Since that time they have increased in number and in variety of testimony; but the examination of this evidence is the central problem of New Testament textual criticism, and must be reserved until the remaining manuscripts and versions have been described.

B_2. **Codex Vaticanus 2066.**— B being defective as regards the Apocalypse, this letter is for that part of the New Testament attached to another MS., also in the Vatican Library, but of less venerable antiquity than its namesake. It is a manuscript of the eighth century, written in somewhat sloping uncials. It was surreptitiously collated by Tischendorf in 1843, published by Mai along with B in 1857, and republished by Tischendorf in 1869. As there are only six uncial copies of the Apocalypse in existence ($אAB_2CP_2ג$), it is of some value, though less important than אAC, and more akin to the cursive MSS. than P_2. Of ג practically nothing is known.

C. **Codex Ephraemi rescriptus.**—As the epithet of its Latin title denotes, this manuscript is a *palimpsest*; that is, the original writing has been more or less completely removed, by washing or scraping, from the surface of the vellum, which has then been used again to receive the transcript of another work. This was a device employed not infrequently at times when vellum was scarce, and not a few manuscripts have come down to us with such double layers of writing, in which, strange as it might appear to the authors of the intruding treatises, the earlier work is almost invariably the one which interests us most at the present day. Perhaps the most valuable of such manuscripts are those which contain the *Institutes* of Gaius and the *De Republica* of Cicero (discovered respectively in 1816 and 1822), since these works were otherwise wholly lost; but the best known of them is probably that which is now before us. It was brought from the East to Italy in the early days of the sixteenth century, when Greek scholars and Greek manuscripts found so warm a welcome in the West, and it became the property of the Medici family. With Catherine de' Medici it travelled from Italy to France, and so entered the Bibliothèque du Roi in Paris, which still (under its changed name of Bibliothèque Nationale) is its home. The first complete collation of the portions of the New Testament contained in it was made for Bentley in 1716 by Wetstein; but this was superseded by the complete publication undertaken by Tischendorf— of the New Testament in 1843 and the Old in 1845. It has been questioned whether his statements as to the various correctors who have worked upon the MS. are always to be trusted; but only an expert who had had something like Tischendorf's experience in the decipherment of uncial MSS. can speak on such a point with any authority; and the precise assignment of corrections is seldom an easy task, even apart from the special difficulties which attend the decipherment of a palimpsest.

Like the three manuscripts already described, the Codex Ephraemi originally contained the whole Greek Bible; but it only survives now in a sadly mutilated form, thanks to the disaster which befell it in the twelfth century, when the original writing was defaced, much of the volume thrown away, and the rest used to receive a Greek version of some treatises by St. Ephraem of Syria. The MS. consists now of 209 leaves, of which 64 contain portions of the Old Testament, while 145 belong to the New. Every book of the New Testament, except 2 Thess. and 2 John, is represented in it, but none is perfect.[1] When complete, the New Testament would have occupied 238 leaves. The leaves measure $12\frac{1}{4}$ inches by 9 inches, and are composed of good, but not especially fine, vellum. Each page contains but one column of writing (thus showing a step in advance since the double

---

[1] For an exact list of the contents of the MS. in its present state, so far as relates to the New Testament, see Scrivener, i. 121, note, or Gregory, p. 367. Specimen facsimile in Omont, *Manuscrits grecs de la Bibliothèque Nationale*, Pl. III.

columns of the Alexandrinus, though the choice of one column or two to the page continued to some extent open till the end of the manuscript period), in a somewhat thick uncial hand of about the same size and character as the Alexandrinus. The superimposed writing having been arranged in double columns, it is often possible to get a fairly clear view of the original hand between the two columns ; but elsewhere it is very difficult, and often impossible, to decipher it. From its resemblance to the Codex Alexandrinus, it may be assigned to about the same date, namely, the first half of the fifth century. Enlarged initials are used, and the Eusebian (or Ammonian) sections are marked in the margins. Tischendorf distinguishes two correctors, one of the sixth, the other of the ninth century, the latter being responsible for the insertion of accents and breathings.

The text of C is more mixed in character than that of any other important MS. It belongs consistently neither to the a-type nor to the β-type. Its transcriber (or the transcriber of some ancestor of it) must have had texts of both kinds before him. Consequently, though its age makes its evidence important, as showing what readings were extant at that early date, it is not of much value in estimating the weight of testimony with regard to particular readings. Hort [1] notices that certain displacements in the text of the Apocalypse show that it was copied from a MS. in which some pages had been disarranged, and that these pages must have been of very small size, only equal to about a quarter of a page of C itself. It cannot, therefore, have been a volume intended for church or library use, but must have been a small pocket volume, either of vellum (such as the cheap copies of literary works which we know were written on vellum in Martial's day, when that material was held in less estimation than papyrus), or, perhaps more probably, of papyrus, such as we have reason to know, from fragments recently discovered, existed during the third and fourth

---

[1] *Introduction*, p. 268.

centuries.[1] In either case it would not be likely to be a copy of high authority with regard to its text, having been intended primarily for private use, and therefore written probably with less attention to precise accuracy of text. How far the same is the case with some other of our earliest copies, we are not in a position to affirm.

D. **Codex Bezae** (Plate VI.).—the most peculiar, and in some respects the most remarkable, of the Greek MSS. of the New Testament. Its modern history begins in 1562, when Theodore Beza, the great biblical scholar of the later Reformation period, obtained it from the monastery of St. Irenaeus at Lyons, as the result of the sack of that city by the Huguenots. It had, however, already been collated by some unknown scholar, by whom a large number of its readings were communicated to Robert Stephanus, which appear in the margin of his Greek Testament of 1550. Since Stephanus speaks of its having been collated for him in Italy, it has been supposed that it was the very ancient copy of the Greek Bible which was taken to the Council of Trent in 1546 as evidence in support of the reading "Si eum volo sic manere" ($\grave{\epsilon}\grave{\alpha}\nu$ $\alpha\grave{\upsilon}\tau\grave{o}\nu$ $\theta\acute{\epsilon}\lambda\omega$ $\mu\acute{\epsilon}\nu\epsilon\iota\nu$ $o\acute{\upsilon}\tau\omega\varsigma$) in John xxi. 22; but this can hardly be regarded as certain. Beza used it slightly in the later editions of his Greek Testament, and in 1581 presented it to the University of Cambridge, in whose keeping it has remained ever since. Considerable use was made of it by Walton, Mill, and Wetstein, and in 1793 a complete edition of it was prepared and issued by Dr. Thomas Kipling for the University of Cambridge. It was again edited by Scrivener in 1864, and quite recently (in 1899) a photographic facsimile of the whole MS. has been issued by the Cambridge University Press. The university has thus always been forward to allow scholars the use of its great treasure, and to make it readily accessible to those who may not be within reach of its library. The peculiar character of the MS. has

---

[1] E.g. the "Logia" and St. Matthew fragments among the Oxyrhynchus papyri; and see above, p. 34.

naturally attracted much attention, and within the last ten years no less than three important studies of its text have been published by Rendel Harris, Chase, and Weiss,[1] to the contents of which we shall have to refer later.

The differences between this manuscript and the four which have been already described begin with its external appearance. They were all copies of the entire Greek Bible ; but there is no sign that D ever contained the Old Testament, and in its present state it includes only the Gospels and Acts (with considerable mutilations, notably the conclusion of the Acts, from ch. xxii. 29 to the end), and a small fragment of the Catholic Epistles (3 John 11–15, in the Latin version), which originally stood between the Gospels and Acts, not, as usual, after the Acts. The Gospels are arranged in the order very early adopted in the Western Church, viz. Matthew, John, Luke, Mark. But a more striking difference is the fact that D contains a Latin text of the New Testament as well as the Greek. The two versions stand side by side, on opposite pages, the Greek holding the place of honour on the left. The pages are somewhat smaller than those of the manuscripts already described, measuring 10 inches by 8. The writing on each page occupies a single column, but is not written in continuous paragraphs but in κῶλα, or short clauses divided according to the sense ; in this way the corresponding words in the two languages are kept more strictly parallel. It is written in rather large uncials, which show a curious resemblance between the Latin and the Greek. No less than nine correctors have been distinguished, ranging from the date of the MS. itself to the twelfth century or later. For the age of the original writing we have the advantage of comparison with both Greek and Latin MSS., from which it is evident that it may be assigned with fair confidence to the sixth century.

[1] Rendel Harris, *A Study of Codex Bezae* (Cambridge, *Texts and Studies*, ii. 1, 1891) ; Chase, *The Old Syriac Element in the Text of Codex Bezae* (London, 1893) ; Weiss, *Der Codex D in der Apostelgeschichte* (*Texte und Untersuchungen*, Neue Folge ii. 1, Leipzig, 1897). Specimen facsimile in *Pal. Soc.* i. 14, 15.

PLATE VI.

CODEX BEZAE. Sixth Century.

(Scale 3 : 8.   The pages shown contain Acts xv. 29-38, beginning with the additional clause inserted in the decision of the Council of Jerusalem in this MS. and in a few minuscules, the Sahidic and Ethiopic versions, and in Irenaeus and Cyprian.)

To face p. 74.

The existence of a Latin text is in itself sufficient evidence that the MS. was originally written in the West. Its presence in the south of France suggests the possibility that this was also its first home; and in such a country, where the Church had been founded by missionaries from Asia Minor, who spoke Greek, but was planted among provincials who spoke Latin, the existence of bilingual copies of the Bible is quite intelligible. Further, it is said that the Latin text of Codex Bezae agrees with the Bible quotations of Irenaeus, even in obvious errors of transcription,[1] which goes far to confirm its connexion with the Church which Irenaeus founded. The main difficulty in the way of this theory is the uncertainty whether bilingual manuscripts would have continued to be produced in southern France as late as the sixth century. It is known that the Greek language and liturgy continued in use there to a relatively late period, but there is no definite evidence carrying them down as late as this. Mr. Brightman,[2] examining the question from the liturgical point of view, and with reference to certain lection-marks which have been supposed to indicate a Gallican use, rejects such an opinion altogether, declaring the lections in question to be of the Byzantine use, and would refer the MS. rather to southern Italy, where the Byzantine rite was regularly used. There is, of course, no difficulty in supposing a bilingual manuscript to have been produced in Magna Graecia; on the contrary, the chief objection to this theory is that Greek was so well known in that region that we should have expected the Greek part of the MS. to be better written than it is. In point of fact, the Greek has the appearance of having been written by a scribe whose native language was Latin; and some of the mistakes which he makes (e.g. writing *l* for λ or *c* for κ) point in the same direction. We want a locality where Latin was the prevalent tongue, but Greek was still sufficiently known to make it desirable

---

[1] Nestle, *Introduction,* Eng. Tr., p. 65.
[2] *Journal of Theological Studies*, i. 446 ff.

to have copies of the Scriptures in their original language as well as in a translation. Southern France may have been such a locality, but clear evidence is lacking for this particular period ; some parts of northern Italy may have been such localities,[1] but we know too little about them ; Sardinia was such a locality, as is shown by the Codex Laudianus (E₂) having had its home, and probably its origin, there ; but southern Italy hardly seems to answer the requirements. The problem, therefore, of the place of origin of D must remain for the present unsolved.

The text of D differs widely from that of any other Greek MS. of the Bible, finding its chief affinities in the Old Syriac and Old Latin versions, described below. It contains remarkable additions to the normal text, such as the passage which it inserts in place of Luke vi. 5 (τῇ αὐτῇ ἡμέρᾳ θεασάμενός τινα ἐργαζόμενον τῷ σαββάτῳ, εἶπεν αὐτῷ· ἄνθρωπε, εἰ μὲν οἶδας ὃ ποιεῖς, μακάριος εἶ· εἰ δὲ μὴ οἶδας, ἐπικατάρατος καὶ παραβάτης εἶ τοῦ νόμου), and a long passage after Matt. xx. 28 (to the same general effect as Luke xiv. 8-11). At the end of St. Luke it has also a remarkable series of omissions, leaving out Luke xxii. 20 (the second mention of the cup in the institution of the Sacrament of the Lord's Supper), xxiv. 12 (Peter's entry into the sepulchre), 36 ("and saith unto them, Peace be unto you"), 40 ("and when he had thus spoken, he showed them his hands and his feet"), 51 ("and was carried up into heaven"), besides minor omissions. In addition there are repeated variants, too many to enumerate here, throughout the text of the Gospels, while in the Acts the variations are so frequent and so remarkable as to give rise to the theory that it represents a different edition of the book, though equally issued by St. Luke himself.

The discussion of this theory, and of the whole type of text of which D is the chief Greek example, and which we have called the δ-text, must be reserved to a later stage, when all the data of the problem have been stated ; but

[1] Prof. Sanday, for instance, has tentatively suggested Ravenna.

there is one subject of controversy which applies to D alone, and which must therefore be mentioned here. This has to do with the relation between the Greek and the Latin texts contained in it. It is clear that these are not wholly independent of one another, so that each would have substantial value, the one as a copy of the Greek Testament, the other as a copy of the Latin version. In many small details, such as the order of words and clauses, the texts have evidently been assimilated to one another; and it is a question whether this assimilation may not extend to some of the larger variants of which this MS. is full, and also whether the Greek has been assimilated to the Latin or *vice versa*. The older view, held by Mill and Wetstein, was that the Greek text had been assimilated to the Latin (in which case the Greek would cease to have independent value, and it might fairly be questioned whether this particular type of text ever existed in Greek at all). The great critic Griesbach, however, maintained the contrary thesis, that the Latin had been assimilated to the Greek; and this view has been generally held down to the present day, when the earlier opinion has been revived and elaborately defended by Mr. Rendel Harris.[1] He points out a number of instances in which small alterations (such as the omission or insertion of the parts of the verb $\epsilon\iota\mu\iota$) have been made in the Greek, in order to produce a more exact verbal parallelism with the Latin; and on the same principle he explains a considerable number of the more important variants of the manuscript. On the other hand Mr. Chase[2] refers these variants, or a large proportion of them, to an original Syriac influence. He would trace back the ancestry of the text of Codex Bezae to a bilingual Greek and Syriac manuscript, produced probably at Antioch, where Greek and Syriac influences met; and he explains many of the readings of Codex Bezae as due

---

[1] *A Study of Codex Bezae* (Cambridge, 1891).
[2] *The Old Syriac Element in the Text of Codex Bezae* (London, 1893); *The Syro-Latin Text of the Gospels* (1895).

to translations from the Syriac. This would account for one of the remarkable characteristics of its text, namely, the apparently aimless substitution of synonyms for words found in the normal Greek text; such as κύριος for θεός, or *vice versa*, μνημεῖον for μνῆμα (Acts ii. 29), πολλούς for ἱκανούς (xiv. 21), τὸ μέσον τῆς νυκτός for τὸ μεσονύκτιον (xvi. 25), τῇ ἐπιούσῃ for τῇ ἑξῆς (xxi. 1), μετεπέμψατο for μετεκαλέσατο (xx. 17), εἶπεν for ἀπεφθέγξατο (ii. 14), εὐαγγελίζοντε (sc. -ται) for καταγγέλλουσιν (xvi. 17), καθεζόμενος for καθήμενος (iii. 10 ; the reverse in vi. 15), and many more of the same type.[1] How far the larger variants are to be explained in the same way is a point which must be considered later ; and even if Mr. Chase's view of the history of the Bezan text is correct, it would not remove the possibility of later accommodations of the Greek to the Latin, such as Mr. Rendel Harris argues for. On the other hand, Scrivener, whose acquaintance with the MS. was minute and extensive, maintains that the Latin is so sensibly accommodated to the Greek as to be deprived of all independent value.

The only possible conclusion derivable from this conflicting testimony, where the evidence on either side is separately convincing, is that assimilation has taken place from *both* sides ; and if this is so, there can be little doubt how the phenomenon is to be explained. The process must not be confined to the scribe of D alone, but must be extended back to some of its ancestors. When the New Testament was introduced into Western lands, it came in its original Greek shape, whence it was translated into Latin for the convenience of local converts ; and when copies were made in which this Latin version was put beside the Greek, it would naturally be assimilated to it in details. But as time went on, and such bilingual MSS. were copied by scribes to whom Latin was more familiar than Greek, it would naturally happen that the Latin version became the predominant partner in the combination, and that in small details, such as the exact parallelism of clauses, the

[1] Cf. Weiss, *Der Codex D in der Apostelgeschichte*, pp. 18 ff.

Greek was modified so as to suit it. Codex Bezae would therefore be a Latinising descendant of a Graecising ancestor ; and (especially if the Syriac element be admitted as an earlier ingredient) its unsupported evidence on purely verbal points will not be regarded as very authoritative. The larger variants, however, and those which are supported by other evidence, would not be affected by these considerations.

One other detail, pointing in the same direction, may be noticed in conclusion. A common form of mistake in the MS. (which is very full of scribal errors) is the use of wrong terminations, such as τήν for τῇ (Acts xiii. 14, xiv. 20), χωρίον for χωρίου (iv. 37), Κλαύδιος for Κλαύδιον (xviii. 2), ἔκαστος for ἔκαστον (iii. 26), αὐτοῦ for αὐτόν (xiv. 20), αὐτῶν for αὐτοῖς (i. 26), κ.τ.λ.[1] Now such mistakes might easily be made, if the scribe were not very careful, in copying from a manuscript in which abbreviations were used. Such manuscripts have been found of late years among the papyri discovered in Egypt ; [2] and where τ‘ stands for τήν and τ‘ for τῆς, αυτ° for αὐτός, αὐτόν, or αὐτοῦ, αυτ for any case of αὐτός, and similarly with other words, it is easy to understand how mistakes arose when they were re-copied. Manuscripts with such abbreviations, however, were never meant for official or library copies, but merely for private use ; and precise purity of text is less to be expected from them. Hence it must be reckoned as a point of discredit to the text of D if a papyrus copy of this type is reasonably to be suspected in its ancestry ; and it may be added that the frequent confusion of ἡμεῖς and ὑμεῖς (and their cases) points in the same direction, since this blunder (odd and inconvenient as it seems) is far from uncommon in papyri of the inferior sort. With this warning it is time to quit Codex Bezae, and to pass on to the consideration of the remaining MSS. of the New Testament.

D₂. **Codex Claromontanus.**—Since Codex Bezae does

---

[1] Weiss, *op. cit.* pp. 21, 23.
[2] Cf. *Palaeography of Greek Papyri*, p. 32 and Appendix IV.

not contain the Pauline Epistles, the letter D is in that group of the New Testament books assigned to another manuscript, which contains the Pauline Epistles and nothing else. It so happens that the manuscript to which the designation falls has several points of resemblance to its comrade of the Gospels and Acts. Both are Graeco-Latin manuscripts; both are of the sixth century; and both belonged in the sixteenth century to the reformer Beza. The manuscript now under notice was acquired by him from the monastery of Clermont, near Beauvais, in northern France, and used in his second folio edition of the New Testament (1582). After his death it passed through a succession of private hands, until about the middle of the seventeenth century it was bought by Louis XIV. for the Royal Library at Paris, in which it still remains. Some use was made of it by New Testament scholars after Beza, notably by Wetstein; and it was fully edited in 1852 by Tischendorf.[1] In size it is slightly smaller than Codex Bezae, each page measuring $9\frac{3}{4}$ inches by $7\frac{3}{4}$ inches; but the writing is considerably superior in point of beauty. As in Codex Bezae, the Greek text occupies the left-hand page, the Latin the right, and the text is divided colometrically. It contains the whole of the Pauline Epistles, save for casual mutilations through which a few verses here and there are lost. Before the Epistle to the Hebrews a list of the books of the New Testament, with the number of στίχοι[2] contained in each, has been written. This list

---

[1] Specimen facsimiles in *Pal. Soc.* i. 63, 64, and Omont, *Manuscrits grecs de la Bibl. Nat.*, Pl. V.

[2] A στίχος, in the bibliographical sense, was the unit of literary measure in ancient times. Originally meaning simply a line, it came to be used to indicate the length of an average hexameter line, i.e. about sixteen syllables, and this was the unit of measurement by which the labours of the copyist were reckoned. Thus when a work is described as containing 1000 στίχοι, it does not mean that it was actually written in 1000 lines, but that it contained about 16,000 syllables. According to the tariff of Diocletian, a copyist received 25 or 20 denarii for 100 στίχοι (according either to quality of writing, or, as Rendel Harris thinks, to the στίχος being taken of the length of a hexameter or an iambic line). At this rate Mr. Rendel Harris has calculated that the cost of production of the Codex Sinaiticus would have been about £36. In the list given in the Codex Claromontanus, the Gospel of St. Luke (the longest of the canonical books) is reckoned at 2900 στίχοι, the Gospel of St. John at 2000, the Epistle to the Galatians at 350, and 2 and 3 John (the shortest books) at 20 each. The

must be derived from an archetype of very early date, since it gives the canonical books in a very unusual order, and adds to them certain uncanonical books. It runs as follows :—Matthew, John, Mark, Luke, Romans, 1 and 2 Corinthians, Galatians, Ephesians, 1 and 2 Timothy, Titus, Colossians, Philemon, 1 and 2 Peter, James, 1, 2, and 3 John, Jude, the Epistle of Barnabas, Apocalypse of John, Acts, the Shepherd (of Hermas), Acts of Paul, Apocalypse of Peter. It will be observed that Thessalonians, Hebrews, and Philippians are omitted, though with regard to the latter there may be some confusion between it and Philemon. Two leaves are palimpsest, the superimposed text being a part of the otherwise lost *Phaethon* of Euripides.

The date of the MS. can be assigned on palaeographical grounds with fair certainty to the sixth century, a period for which we have a datable example in the Vienna Dioscorides.[1] According to Tischendorf, the hands of nine correctors can be traced in it, the most active being D** of the seventh century and D*** of the ninth or tenth. With regard to the text, the controversies which beset Codex Bezae fortunately do not arise, owing to the fact that the Pauline Epistles afford much less ground for debate than the Gospels and Acts. But the text of Codex Claromontanus belongs (as is natural in a Graeco-Latin MS.) to the type prevalent in the West, and is akin to that of $E_3F_2G_3$, which are likewise Graeco-Latin. All probably go back to one common archetype, the origin of which is attributed to Italy ;[2] and the excellence of the Greek hand in which it is written is a point in favour of this attribution. The Latin text has not been adapted to the Greek, as in Codex Bezae, but is practically independent, representing an early type of the Old Latin version which

principal authorities on stichometry are Graux (*Revue de Philologie*, 1878, pp. 97 ff.), Diels (*Hermes* xvii. 377 ff.), and Rendel Harris (*Stichometry*, Cambridge, 1893). The unit of a sixteen-syllable hexameter line is expressly stated by Galen, and confirmed by the author of a stichometrical catalogue of the Biblical books and the works of Cyprian in a MS. in the Phillipps Library at Cheltenham.

[1] See above, p. 54.

[2] So Corssen, the chief elaborator of this theory, approved by Sanday (*Romans*, introd. p. lxx.).

preceded the Vulgate.   The consideration of the position which this manuscript holds in the textual criticism of the New Testament belongs to a later chapter.

E. Codex Basiliensis.—The remaining manuscripts of the New Testament are of less importance than those which have hitherto been described, some on account of their fragmentariness, and others on account of their comparatively late date.   The manuscript now to be described contains the four Gospels, except for some mutilations in St. Luke, which have been, for the most part, supplied in a cursive hand.   Some fragments of the Apocalypse are attached to the end of it, also in a cursive hand.   It was probably brought from Constantinople by Cardinal John de Ragusio about 1431, and given by him to the Dominicans in Basle, whence it passed in 1559 to the University library of that town.   It was collated for Mill, and afterwards by Wetstein, Tischendorf, and Tregelles, but has never been published in full.   It appears to be of the eighth century, and is written with only one column to the page, in a rather square and thick hand of medium size.   In character its text belongs to the *a*-family.

E₂. Codex Laudianus.—This is a much more interesting manuscript than its colleague of the Gospels.   It is a Graeco-Latin copy of the Acts in the Bodleian Library at Oxford, differing, however, from D and D₂ in having the Latin text in the place of honour on the left.   This in itself points to a later date, when the natural primacy of the Greek, as the original language of the New Testament, had been overcome by the greater prevalence of Latin in the West ; and the character of the writing confirms this supposition.   It is written in a large coarse hand, which is sometimes assigned to the latter part of the sixth century ; but the first half of the seventh century is perhaps a more probable date.   About the end of that century it was in England, since it is practically certain that it was used by Bede in his commentary (*Expositio Retractata*) of the Acts ; and it is very probable that it was brought to this country, like the original of the Lindisfarne Gospels and (probably) that of the Codex Amiatinus,[1] by Theodore of Tarsus, when he came to be Archbishop of Canterbury in 669. At an earlier date it was in Sardinia, since the first words of an edict of Flavius Pancratius, "Dux" of Sardinia, are written on a fly-leaf at the end.[2] Officials with this title administered Sardinia from 534 to 749, but the precise date of Pancratius is not known. The actual place of origin of the MS. cannot be demonstrated; but the margin of time between its production and its probable arrival in England is not great enough to allow for much travelling, in the ordinary course of things, and Sardinia, as an island in which Greek and Latin elements met, would be a very natural birthplace for it. When Bede used it, it must have been in the north of England, but its precise history is unknown until 1636, when Archbishop Laud presented it to the Bodleian Library at Oxford. It was published in full by Hearne in 1715; and again (more accurately) by Hansell in 1864 and Tischendorf in 1870.[3] It contains the Acts, complete except from xxvi. 29 to xxviii. 26, the text being arranged colometrically, as in D and D$_2$, but with much smaller κῶλα, often consisting only of a single word. A peculiar chapter-division, containing fifty-eight chapters up to ch. xxvi. 24, has been added by a corrector of the seventh century. The Latin text, in spite of its holding what is supposed to be the place of honour, has been accommodated to the Greek, so that it is of little value as evidence of the Latin version of the Acts. The Greek text, on the other hand, is of considerable value, having affinities with Codex Bezae, but not going so far as that MS. in the way of peculiar readings. It is the earliest MS. (D being imperfect here) containing Acts vii. 37 (the confession of faith demanded by Philip of the eunuch before baptism), though there is evidence that that verse was known to Irenaeus.

---

[1] See below, p. 192.

[2] This, and other scribblings on the same leaf, are in Greek, in hands that might be of the late sixth or seventh century.

[3] *Monumenta Sacra Inedita*, Nov. Coll., vol. ix.; specimen facsimile in *Pal. Soc.* i. 80.

E$_3$. Codex Sangermanensis.—In the Pauline Epistles the letter E is assigned to this MS., which is again a Graeco-Latin book, but arranged with two columns on each page, the Greek being on the left hand. In the eighteenth century it belonged to the abbey of St. Germain des Prés, near Paris, which was burnt during the Revolutionary period, when many of its books disappeared. This MS. found its way to St. Petersburg, where it was discovered by Matthaei in 1805, and where it now is. It is written in a large, coarse hand, said to be not unlike that of E$_2$, but of later type, and is assigned to the ninth or tenth century. It is of no independent value, being a transcript of the Codex Claromontanus (D$_2$), made at a date later than that of the fifth corrector of that MS. (D^d).

F. Codex Boreeli; formerly the property of John Boreel, Dutch Ambassador at the court of James I., but since 1830 in the University Library at Utrecht. Examined by Tregelles and Tischendorf; a full collation by Heringa, published after his death by Vinke in 1843, with a facsimile. The MS. originally contained the Gospels, but it is now seriously mutilated, beginning at Matthew ix. 1 and ending at John xiii. 34, besides having many gaps in other places. It is written with two columns to the page, in tall, thick uncials of the latest type, apparently of the ninth century, though it has also been assigned to the eighth and tenth. The text is of the usual *a*-type, and the late date of the MS. gives it comparatively little authority.

F^a. Codex Coislinianus 1.—This is not, properly speaking, a copy of the New Testament at all, and consequently does not have a distinguishing letter all to itself. It is a manuscript of the Septuagint, of the seventh century (now in the Bibliothèque Nationale at Paris), in the margin of which the original scribe has inserted some verses (twenty-six in all) from the New Testament, the Gospels, Acts, and Pauline Epistles all being represented.

F$_2$. Codex Augiensis.—This is yet another Graeco-Latin manuscript, containing the Pauline Epistles, with a few mutilations, the principal loss being Romans i. 1-iii. 19. It belonged to the monastery of Reichenau (Augia Dives, whence its name), on an island in Lake Constance; and Scrivener suggests that it may have been actually written there. At the beginning of the eighteenth century it was in private hands, and was bought by Bentley, whereby it passed into the possession of Trinity College, Cambridge, where it still remains. The text is written with two columns to the page, the Greek being on the inside of each page, the Latin on the outside. It was collated by Bentley and Wetstein, examined by Tischendorf and Tregelles, and published in full by Scrivener in 1859.[1] It is neatly written, the Latin better than the Greek, as was natural in the West at the date to which it probably belongs, which is the ninth century. The Epistle to the Hebrews is given in Latin only. The text of this MS. is closely connected with that of G_3 (see below), and both form one group with the other Graeco-Latin MSS., D_2, E_3, representing the δ-type of text for the Pauline Epistles.

G. **Codex Wolfii A.**—This MS. was brought from the East by A. E. Seidel, and acquired by J. C. Wolf, who published extracts from it in 1723. Half a leaf of it was sent by him to Bentley, and is now among his papers in the library of Trinity College, Cambridge; but the bulk of it was bought by Edward Harley, second earl of Oxford,[2] and came with the rest of the Harleian library into the British Museum, where it is now Harl. MS. 5684. It was collated by Tischendorf and Tregelles. It contains the Gospels in a mutilated state, 372 verses in all being lost, including the beginning of Matthew as far as chap. vi. 6 (the Cambridge fragment contains part of v. 29-43). It is written with two columns to

---

[1] Specimen facsimiles in Scrivener, *op. cit.*, and in *Pal. Soc.* i. 80.
[2] Gregory (*Prol.* p. 376) questions whether the MS. was bought by the first or the second Lord Oxford. Wanley's Diary shows that the first lord tried to buy it in 1722, but Wolf would not sell at any price; and there is no further mention of it in the Diary, which extends till 1726, two years after the first lord's death in 1724 (not 1729, as Gregory states).

the page, in medium-sized uncials of the Slavonic type, apparently of the ninth century.

G_2. The letter G is assigned by Tischendorf in the Acts to a single leaf of the seventh century, now at St. Petersburg, containing Acts ii. 45-iii. 8, with some remarkable readings.

G^b : see M_2.

G_3. **Codex Boernerianus.**—This is the companion to F_2, spoken of above, and derives its name from C. F. Boerner of Leipzig, who bought it in 1705, and lent it to Bentley, who showed his appreciation of it by refusing to part with it for five years. Having failed to buy it, he at last returned it, and it is now in the Royal Library at Dresden. It contains the Pauline Epistles, with the exception of the Epistle to the Hebrews. It was published by Matthaei in 1791, with facsimiles. It has since been shown that it was originally part of the same MS. as Δ of the Gospels (see below), and it may have been written at St. Gall, where Δ now is. St. Gall was much frequented by Irish monks, and some curious Irish verses have been written on one of the pages of G_3. It is written in a peculiar hand, probably of the ninth century, with a Latin version between the lines ; and the mistakes in the Greek writing show that Latin was a more familiar language to the scribe or scribes. Besides being thus connected with Δ, G_3 is also closely akin to F_2. Dr. Hort was inclined to believe that G_3 was actually copied from F_2 ; but the commoner view, held by Scrivener and Corssen, is that both were taken from the same exemplar, F_2 being perhaps slightly the earlier of the two. In any case the connection is so close that the two manuscripts only have the force of a single authority.

H. **Codex Wolfii B.**—This manuscript was brought from the east with G, and passed with it into the possession of J. C. Wolf, who sent a fragment of it (as of G) to Bentley at Cambridge, where it still remains. Its subsequent history is unknown until 1838, when it reappeared in the Public Library at Hamburg. It was collated by both Tischendorf and Tregelles, who assign it to the ninth century. When perfect it contained the four Gospels, written with a single column to the page, in rather small and ill-formed uncials; but it is now seriously mutilated, wanting (according to Scrivener) 679 verses out of the 3780 of which the Gospels consist, the most notable loss being Matt. i. 1-xv. 30. The text is of the *a*-type.

H₂. **Codex Mutinensis.**—A ninth-century copy of the Acts (with some defects), with the Epistles (Catholic and Pauline) added in a cursive hand. It is in the Grand Ducal Library at Modena, and has been collated by Tischendorf and Tregelles, but is not of much importance.

H₃. **Codex Coislinianus** 202.—This, on the other hand, is a very interesting manuscript, containing an important text of the Pauline Epistles. Originally in the monastery of the Laura on Mt. Athos, it was there used to supply materials for the binding of several volumes, which have since been scattered in various parts of the world. Forty-one leaves are at present known to exist, of which eight are still on Mt. Athos, twenty-two at Paris, three at St. Petersburg, three at Moscow, three at Kieff, and two at Turin. They are written in very large, square uncials, probably of the sixth century, the text being arranged colometrically. The letters have been retraced in a dark ink of corrosive character, which has eaten through the vellum in many places. The text has been edited by Omont (*Notices et extraits*, vol. xxxiii. pt. 1, p. 141 ff.), with two facsimiles. It contains scattered portions of most of the Pauline Epistles (but not Romans, Philippians, Ephesians, 2 Thessalonians, or Philemon). A note appended to the Epistle to Titus states that it (or possibly one of its ancestors) was corrected from the copy in the library at Caesarea, written by the hand of the holy Pamphilus himself (cf. p. 52, above). Further, it has been shown that it represents (perhaps in a modified form) the edition of the Pauline Epistles, colometrically arranged, which we know to have been prepared, about the middle of the fourth century, by Euthalius of Sulca, whose work, especially as the author of a division of the Acts and Catholic Epistles into sections, has been mentioned above (p. 67). Traces of the Euthalian text (for which we also have the evidence of some minuscule MSS., mentioned below, pp. 118-120) have been found in the Armenian version, but it is still uncertain whether there is any intimate connexion between them ; and the whole subject of the edition of Euthalius is still involved in much obscurity.[1]

I. Codex Tischendorfianus.—This letter is assigned to twenty-eight palimpsest leaves which Tischendorf obtained from the convent of Mar Saba, between Jerusalem and the Dead Sea ; but they belong to no less than seven manuscripts. Four of these were copies of the Gospels, I^1 (fifth century) containing fragments of St. John, I^3 (fifth century) of Matthew and Mark, I^4 (sixth century) of Matthew, Luke, and John, and I^7 (sixth century) of Luke. I^2 (fifth century) contains some verses of the Acts and Pauline Epistles, I^5 and I^6 (both seventh century) of the Acts. The seven fragments only contain 255 verses in all, of which 190 are from the Gospels. All are edited by Tischendorf (*Monumenta Sacra Inedita*, i. 1-48), with facsimiles. The later writing above them is Georgian.

I[b]. Codex Musei Britannici 17136.—Tischendorf gives this letter to a fragment brought about the middle of the present century from the convent of Nitria (in Egypt) to the British Museum. It is a double palimpsest, containing two layers of Syriac writing above Greek, which has been made out by Tischendorf and Tregelles to be sixteen verses of St. John, in a hand of the fourth or

---

[1] Euthalius' work was first edited by Zacagni (*Collectanea monumentorum veterum ecclesiae*, 1698). The connexion of his text with the Armenian version has been pointed out and partially examined by Corssen, Bousset, Rendel Harris, and Conybeare ; but by far the most important treatment of the subject is that given by Canon Armitage Robinson (*Texts and Studies*, iii. 3), in which, among other things, he fixes for the first time the true date of Euthalius, who had previously been assigned to the fifth century. He also gives the text of sixteen lost pages of H_3, which he recovered from the "sets-off" left on the pages opposite to them.

PLATE VII.

CODEX REGIUS. Eighth Century.
(Scale 2 : 3. Shows the alternative endings to St. Mark.)

To face p. 89.

fifth century.   Scrivener calls this fragment N[b], as Tischendorf also did in his penultimate (seventh) edition.   Published by Tischendorf.[1]

I$_2$.—See O$_2$, below.

K. Codex Cyprius.—Brought from Cyprus in 1673 ; now in the Bibliothèque Nationale.   Used by Mill and Scholz ; thoroughly collated by that indefatigable pair of scholars, Tischendorf and Tregelles.   It is one of the seven extant complete uncial copies of the Gospels, the others being אBMSUΩ ; but as it is as late as the ninth century, and contains the normal *a*-text, it is not of remarkable value.   It is written in compressed uncials of a late type, rather irregular, in one broad column to the page.

K$_2$. Codex Mosquensis.—Brought from Mt. Athos to Moscow.   It contains the Catholic and Pauline Epistles, but not the Acts, and is assigned to the ninth century. It has been collated by Matthaei alone.

L. Codex Regius (Plate VII.).—This is a manuscript of the Gospels, nearly complete, in the Bibliothèque Nationale at Paris, where it was used by Stephanus in the sixteenth century, and subsequently by Wetstein, Griesbach, and Tischendorf, the latter of whom published it in full.[2] This honour was due, not to its age, but to its character. It is nearly as late as the two MSS. last mentioned, being written in compressed uncials which cannot be earlier than the eighth century ; but its text differs very markedly from the type which had long before that date established itself as predominant in the Church.   On the contrary, it agrees in very many places with B, and has clearly been copied from a manuscript of the same type.   It is badly written, containing many ignorant blunders.   Its most notable feature is in regard to the conclusion of St. Mark, where it gives, after xvi. 8, first the shorter conclusion and then the longer (the ordinary last twelve verses), prefixing to each a note to say that these passages are current in some

---

[1] *Monumenta Sacra Inedita*, Nov. Coll., ii. 311-12, with facsimile.
[2] *Ib.* (1846), i. 57-399, with facsimiles.

quarters, but evidently not recognising either as authoritative. The text is generally regarded as having an Egyptian origin.

L₂. Codex Bibliothecae Angelicae A. 2. 15.—Belongs to the Augustinian monastery at Rome. It contains the Acts from viii. 10, the Catholic Epistles, and the Pauline Epistles as far as Hebrews xiii. 10. It is assigned to the ninth century, and has been collated by Tischendorf and Tregelles, besides earlier scholars. A facsimile is given by Montfaucon (*Palaeographia Graeca*, p. 514).

M. Codex Campianus.—Presented to Louis XIV. in 1706, and now in the Bibliothèque Nationale; but that it formerly had a home, and perhaps its origin, in the East is shown by some notes in Arabic and Slavonic which its pages contain. It is a complete copy of the Gospels, written with two columns to the page, in small compressed uncials of the ninth century. It has been collated by Wetstein, Scholz, and Tregelles, and transcribed in full by Tischendorf. Its text is of the normal *a*-type. Facsimiles in Montfaucon (*op. cit.* p. 260) and Silvestre (*Paléographie universelle*, pl. 76).

M₂.—Palimpsest fragments, formerly at Grotta Ferrata, now in the Vatican, consisting of five leaves, containing portions of Acts xvi. 30-xviii. 26 in a hand of the eighth or ninth century. Published by Cozza in 1877 (*Sacrorum Bibliorum vetustissima fragmenta*, pt. iii.), with the exception of one leaf, discovered in 1886 by Gregory. Called Gᵇ by Gregory.

M₈. Codex Ruber; so called from the red ink in which it is written. It consists of but four leaves, of which two, containing Heb. i. 1-iv. 3, xii. 20-xiii. 25, are in the Public Library at Hamburg, and two, containing 1 Cor. xv. 52-2 Cor. i. 15, 2 Cor. x. 13-xii. 5, in the British Museum (Harl. MS. 5613*), having been extracted from the binding of a minuscule copy of the Gospels written in 1407. Collated by Tregelles and published by Tischendorf (*Anecd. sacr. et profan.*, 1855). It is written in small uncials, of a type so late as to verge on being cursive, and is probably not earlier than the tenth century. The text, so far as it goes, is of the β-type.

N. **Codex Purpureus Petropolitanus.**—A few years ago this manuscript (with the omission of the final adjective of its title, to which it had then no claim) might have been briefly described as consisting merely of forty-five leaves of purple vellum, divided between four different libraries (thirty-three at Patmos, six in the Vatican, four in the British Museum, and two at Vienna), and containing portions of each of the four Gospels, especially St. Mark. Within the last five years, however, the position has been wholly altered. So far back as 1883, a purple manuscript of the Gospels was reported to have been seen in Cappadocia, and various travellers in the East since that date had heard of it, and even tried to purchase it ; but nothing came of these efforts until 1896, when it was announced that the manuscript had been secured by the Tsar of Russia. It was conjectured almost immediately, from the fragmentary descriptions of it that reached this country, that it might be a further part, if not the whole remainder, of N ; and this conjecture was verified when the manuscript was examined by competent hands. By the courtesy of the authorities of the Imperial Library at St. Petersburg, the first publication of the newly-acquired treasure was committed to an English scholar, Mr. H. S. Cronin, of Trinity Hall, Cambridge ; and it is from his careful and thorough edition of it that the following description is taken.[1]

The portion of the manuscript thus acquired does not indeed complete the whole volume, but it adds 182 leaves to the forty-five previously known, making a total of **227** leaves. It can be calculated that the original volume, when complete, contained 462 leaves, so that we have even now slightly less than half of it ; but this is quite sufficient to show its general character. All four Gospels are substantially represented, St. Matthew proportionately

---

[1] *Codex Purpureus Petropolitanus*, by H. S. Cronin, M.A. (*Texts and Studies*, vol. v. No. 4, Cambridge, 1899).

the least (Matthew forty-seven leaves, Mark forty-four, Luke seventy-three, John sixty-three). The leaves measure about 13 inches by 10½ inches, and contain two columns to the page, with sixteen lines in each. The writing is in silver, with gold for the abbreviations of the sacred names, and the letters are unusually large. The date appears to be in the sixth century.[1] Of its *provenance* nothing is known, but Mr. Cronin suggests Constantinople, alike from the magnificence of its appearance and the character of its text. Mr. Cronin has very carefully and ingeniously worked out the history of the MS., from such indications as its present state provides, and concludes that it was dismembered about the twelfth century, possibly by Crusaders, some of its leaves being brought to Europe, and reaching their present homes in the sixteenth and seventeenth centuries. The rest was again subdivided, part finding its way to Patmos, and part to Ephesus, where it appears to have been seen in the eighteenth century by the writer of a note in the similar Codex Beratinus (Φ). This latter part, possibly increased by some other leaves from the same neighbourhood, was carried between 1820 and 1847 to Sarumsahly, the ancient Caesarea in Cappadocia, whence it was acquired in 1896 by the Russian Government.[2]

The text (as had already been gathered from the previously extant fragments) proves to be predominantly of the *a*-type, though it also shares some readings with authorities of the opposite class. It is, in fact, a mixed text, marking a stage in the evolution of the Textus Receptus. In this character it is associated with the two other purple manuscripts of the Gospels, Σ and Φ, described below ; and Mr. Cronin shows that its connexion with Σ is very

---

[1] The oval shape of some of the letters in the prefatory matter (which is in a different but necessarily contemporaneous hand) does not appear to militate against this date, since it is found in other hands of the sixth century, e.g. the Codex Marchalianus.

[2] Fuller details of the various dismemberments and re-collections of the manuscript will be found in Mr. Cronin's book. A facsimile of one of the London leaves is given in *Facsimiles from Biblical MSS. in the British Museum*, Pl. IV. (1900).

close indeed. Both must have proceeded from the same workshop, and probably they were copied from the same original. Now Σ contains only St. Matthew and St. Mark ; and as N now gives us more than half of St. Luke and St. John, we have by far the greater part of the Gospels in this type of text, derived from a common original not later than the early part of the sixth century. Φ is of similar character, but its relationship is not so close as that between N and Σ.

N^a.—This letter is assigned by Gregory to two fragments of purple vellum with letters of gold, seen in Egypt by Bishop Porphyry Uspensky in 1850. They contain Mark ix. 14-22, x. 23-29, mutilated. They are now in the Imperial Library at St. Petersburg (no. 275). Facsimiles in Bishop Porphyry's *Christiansky Vostok*, 1857, pl. 13, 14.

N_2.—Two leaves, extracted from the binding of another MS., now at St. Petersburg, containing Gal. v. 12-vi. 4, Heb. v. 8-vi. 10, in a hand of the ninth century.

O.—A ninth-century fragment at Moscow, containing portions of John i. 1-4, xx. 10-24.

O^{a-b}.—Manuscripts containing the *Magnificat, Benedictus*, and *Nunc Dimittis*, or some of these, generally in connexion with Psalters, which are often followed by collections of Canticles, among which these three are included. As they represent merely liturgical tradition, they do not rank high for critical purposes.

O_2.—The fragments of Hebrews x., described by Tischendorf (7th ed.) as N^c and by Scrivener as O of the Pauline Epistles, are really part of H_3 (Gregory, *Prol.* p. 438), and are included in the enumeration of the leaves of that MS. given above.

$O_2^{a, b}$.—Some small fragments, at St. Petersburg and Moscow, of the sixth century, containing a few verses of 2 Corinthians (i. 20-ii. 12) and Ephesians (iv. 1-18). The first is doubly described by Scrivener, as I and O^a.

P. **Codex Guelpherbytanus A.**—A palimpsest in the Ducal Library at Wolfenbüttel, first published by the discoverer, F. A. Knittel, in 1762; re-published more fully by Tischendorf.[1] It contains portions of 518 verses, all the Evangelists being represented; and is assigned by Tischendorf to the sixth century. It contains a considerable number of early readings, but agrees with the *a*-type oftener than with the *β*-type.

P_2. **Codex Porphyrianus.**—A palimpsest found by Tischendorf among the MSS. of Bishop Porphyry at St. Petersburg, and published by him in full.[2] It is written in sloping uncials of the ninth century, and contains (with some mutilations) not only the Acts and Catholic and Pauline Epistles, but also the Apocalypse, for which it is a useful authority, uncial manuscripts of that book being so rare that only five others are known ($\aleph AB_2 C_2$). It shares with B_2 the representation of the later stage in the textual tradition of that book. The upper writing, which is cursive, written in 1301, is stated by Tischendorf to represent the Euthalian edition of the Acts and Pauline Epistles (see above, pp. 67, 88), and consequently has an independent value of its own; but it has not yet been published.

Q. **Codex Guelpherbytanus B.**—This MS. shared the fortunes of P, having been used, together with it and with a fragment of a copy of Ulfilas' Gothic Gospels, to receive a later text; and it was discovered and published by the same persons. It contains only 247 verses, from SS. Luke and John. It is probably of the fifth century, written in double columns in moderate-sized uncials. Its text is of a similar character to that of P, but with a larger infusion of readings of the *β*-type.

$Q_2 = Pap.^9$ (above, p. 37).

R. **Codex Nitriensis** (Plate VIII.).—An imperfect palimpsest copy of St. Luke, now in the British Museum, having been brought thither from the convent of St. Maria Deipara, in the Nitrian desert. The upper writing is a

---

[1] *Mon. Sac. Ined.*, Nov. Coll., vol. vi. 249-338; facsimile in vol. iii. where Cod. Q is edited (Pl. II.).

[2] *Ibid.* vols. v. and vi., with facsimiles.

PLATE VIII.

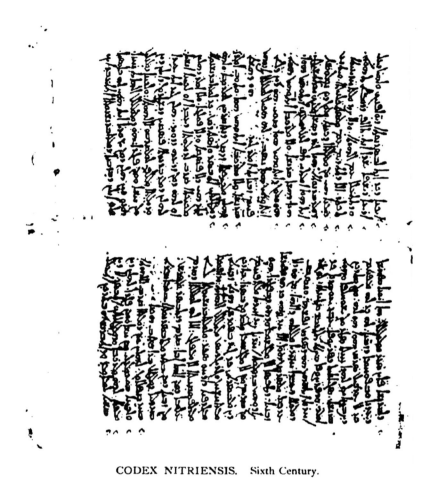

CODEX NITRIENSIS.   Sixth Century.

(Scale 2 : 5.   A palimpsest, having Syriac writing above the original Greek.   The
page shown contains Luke xxiii. 38-45.)

To face p. 95.

Syriac treatise, for the transcription of which the Nitrian monk had taken, not only a copy of the Gospels, but also an equally early MS. of the *Iliad* and a somewhat later copy of Euclid's *Elements*. The Gospel MS. is written in a large, plain hand, probably of the sixth century, with two columns to the page. About half the text of St. Luke is preserved, in detached portions. The decipherment of it is due to Tregelles and Tischendorf, the latter of whom published it in full.[1] The text is of an early type, belonging to the β-family rather than to its more prevalent rival.

R_2. **Codex Cryptoferratensis.**—A single leaf containing 2 Corinthians xi. 9-19, palimpsest, of the seventh or eighth century, in the monastery of Grotta Ferrata. Edited by Cozza-Luzi (*Sacrorum Bibliorum vetustissima fragmenta*, 1867).

S. **Codex Vaticanus** 354.—A complete copy of the Gospels, mainly noticeable as bearing a precise date, having been written by a monk named Michael in A.D. 949. It is written in the large compressed Slavonic characters which were the latest phase of uncial writing. It has been collated by Birch and Tischendorf, but its text is not of a remarkable character, being mainly of the usual a-type.

S_2. **Codex Athous.**—A manuscript in the monastery of the Laura on Mt. Athos, containing the Acts, Catholic Epistles, Romans, and parts of 1 and 2 Corinthians and Ephesians. It is assigned to the eighth or ninth century. Examined by Gregory in 1886, but not fully collated.

T.—Under this letter are grouped a number of fragments from Egypt, many of them being bilingual, containing the Coptic version (of the Sahidic type, see below, p. 159) side by side with the Greek. The principal member of this group, **Codex Borgianus,** is in the library of the Propaganda at Rome, and consists of

---

[1] *Mon. Sac. Ined.*, Nov. Coll., vol. ii. 1-92. A page is reproduced in *Facsimiles of Biblical MSS. in the British Museum,* Pl. III.

seventeen leaves from the Gospels of St. Luke and St. John, the Greek text being on the right-hand page, the Sahidic on the left, with two columns to the page. Giorgi, who first edited part of it in 1789, assigned it to the fourth century; Tischendorf, with more probability, to the fifth. Its text is decidedly of the β-type, being ranked by Hort next after B and ℵ in this respect.

T^{b-h} and T^{woi} are smaller fragments of Graeco-Sahidic MSS., ranging from the fifth to the ninth centuries. T^{i-r} are fragments found by Amélineau among the Coptic MSS. from the great White Monastery in Upper Egypt (published in *Notices et Extraits des manuscrits de la Bibl. Nat.* xxxiv. 1895), and attributed by him to the eighth to tenth centuries. Three of them are Graeco-Sahidic, six Greek only, though in hands of Coptic character. One of them, T^l, has the double ending to St. Mark, as in L. The designation T^s may be assigned to another bilingual fragment, in the British Museum, containing John iii. 5-iv. 18, iv. 23-35, 45-49, in Greek and Middle Egyptian, of the sixth century.[1] T^{t-v} are at Vienna, and are published for the first time in Gregory's *Textkritik*, vol. i. (1900). T$_2$^{a} and T$_2$^{b} are Graeco-Sahidic fragments of the Pauline Epistles, both at Paris, the latter among Amélineau's discoveries. The former is assigned to the fifth century, the latter to the ninth or tenth.

U. **Codex Nanianus.**—In the Biblioteca Marciana at Venice; an entire copy of the Gospels, written with two columns to the page, in large, well-rounded uncials, showing an attempt to revive the hands of the fifth and sixth centuries, but without possessing their firmness and retaining certain details of the "Slavonic" type. It probably belongs to the latest age of uncial writing, in the tenth century. It was collated by Tregelles and Tischendorf; its text is of the a-type.

V. **Codex Mosquensis.**—A copy of the Gospels,

---

[1] Published by Crum and Kenyon, in *Journ. of Theol. Studies*, i. 415-433 (1900). Gregory calls this fragment T^w, having assigned T^s to the papyrus MS. from Oxyrhynchus described above as Pap.[1]

formerly at Mt. Athos, now at Moscow, written in uncials of the eighth (Scrivener) or ninth (Gregory) century as far as John vii. 39, and thence continued in a cursive hand, which, according to Bengel, bore a date in the year 1000, but which (the end of St. John, with the colophon which presumably contained this date, having been since lost) is assigned by Matthaei and Gregory to the thirteenth century. It was collated by Matthaei.

W. This letter includes a number of small fragments, ranging from W^a to W^o. The largest is W^b, at Naples, which contains palimpsest portions of SS. Matthew, Mark, and Luke in a text of good quality. None of them is earlier than the seventh century, and most of them are palimpsests. W^g of Gregory's notation is called T by Scrivener (see below.)

X. **Codex Monacensis.** — A considerably mutilated copy of the Gospels at Munich, written in small thin uncials of the tenth century, approaching the minuscule type, and accompanied by a marginal commentary in a contemporary minuscule hand. Collated chiefly by Tischendorf and Tregelles. It occasionally contains readings of an early type, akin to the β-family.

X^b. **Codex Monacensis II.** — Fourteen uncial leaves at the end of a MS. at Munich, containing Luke i. 1-ii. 40, written with three columns to the page. Gregory, who was the first to notice them, assigns the writing to the ninth or tenth century. The rest of the MS. contains discussions on Mt. and Jn., in a minuscule hand, and the MS. consequently appears in Scholz's and subsequent lists of minuscule MSS. as Evan. 429.

Y. **Codex Barberini,** in the Barberini Library at Rome. A fragment, consisting of six leaves, containing John xvi. 3-xix. 41, assigned by Tischendorf, who edited it,[1] to the eighth century.

Z. **Codex Dublinensis.** — An interesting palimpsest fragment, in the library of Trinity College, Dublin, containing less than a third of St. Matthew (295 verses) in

---

[1] *Mon. Sac. Ined.* 1846, i. 37-50, with facsimile.

detached portions, underlying a cursive text of the tenth century. It was discovered by Dr. Barrett in 1787, and published in full by him in 1801, and again (with additional decipherments and facsimiles) by Dr. T. K. Abbott in 1880. It is written in large and broad uncials, with strongly marked Egyptian characteristics, especially in the shapes of a and μ. It is probably of the sixth century, though Dr. Abbott is inclined to put it as high as the fifth. The text is of the β-type, with considerable resemblances to א.

Γ. **Codex Tischendorfianus** IV.—The Latin alphabet being now exhausted, it is necessary to have recourse to those letters of the Greek alphabet which differ from the Latin in form. The first of these is a considerable fragment in the Bodleian Library, bought out of the spoil brought back by Tischendorf from his second campaign in the East. It consists of 158 leaves, and contains the whole of SS. Mark and Luke (except Mark iii. 35-vi. 20), with portions of SS. Matthew and John. A further portion of the same MS., completing it with the exception of the hiatus in St. Mark and a few verses of St. Matthew, was secured by Tischendorf on his third Eastern expedition, and is now at St. Petersburg. This latter portion contains a colophon, stating that the MS. was completed at a date which can probably be identified with A.D. 844. The hand is a very thick, heavy uncial of the Slavonic type, sloping slightly backwards. The text has been collated by Tischendorf and Tregelles ; it is usually of the standard a-type.

Δ. **Codex Sangallensis.**—This manuscript, as has been stated above, originally formed one volume with the MS. known as G$_3$, the latter containing the Pauline Epistles, while Δ contains the four Gospels, practically complete. It is a Graeco-Latin manuscript, the Latin version being written between the lines of the Greek. The frequent misdivisions of the Greek words seem to show that it was written by a scribe imperfectly acquainted with Greek, who was copying from a MS. in which the words were not

separated.   It was evidently written in the West, probably
at St. Gall, where it now is.   The writing is rough and
ugly, of the ninth century or later.   It was fully edited in
1836 by Rettig, who was the first to identify it with G_3.
In three out of the four Gospels, the text is of the usual
a-type; but in St. Mark it has evidently been copied
from a different original, belonging to the β-family.   The
Latin version is of little value, being an amalgamation of
the Old Latin and the Vulgate, with modifications to suit
the Greek.[1]

Θ[a-h].—These are eight small fragments of MSS. of the
Gospels, now at St. Petersburg, with the exception of four
out of the five leaves of Θ[a], which are at Leipzig.   Θ[h] has
been shown to be part of a MS. now at Mount Sinai (see
Mrs. Lewis' Catalogue in *Studia Sinaitica*, pt. i. p. 105, and
Burkitt in *Journ. of Theol. Studies*, ii. 176).   Their dates
vary from the sixth to the ninth or tenth century; but
they are so small as to be of little importance, though
Θ[c, e, g] (all of the sixth century) appear to have belonged
to MSS. containing the β-type of text.

Λ. **Codex Tischendorfianus III.**—This was brought
by Tischendorf from the East with Codex Γ, and like it is
now in the Bodleian Library at Oxford.   It contains the
Gospels of SS. Luke and John complete, written with two
columns to the page in sloping Slavonic uncials of the
ninth century.   There is good reason to suppose that the
earlier portion of this MS. is at St. Petersburg, Tischendorf having deposited there a copy of SS. Matthew and
Mark (Evan. 566 in Gregory's list) which corresponds
in size and contains marginal matter in the same hand.
Moreover the St. Petersburg MS. has not got the subscription to St. Mark, which is preserved at the beginning of
the Oxford part, while the subscription to St. Matthew
is of the same rather unusual type as the three in the
Oxford MS.   It is true that the St. Petersburg part is

---

[1] Cf. J. Rendel Harris, *The Codex Sangallensis* (Δ), Cambridge, 1891, in
which the Latin text is discussed.   Its main value is for the relics of the Old
Latin version which can be extracted from it.   A facsimile is given in *Pal.
Soc.* i. 179.

written in minuscules, while the Oxford part is in uncials;
but this combination of hands can be paralleled by Codex
E of the Septuagint, which Tischendorf divided between
Oxford, London, and St. Petersburg, while retaining in
his own hands the tell-tale leaf containing the transition
from the uncial to the cursive hand.   In the case of Λ,
however, the identification of the two portions is due to
Tischendorf himself, who is very likely to have known
that they were derived from the same source.   Its text is
said to be rather unlike the received type, and to form
one group with the cursive MSS. numbered 20 (as revised
by its corrector), 157, 164, 215, 262, 300, 376, 428,
473, 573, 736, 1071,[1] all of which have (like Λ) subscriptions stating that their text was derived "from the
ancient copies at Jerusalem."

Ξ. **Codex Zacynthius.**—A palimpsest in the possession
of the British and Foreign Bible Society in London, containing the greater part of Luke i. 1-xi. 33, with marginal
commentary.   Such marginal commentaries, or catenae,
are common enough in later MSS., especially of the Latin
Bible; but this is, with the exception of X, the only
example of one attached to an uncial text of the New
Testament.   It was brought from Zante in 1821, and
published by Tregelles (with a facsimile) in 1861.   It is
assigned to the eighth century.   Its text is of the
β-type, and it is notable as containing a system of
chapter-division, elsewhere known only in Codex B.
The upper writing is an Evangeliarium of the thirteenth
century.

Π. **Codex Petropolitanus.**—A nearly complete copy
of the Gospels, formerly at Smyrna, now (through the
intervention of Tischendorf) at St. Petersburg.   It is of
the ninth century, and its text is of the a-type, agreeing
especially with K.   Tischendorf appears to be the only
scholar who has made use of it.

---

[1] The numbers used here (and elsewhere) are those of Scrivener's list of the
minuscule MSS., which, as explained in the next chapter, differ in places from
those of Gregory.

Σ. **Codex Rossanensis.**—This copy of the Gospels is remarkable for its external appearance. It is written in silver letters on purple-stained vellum, and is adorned with miniatures in water-colour. The writing is of the sixth century, and it therefore shares with the manuscript next to be mentioned, and with the Vienna Genesis and Dioscorides, the Cottonian Genesis and the Vatican Virgil, the honour of being the earliest illustrated MS. in existence (apart from Egyptian papyri), and of representing more faithfully than later MSS. the characteristics of classical painting. Its present home is at Rossano in Calabria, where it was observed in 1879 by Gebhardt and Harnack, who edited it in full. Quite recently, a study of it in its artistic aspect, with photographic reproductions of all the miniatures, has been published by A. Haseloff,[1] who regards it as exhibiting pictorial characteristics of an earlier type than any of its competitors. It contains the Gospels of SS. Matthew and Mark only, the others (with the last seven verses of St. Mark) being lost. The hand is large and square. As has been stated above, it is a sister MS. of N, and its text is of the a-type, in a comparatively early stage of its development.[2]

Σ[b]. **Codex Sinopensis.**—It will be useful to give this letter and designation, at least provisionally, to the last discovered uncial MS. of the Gospels, which is closely akin to the Codex Rossanensis. It consists of forty-three leaves of purple vellum, written throughout in letters of gold (in which respect it is unique among all purple uncials, with the exception of the fragment N[a]), and contains portions of Matthew, mainly from chapters xiii. to xxiv., with five illustrations in the lower margins.[3] The hand is a large one, resembling those of N and Σ, and the illustrations are of the same general character as those of Σ. Its

---

[1] *Codex Purpureus Rossanensis* (Berlin and Leipzig, 1898).

[2] See Sanday, *Studia Biblica*, i. 103 ff.

[3] Since this MS. does not appear in the lists of Scrivener and Gregory, it may be convenient to state its contents precisely : Matthew vii. 7-22, xi. 5-12, xiii. 7-47, xiii. 54-xiv. 4, xiv. 13-20, xv. 11-xvi. 18, xvii. 2-24, xviii. 4-9, 16-30, xix. 3-10, 17-25, xx. 9-xxi. 5, xxi. 12-xxii. 7, xxii. 15-24, xxii. 32-xxiii. 35, xxiv. 3-12.

date is presumably the same, namely the sixth century. It was discovered at Sinope in 1899 by a French naval officer, and is now in the Bibliothèque Nationale. A preliminary description of it, with a facsimile, was published by M. Omont (*Journal des Savants*, 1900, pp. 279-285), and a full publication of its text, with facsimiles of four of the illustrations, is given in *Notices et Extraits des Manuscrits de la Bibl. Nat.* xxxvi. (1900) by the same scholar. M. Omont's collation shows that the text is closely akin to that of N and Σ.

T. Codex Blenheimius.—Formerly in the Sunderland Library at Blenheim Palace, now in the British Museum (Add. MS. 31919). It is a palimpsest of the ninth century, containing scattered passages from all four Gospels; first recognised by Professors Abbott and Mahaffy in 1881, while it was still at Blenheim. It has not been fully collated, and is not easy to decipher.

Φ. Codex Beratinus.—This, like N and Σ, is a sumptuous purple and silver copy of the Gospels; and it is curiously like the latter of these, and the former until quite recently, in having its home in a comparatively obscure locality. It is at Berat, or Belgrade, in Albania (where it has been since 1356), and was first made known in 1868 by the archbishop of the diocese, Anthymius Alexoudi, whose mention of its existence led to a fuller examination of it being made by the Abbé (now Mgr.) Batiffol in 1885, followed by a complete edition, with facsimile, in 1886. It consists of 190 leaves, about the same size as those of the Codex Alexandrinus, and having, like that MS., two columns to the page; but the letters are much larger. Its date is probably in the sixth century. It contains only St. Matthew and St. Mark, and these are slightly mutilated. A note in the MS. states that the loss of the other two Gospels is due to "the Franks of Champagne," i.e. probably some of the Crusaders, who may have seen it at Patmos, where it is believed formerly to have been. In text, like N and Σ, it belongs to the received a-type, though with some variations; as for instance, the inclusion of the long passage after Matthew xx. 28, which is also found in D.

Ψ.—A copy of the New Testament in the monastery of the Laura on Mount Athos, beginning at Mark ix. 5, and containing the remainder of the Gospels, the Acts, the Catholic Epistles, and the Pauline Epistles, with the exception of a leaf of Hebrews. It is assigned to the eighth or ninth century. It is especially interesting as agreeing with L in inserting the alternative conclusion to St. Mark before the ordinary last twelve verses. The MS. was seen by Gregory in 1886, but the first full examination of it has been made quite recently by the Rev. K. Lake, who states that the text of Mark is far more valuable than that of Luke or John. In this Gospel its text is emphatically of an early type, including readings of the β and δ-types, without ranging itself definitely with either family. Mr. Lake is inclined to look to Alexandria for its home, and to connect it with the group of authorities אCLΔ and the quotations in Clement of Alexandria, in which we find just this comprehensive form of ancient text.[1]

Ω.—A complete copy of the four Gospels in the monastery of Dionysius on Mount Athos, of the eighth or ninth century. It was cursorily examined by Gregory in 1886, but has not been fully collated.

With this MS. the letters of the Greek alphabet are exhausted. There remain a few manuscripts, or fragments of manuscripts, which have been discovered of late years, and of which (as of the last mentioned) not much is yet known. To these the letters of the Hebrew alphabet are applied, with the exception, of course, of א, which has already been appropriated to the Codex Sinaiticus. Very brief details, however, can be given of them.

ב (Beth).—The Gospels, with some lacunae, of the ninth or tenth century, in the monastery of St. Andrew on Mount Athos.

---

[1] See *The Text of Codex Ψ in St. Mark*, by the Rev. K. Lake (*Journal of Theological Studies*, i. 290).

ב₂.—A palimpsest of the fifth century, formerly in the monastery of St. Mary of Patirium, a suburb of Rossano in Calabria, whence it was taken about the end of the seventeenth century to the Vatican Library at Rome. Here, having been lost to sight for a long time, it was rediscovered by M. Batiffol in 1887.[1] It contains fragments of the Acts, Catholic and Pauline Epistles, written (like B) with three columns to the page. In text it is said to be akin rather to A.

ג (Gimel).—The New Testament (the Apocalypse preceding the Pauline Epistles), of the tenth century, at Kosinitsa.[2]

ד (Daleth).—This letter is assigned to some fragments found by Mr. Rendel Harris in the monastery of St. Catherine on Mount Sinai, formerly the home of א. The texts of all have been published by him,[3] and his descriptions may be summarised as follows: (1) A fragment containing only Matthew xi. 27, 28, of the eighth century; (2) Matthew xiv. 28-31, of the fifth century; (3) Four mutilated leaves of Matthew xiii.-xv., of the eighth or ninth century; (4) Matthew xiii. 46-52, of the ninth century, having Greek and Arabic in parallel columns; (5) Ten palimpsest leaves of the fifth century, containing about a hundred verses from the later chapters of St. Matthew and the earlier of St. Mark; (6) Two leaves of the sixth century, with a few verses from the same Gospels; (7) Three leaves from the end of St. Mark, of the sixth or seventh century, which are important as containing the alternative endings of the Gospel, as in L. There is also a fragment on papyrus, which has been described above (Pap.¹⁰, p. 38), and six Old Testament

---

[1] See full description in Batiffol, *L'Abbaye de Rossano*, pp. 71-74 (1890).

[2] ג in Gregory and Scrivener, described as being a MS. of the sixth century, written in gold and silver letters on purple vellum, with two columns to a page, etc., but of which the locality was unknown, is presumably the part of N which was then in Asia Minor, and of which some portions had been seen by travellers, but which is now at St. Petersburg.

[3] *Biblical Fragments from Mount Sinai* (Cambridge, 1890). Some corrections and amplifications of his text are made by Mrs. A. S. Lewis in an appendix to her catalogue of the Syriac MSS. at Mount Sinai (*Studia Sinaitica*, i.) with a facsimile of No. 7.

MSS., which do not concern our present subject.[1] To this list Mrs. Lewis adds (8) a fragment of the Acts (xiii. 28, 29), probably of the fifth century; and (9) another fragment of the Acts is likewise mentioned in her list (No. 41), without any details being given, except that it is in uncials of the tenth century.

ד‎[b].—The Gospels, wanting Matthew i. 1-ix. 1, of the ninth or tenth century, at Kosinitsa.

ה‎ (He)[a-d].—Fragments of four MSS. of the sixth century, at Mount Athos, containing portions of the Gospels attached to other theological works.

---

[1] Gregory's notation of the New Testament fragments as ד‎[6-14] (adopted from Harris's continuous numeration of his fragments from 1 to 14) is illogical, as he has nothing to do with the Old Testament MSS. which form Nos. 1-5 of the series.

CHAPTER IV

THE MINUSCULE MANUSCRIPTS

[**Authorities**: Gregory, *opp. citt.* ; Scrivener-Miller, *op. cit.* ; Westcott and Hort, *op. cit.* ; Nestle, *op. cit.*]

THE uncial period of vellum manuscripts, as will have been seen from the foregoing chapter, extends from the fourth century to the tenth ; but for the last two centuries of its course it overlaps with another style of writing, which was destined to supersede it. As the demand for books increased, the uncial method, with its large characters, each separately formed, became too cumbrous. A style of writing was needed which should occupy less space and consume less time in its production. For everyday purposes such a style had existed as far back as we have any extant remains of Greek writing, and (as we have seen in Chapter II.) it had not infrequently been employed in the transcription of literary works ; but it never had become the professional hand of literature, and books intended for sale or for preservation in a library were always written in the regular uncial hand. In the ninth century, however, the demand for a smaller and more manageable literary hand was met by the introduction of a modified form of the running hand of everyday use. The evolution cannot now be traced in all its details, since the extant specimens of non-literary hands (on papyrus) do not come down much later than the seventh century ; but in these we can see all the elements of the hand which was taken into literary use in the ninth century, and which is commonly called "minuscule," as opposed to the majuscule (uncial or capital) hands of the earlier period. In the true minuscule hand, not only is the writing considerably smaller than the average uncial, but the forms of the letters are different. We have γ, δ, ζ, μ, ξ, σ, v, instead of Γ, Δ, Z, M, Ξ, C, Υ, with lesser variations in the case of the other letters. Also the new forms of the letters lend themselves to combination by means of ligatures into a running hand, in which several letters are written continuously, without lifting the pen ; from which fact minuscule hands are commonly described as "cursive," and it is usual to classify Greek MSS. as "uncials" or "cursives." The description, however, is not accurate, since not every minuscule hand is cursive and (on papyrus at any rate) there is nothing to prevent uncial letters being, to some extent, linked together by ligatures. Broadly speaking, however, and with reference to vellum MSS. alone, the distinction holds good. Most minuscule MSS. are also cursive, and the tendency increases as time goes on, until we find books written in hands almost as cursive as those of non-literary papyri.

Another change in the external characteristics of manuscripts falls within the minuscule period, namely, the introduction of paper by the side of vellum as the material for the reception of writing. Though its manufacture in Asia can be traced back to the eighth century, and its importation into Europe to the tenth, it was not manufactured in this continent until the twelfth century, and does not appear in common use until the thirteenth.[1] Even then it does not supersede vellum. The two materials continue in use side by side through the rest of the period during which books were normally written by hand ; and it was only the invention of printing which finally secured the victory of paper. During the manuscript period the best work could only be produced on vellum ; consequently, though copies of the Scriptures on paper are common enough, the finer

[1] See Thompson, *Greek and Latin Palaeography*, p. 43.

and generally the better, volumes are still those which are written on the older material.

The notation of minuscule MSS. for purposes of reference is simply numerical; but, as in the case of the uncials, separate series are arranged for each of the four principal divisions of the New Testament—the Gospels, Acts and Catholic Epistles, Pauline Epistles, and Apocalypse. Thus the first MSS. in these four groups would be known respectively as Evan. 1, Act. 1, Paul. 1, Apoc. 1. This arrangement keeps the numbers within a more manageable compass, since most MSS. contain only one of these groups, and it also shows what bulk of testimony is available for each part of the New Testament; but it has this disadvantage, that where a volume contains more than one of the groups, it will appear under different numbers in each of the groups concerned. Thus, to take an example at random, a certain MS. in the British Museum, which contains three groups, is known as Evan. 582, Act. 227, Paul. 279; while another, which possesses all four groups, is Evan. 584, Act. 228, Paul. 269, Apoc. 97.

Catalogues of the known minuscule MSS. of the New Testament are given in Scrivener's and Gregory's books, which are the recognised works of reference on this subject. So far as Evan. 449, Act. 181, Paul. 229, and Apoc. 101, the two lists are identical, both being derived from earlier catalogues, ultimately that of Scholz. But from this point they diverge, Gregory having elected not to follow the order adopted by Scrivener [1] in dealing with the MSS. of which the existence had been made known since the work of Scholz; and as far as Evan. 774, Act. 264, Paul. 341, Apoc. 122, the numerations are wholly different. After this point Gregory had the first word, the subsequent MSS. having been first catalogued by him; and Scrivener's latest editor, Mr.

[1] Scrivener's numbers were taken from those assigned by Dean Burgon in a series of letters to the *Guardian* in July 1882, in which he described a considerable number of MSS. which had not previously been included in the extant lists.

E. Miller, has wisely been content to follow his order and adopt his numbers as far as possible. This is clearly the right principle, and in future it may be hoped that the editor who first includes a new MS. in either of the recognised lists will be allowed the right of assigning it a number which will be accepted in subsequent editions of the other list.

The number of minuscule copies of the New Testament hitherto known is given in the latest list of Gregory (*Textkritik*, 1900), as follows :

Gospels	1420
Acts and Catholic Epistles . . .	450
Pauline Epistles	520
Apocalypse	194
	2584

If, however, it is desired to know the number of separate MSS., a deduction must be made from this total in the case of those MSS. which contain more than one of the four groups, and in this way the total is reduced to 1945 ; while a further scrutiny of the lists, to remove duplicate or erroneous entries, reduces the figure to 1825.

On the other hand, there is a whole class of authorities not yet mentioned, of less value than those already described, but serving to swell the total. These are the *Lectionaries*, or volumes containing the Gospels and Epistles appointed to be read throughout the year. They are grouped in two classes, known respectively as Evangeliaria (Evl.)[1] when they contain lessons from the Gospels, and Apostoli or Praxapostoli (Apost.) when they contain the Acts or Epistles. In the catalogues of these MSS., uncials and minuscules are reckoned together ; but the uncials are never of very early date, being almost invariably of the ninth century or later. The number of extant MSS. of these classes is given by Gregory as follows:

---

[1] Scrivener and others use the term *Evangelistarium*, but this properly means only a table of lections, not the lections themselves ; cf. Brightman, *Journal of Theological Studies*, i. 448.

Evangeliaria	.	.	.	.	.	1072
Praxapostoli	.	.	.	.	.	300
						1372

or, after making allowance, on the one hand, for the cases where the same MS. contains both classes, and on the other for erroneous entries or for entries of more than one MS. under the same number, a total of 1255 separate MSS.

Adding up all the figures which have now been presented, we get the following list of Greek authorities for the text of the New Testament, the first column giving the figures arrived at when each group of books is regarded as a distinct MS., the second allowing for duplicates, and giving the sum of separate volumes or fragments of volumes.

Papyri	.	.	.	12	12
Uncials	.	.	.	156	129
Minuscules	.	.	.	2584	1825
Lectionaries	.	.	.	1372	1255
				4124	3221

These figures may not be absolutely correct in all details, but they serve at least to give an approximate idea of the amount of evidence available for the text of the New Testament. Not all of it has been fully examined hitherto. Many of the minuscule MSS. (especially those which are still preserved in the monasteries of the East) have been only superficially studied ; and the lectionaries have been even more neglected than the minuscules. Also there are, no doubt, many MSS. in existence which have not yet found a place in the recognised lists.[1] It is not, however, to be expected that any considerable accession to our knowledge is to be derived from further collection or examination of minuscule MSS. or lectionaries, beyond what is

---

[1] For example, Mr. Lake (*Journal of Theological Studies*, i. 442) mentions that there are more than 120 vellum codices of the Gospels in the library of the Laura on Mount Athos, of which only ten are included in Gregory's list.

already available.   The bulk of evidence is ample ; what is now needed is its proper organisation and digestion.

It is obviously impossible to describe all these 3000 MSS. individually ; but it may be useful to point out those which, so far as our present knowledge goes, are the most notable, and especially those which have been shown to be connected with one another, and thereby to point back to some common ancestor.   Notability, in a minuscule MS., is chiefly to be achieved by departure from the normal type ; and since the normal type of text is that which in the last chapter has been called the *a*-text, the MSS. now to be described are those which, in a greater or less degree, represent the β or δ-texts.   To select these for special mention is not necessarily to assume the superiority of their text ; it is merely to indicate their divergence, whether for better or for worse, from the common norm.   In a future chapter we shall have to consider whether the truth is likely to rest with the majority or the minority.

In the following list Scrivener's numbers are followed, Gregory's being also given when they differ.

Evan. 1 (Act. 1, Paul. 1): an eleventh century MS. at Basle, with illuminations.   Used by Erasmus, and collated by Wetstein and Tregelles.   Its text frequently agrees with that of אBL, while among minuscule MSS. it is closely connected with Evan. 209, and somewhat less closely with 118 and 131.   A study of this group is in preparation by the Rev. K. Lake.

Evan. 2 : a late MS. (fifteenth century) at Basle, only noticeable as having formed the basis of the first printed edition of the New Testament, published by Erasmus in 1516.

Evan. 13 : twelfth century, at Paris.   This MS. was brought into prominence by Professor W. H. Ferrar, of Trinity College, Dublin, who showed that it is closely connected with Evann. 69, 124, and 346.[1]

[1] *A Collation of Four Important Manuscripts of the Gospels*, by W. H. Ferrar and T. K. Abbott (Dublin, 1877).   Professor Abbott carried on and completed Ferrar's work after the death of the latter in 1871.

By a comparison of these four MSS. (which from him are generally known as "the Ferrar group"), Professor Ferrar showed that they are descended from one not very distant ancestor, which he held must have been an uncial MS. of good character; and he and his coadjutor sought to recover the text of this archetype by a collation of its descendants. The Abbé Martin added the observation that three at least of the four (13, 124, 346) were written in Calabria, which must therefore have been the home of the archetype in the twelfth century; also that Evann. 348 (this, however, is doubtful) and 556 are related to the same group. Other scholars have pointed out traces of relation in Evann. 561, 624, 626, 788, and it is probable that further investigations would lead to the identification of other members of the family. With regard to the text represented by this group, it is clear that it is predominantly of the a-type, but it also contains many readings of the β or δ-type. Mr. Rendel Harris, on the ground of certain affinities with the Old Syriac version (see next chapter), sought to establish a Syriac origin for the most characteristic readings of the group,[1] while in a more recent study[2] he argues for an Arabic medium of transmission for this Syriac influence; but this is part of a very large question which cannot here be discussed.

Evan. 18 (Act. 113, Paul. 132, Apoc. 51): a complete New Testament, written in 1364, now at Paris. Only thirty-five complete minuscule copies of the New Testament are known, viz. Evann. 18, 35, 61, 69, 141, 149, 175, 180, 201, 205, 206, 209, 218, 241, 242, 296, 339, 367,

[1] *On the Origin of the Ferrar Group* (Cambridge, 1893). One of the most notable examples of Syriac affinity occurs in Matthew i. 16, where the Ferrar archetype evidently had the same reading as the Curetonian Syriac. See below, p. 131. Evan. 346 preserves this reading now. Another noticeable feature of the Ferrar group is that they place the section John vii. 53-viii. 11 after Luke xxi. 38, while Luke xxii. 43, 44 is transferred to Matthew xxvi. 39, as is also the case in some lectionaries.

[2] *Further Researches into the History of the Ferrar Group* (Cambridge, 1900). In this work Rendel Harris works out the Calabro-Sicilian origin of the group in great detail, concluding that part, at least, of it is descended from a Graeco-Arabic archetype in Sicily in the twelfth century.

386, 451, 472, 488, 492, 503, 531, 584, 603, 605, 622, 698, 922, 1072, 1075, 1094, 1262. Of these, nine (61, 69, 201, 488, 492, 503, 531, 584, 603) are in England or Ireland.

Evan. 28: eleventh century, at Paris. Carelessly written, but containing many noticeable readings, chiefly of the δ-type of text.

Evan. 33 (Act. 13, Paul. 17): ninth century, at Paris. Examined by many scholars, and fully collated by Tregelles. Its text is more of the β-type than that of any other minuscule MS. of the Gospels. It was called by Eichhorn "the queen of the cursives"; and Hort considered it to rank in antiquity of text next to Act. 61 alone among the cursives.

Evann. 54 (Bodleian Library, Oxford), 56 (at Lincoln College, Oxford), 58 (at New College, Oxford), and 61 (at Trinity College, Dublin), the first named written in 1338, the rest in the fifteenth century at earliest, are very closely connected, but not of special importance except for their association with the last named. Evann. 47, 109, and 171 also belong to this group.

Evan. 59: twelfth century, at Caius College, Cambridge. Contains some notable readings of the β-type.

Evan. 61 (Act. 34, Paul. 40, Apoc. 92): fifteenth or sixteenth century, at Trinity College, Dublin. This MS. is historically important, because it was the first Greek MS. discovered which contained the passage relating to the Three Heavenly Witnesses (1 John v. 7, 8), and thereby was the cause of that passage being inserted in Erasmus' third edition (1522), in fulfilment of a pledge given to those who criticised his omission of it in his earlier editions. It is now known to occur also in Act. 162. The Apocalypse is a later addition, probably copied from Evan. 69.

Evan. 69 (Act. 31, Paul. 37, Apoc. 14): fourteenth to fifteenth century, at Leicester, written partly on vellum and partly on paper, the vellum forming the inner and outer sheet in each gathering. Collated by Tregelles

I

and Scrivener. It belongs to the Ferrar group (see Evan. 13, above).[1]

Evan. 71 : a well-written copy, in the Lambeth Library, transcribed in A.D. 1160, and containing a good text.

Evan. 102 : this item illustrates the difficulty of making a complete and accurate catalogue of the authorities for the text of the New Testament. This number has been assigned to some readings which Wetstein found noted in the margin of a New Testament in the library of J. Le Long. These readings were of good character, and well deserved notice ; but it is now recognised that they must have been taken from the great Codex Vaticanus (B), and the number assigned to them is consequently left vacant.

Evann. 113, 114 : two early cursives, of the eleventh and tenth centuries respectively, now in the British Museum, well written and with good texts.

Evan. 118 : thirteenth century, in the Bodleian Library at Oxford. A palimpsest, with the Gospels uppermost. Akin to Evan. 1 (q.v.).

Evan. 124 : twelfth century, at Vienna. One of the Ferrar group (see Evan. 13).

Evan. 131 (Act. 70, Paul. 77) : fourteenth or fifteenth century, in the Vatican at Rome. Akin to Evan. 1 (q.v.). Probably employed for the Aldine edition of the New Testament in 1518.

Evan. 157 : twelfth century, in the Vatican. Written for John II. Comnenus (1118-43). A handsome copy, with a remarkable text. Hort describes it as "the best example of the few cursives which more nearly resemble 33" in the ancient elements of its text, "though not connected with 33 by any near affinity." Zahn states that its text sometimes approaches that of Marcion. Belongs to the same group as Λ (q.v.).

Evan. 201 (Act. 91, Paul. 104, Apoc. 94) : A.D.

---

[1] See special studies of this MS. in Scrivener's *Codex Augiensis*, appendix, and Rendel Harris' *Origin of the Leicester Codex* (1887).

1357, in the British Museum. A large and handsome copy of the whole New Testament ; collated by Scrivener.

Evan. 205 (Act. 93, Paul. 106, Apoc. 88): fifteenth century, at Venice. Written for Cardinal Bessarion. Closely akin to, if not copied from, Evan. 209. It contains both Testaments, as also do Evann. 206 and 218, while Evan. 605 did so when complete.

Evan. 209 (Act. 95, Paul. 108, Apoc. 46): variously assigned to the eleventh and fourteenth centuries, at Venice, formerly the property of Bessarion. Akin to Evann. 1 (q.v.), 118, 131.

Evan. 211 : twelfth century, at Venice. A bilingual Graeco-Arabic MS., probably executed in Calabia or Sicily, and containing much of the additional matter often found in MSS. of the Ferrar group, but not having itself a Ferrar text (cf. Lake, *Journ. Theol. Studies*, i. 117-120).

Evan. 218 (Act. 65, Paul. 57, Apoc. 33): thirteenth century, at Vienna. Contains both Testaments, and has many noticeable readings in the New Testament. It came to Vienna from Constantinople, and was published in full by F. K. Alter (1786-7).

Evan. 235 : A.D. 1314, at Copenhagen. Contains many readings of the δ-type.

Evan. 262: tenth century, at Paris. Probably written in Italy. Belongs to the same group as Λ (q.v.), and has many noticeable readings.

Evan. 274 : tenth century, at Paris. Only noticeable as containing (in the margin) the shorter ending to St. Mark, found also in L and Ψ.

Evan. 346 : twelfth century, at Milan. One of the Ferrar group (see Evan. 13). In Matthew i. 16 this MS. (alone of Greek MSS.) has substantially the same reading as the Curetonian Syriac (see below), Ἰωσὴφ ᾧ μνηστευθῆσα (sic) παρθένος Μαριὰμ ἐγέννησεν Ἰησοῦν τὸν λεγόμενον Χριστόν.

Evan. 431 (Act. 180, Paul. 238): twelfth to thirteenth century, in the Catholic Seminary at Strassburg (wrongly stated by Gregory and Scrivener to have perished in the bombardment of 1870 ; see Valentine-Richards, *Journ. Theol. Studies*, i. 608. Its text is partly of the δ-type and partly of the β-type, and it appears to be akin to Act. 137.

Evan. 473 [Greg. 565]: ninth to tenth century, at St. Petersburg. A beautiful MS., written in gold letters on purple vellum, and containing a remarkable text. Hort (who assigns it the number 81) considers it the most valuable cursive for the preservation of readings of the δ - type, especially in St. Mark, which has been separately edited by Belsheim (1885), and re-collated by Cronin (Cambridge, *Texts and Studies*, v. 4, 1899). It has the same subscriptions as Λ (q.v.).

Evan. 481 [Greg. 461]: A.D. 835, at St. Petersburg. Notable as the earliest dated Greek MS. on vellum in existence, and known as the "Uspensky Gospels," from its former owner, Bishop Porphyry Uspensky of Kiew.

Evann. 510, 511 [Greg. 471, 472]: two MSS. at Lambeth, of about the twelfth century, collated by Scrivener, who states that they have valuable readings.

Evan. 556 [Greg. 543]: twelfth century, in the possession of the Baroness Burdett-Coutts. Akin to the Ferrar group ; see description of Evan. 13.

Evan. 561 [Greg. 713]: eleventh to twelfth century, in the possession of Miss A. Peckover, of Wisbech. Identified in 1877 by Mr. Rendel Harris as akin to the Ferrar group ; but in his recent study of the group he makes no mention of it.

Evan. 565 [Greg. 716]: twelfth century, in British Museum. A well-written copy, with many interesting readings.

Evan. 582 (Act. 227, Paul. 279) [Greg. 496]: thirteenth to fourteenth century, in British Museum. Contains several readings of the β-type.

Evan. 603 (Act. 231, Paul. 266 and 271, Apoc. 89) [Greg. 699]: tenth or eleventh century, partly in British Museum, partly at Sir R. Cholmeley's School, Highgate,

PLATE IX.

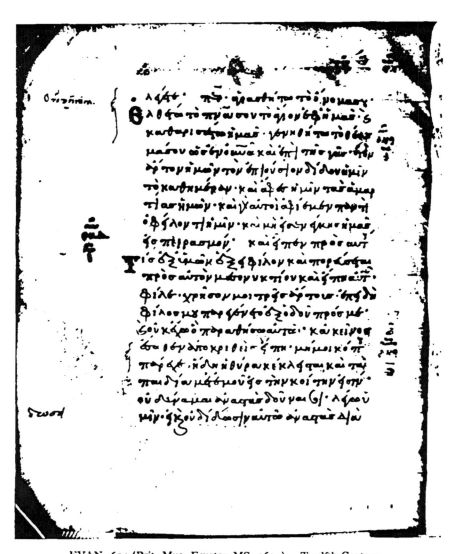

EVAN. 604 (Brit. Mus. Egerton MS. 2610).   Twelfth Century.
(Scale nearly 1 : 1.   The page shown contains Luke xi. 2-8, with the abbreviated
form of the Lord's Prayer.)

To face p. 117.

the latter portion having been bought in Epirus by the Baroness Burdett-Coutts. A very handsome manuscript.

Evan. 604 [Greg. 700]: twelfth century, in British Museum (Plate IX.). Contains a large number of very interesting readings, 270 being unique, while in several others it represents the δ-type of text. Collated by Mr. H. C. Hoskier (*A Full Account and Collation of the Greek Cursive Codex Evan.* 604, London, 1890).

Evann. 624, 626 [Greg. 826, 828]: both eleventh to twelfth century, at Grotta Ferrata. Belong to the Ferrar group. Both written in Calabria. Described by the Rev. K. Lake in *Journ. Theol. Studies*, i. 117-120.

Evan. 743 [Greg. 579]: thirteenth century, at Paris. Has the double termination to St. Mark, as in L.

Evan. 892: tenth century, in the British Museum. Contains many remarkable readings of an early type. Collated by J. Rendel Harris in *Journal of Biblical Literature* (1890).

Evan. 1071: twelfth century, in the monastery of the Laura on Mount Athos, but written probably in South Italy. It has the same subscriptions as Λ, etc., and is remarkable for having a text of the section relating to the woman taken in adultery practically identical with that in D (cf. Lake, *Journ. Theol. Studies*, i. 441).

Evann. 775-811, 846-869 (with a few exceptions) are at Athens, 905-1140 in the monasteries of Mount Athos, 1160-1181 at Patmos, 1185-1256 in the monastery of St. Catherine on Mount Sinai; and of these, as of most of the MSS. belonging to the latter half of the list, little is known beyond the mere fact of their existence. There may be many MSS. among them as important as the best of those we have described; but at present, for the most part, they have not been sufficiently examined, and merely hold a nominal place in the list of authorities for the Gospel text.

We come now to MSS. of the second group, the Acts and Catholic Epistles. Several of them, which also contain the Gospels, have been described above.

Act. 1 = Evan. 1, q.v.   Has the Euthalian apparatus here and in the Pauline Epistles.

Act. 2 (Paul. 2): variously dated in the twelfth, thirteenth, or fourteenth century, at Basle.   The principal source of the text of the Acts and Epistles in Erasmus' *editio princeps* of the New Testament.

Act. 9 (Paul. 11): eleventh century, at Cambridge. Used by Stephanus, and contains several notable readings in the Catholic Epistles.

Act. 13 = Evan. 33, q.v.

Act. 15: eleventh century, at Paris.   Has colophon stating that it (i.e. an ancestor) was collated with the MS. of Pamphilus at Caesarea (cf. ℵ and H$_8$).

Act. 25 (Paul. 31, Apoc. 7): A.D. 1087, in the British Museum (from Asia Minor).   Contains a good text.

Act. 31 = Evan. 69, q.v.   Hort quotes it as containing many ancient readings in this part of the New Testament, in spite of the late date of the MS. itself.

Act. 34 = Evan. 61, q.v.

Act. 40 (Paul. 46, Apoc. 12): eleventh century, in the Vatican.   Contains the apparatus of Euthalius (prologues, etc.) to the Acts and Epistles, and is the basis of Zacagni's edition of them (see description of Cod. H$_8$). The Apocalypse is a later addition, of the fifteenth century.

Act. 58: thirteenth century, in the Bodleian Library. Has many readings of the δ-type in Acts xiii.-xxii. (cf. A. Pott, *Der abendländische Text der Apostelgeschichte*, Leipzig, 1900).

Act. 61: A.D. 1044, in British Museum (Add. MS. 20003 ; Plate X.).   A roughly written copy, but of great importance.   Agrees in many respects with the β-type of text.   Hort regards it as by far the best of the cursives in respect of freedom from late readings, and as containing a very ancient text.   Collated by Tischendorf (who brought it from Egypt in 1853), Tregelles, and Scrivener.

Act. 65 = Evan. 218, q.v.

Act. 70 = Evan. 131, q.v.

PLATE X.

ACT. 61 (Brit. Mus. Add. MS. 20003). A.D. 1044.

(Scale 6 : 7. The page shown contains Acts. xvi. 3-9. In verse 7 the MS. originally
had Ἰησοῦ after πνεῦμα, as in ℵABC²DE etc. The word has been partially erased
by a corrector.)

To face p. 118.

Act. 83 (Paul. 93, Apoc. 99): tenth century, at Naples. Like Act. 15, has colophon referring to the MS. of Pamphilus at Caesarea.

Act. 95 = Evan. 209, q.v.

Act. 96 (Paul. 109): eleventh century, at Venice, whither it was brought from Sicily. Has a good text, accompanied by Latin and Arabic translations.

Act. 137 (Paul. 176): eleventh century, at Milan (previously at Corfu). The text is of the δ-type, and especially useful for the end of Acts, where D, the principal Greek authority of this type, is mutilated.

Act. 162 (Paul. 200): fourteenth to fifteenth century, in the Vatican. A bilingual MS., having the Vulgate text parallel with the Greek. This is the only MS. besides Act. 34 (= Evan. 61) which contains the passage relating to the Three Heavenly Witnesses; and as 34 has been sometimes suspected of having been expressly written for the purpose, after the controversy with Erasmus, 162 is the only unsuspected Greek witness to the passage. As, however, it is stated that in other passages the Greek text has been accommodated to the parallel Latin, its authority is not great.

Act. 178 (Paul. 242, Apoc. 87): eleventh or twelfth century, at Berlin, formerly in the Phillipps Library at Cheltenham. The text is said to be valuable in the Apocalypse.

Act. 180 = Evan. 431, q.v.

Act. 184 (Paul. 254) [Greg. 216]: fifteenth century, formerly at Lambeth, but given in 1817 to the Patriarch of Jerusalem. Its text is akin to that of Act. 137, 221. Hort denotes it by the number 112.

Act. 220 (Paul. 264) [Greg. 223]: eleventh or twelfth century, in the library of Baroness Burdett-Coutts. Said to be one of the handsomest copies of the latter part of the New Testament in existence.

Act. 221 (Paul. 265) [Greg. 224]: twelfth century, in the library of Baroness Burdett-Coutts. The text is of the same type as D and its colleagues (137, 184, etc.).

Act. 231 [Greg. 256] = Evan. 603, q.v.

Act. 232 (Paul. 271, Apoc. 107) [Greg. 205]: A.D. 1111, in the British Museum. A handsome copy, with Euthalian apparatus.

Act. 243 (Paul. 291) [Greg. 317]: tenth century, at Grotta Ferrata. Has the Euthalian apparatus.

Act. 334 (Paul. 319) [Greg. 328]: tenth century, in the Vatican. Another Euthalian MS. Other Euthalian MSS. are Act. 256 (in the Vatican) and 393 (at Thessalonica), both of the eleventh century.

Act. 270-287, 336-379 are in the monasteries of Mount Athos, 289-300, 394-414 at Sinai.

In the third section, that of the Pauline Epistles, most of the important MSS. have been already mentioned.

Paul. 1 = Evan. 1, q.v.

Paul. 2 = Act. 2, q.v.

Paul. 17 = Evan. 33, q.v.   The best Pauline cursive.

Paul. 31 = Act. 25, q.v.

Paul. 37 = Evan. 69, q.v.

Paul. 40 = Evan. 61, q.v.

Paul. 47 : eleventh century, in the Bodleian (formerly on the island of Chalcé). Has a text akin to that of A and B (which, it will be remembered, are nearer to one another in the Epistles than in the Gospels).

Paul. 67 (Act. 66): A.D. 1064-68, at Vienna. Valuable on account of some marginal readings, which must have been taken from an ancient MS. Hort states that this MS. must have been nearly akin to M_3,[1] though it cannot have been M_3 itself.

Paul. 80 (Act. 73): eleventh century, in the Vatican. Akin to Paul. 37 (Evan. 69).

Paul. 81 : twelfth century, in the Vatican. Has the Euthalian apparatus, as also have Paul. 83, 379, 381.

Paul. 93 = Act. 83, q.v.

Paul. 108 = Evan. 209, q.v.

Paul. 238 = Evan. 431, q.v.

---

[1] Hort says M_2 (*Introd.* p. 155) ; but the previous page (as well as the context here) shows that he means Mpaul, which is described above as M_3.

Paul. 266 + Paul. 271 [Greg. 306] = Evan. 603, q.v.

The list ends, like the others, with a number of MSS. from Athos (Paul. 423-468, with a few exceptions) and Sinai (481-485).

There remain only the MSS. of the Apocalypse.

Apoc. 1 : twelfth century, at Mayhingen in Bavaria. The only MS. used by Erasmus for the Apocalypse in his *editio princeps* ; and since it is defective at the end (xxii. 16-21) this part of his Greek text was supplied by re-translation from the Latin, whence it has happened that some words still hold their ground in our Textus Receptus, for which there is no authority in any Greek MS. whatever. Hort describes this MS. as above the average in quality, containing a large and good ancient element.

Apoc. 7 = Act. 25, q.v.

Apoc. 14 = Evan. 69, q.v.

Apoc. 28 : fifteenth century, in the Bodleian. According to Scrivener, it is akin to 7 and 96 ; while Gregory, following Delitzsch, states that it appears to be copied from Apoc. 79.

Apoc. 38 : thirteenth century, in the Vatican. Akin to Apoc. 1, with good readings of an early type; according to Scrivener it closely resembles A and C.

Apoc. 68 : eleventh century, in the Vatican. A fragment, with text akin to A and to Apoc. 35 and 87.

Apoc. 79 : fourteenth century, in the Vatican. Cf. Apoc. 28 above.

Apoc. 87 = Act. 178, q.v. A good text of the Apocalypse, to which Apoc. 35 and 68 are akin.

Apoc. 91 : fifteenth century, in the Vatican. The late supplement to B, which is defective here.

Apoc. 92 = Evan. 61. Probably a later addition, copied from Apoc. 14.

Apoc. 95 : twelfth century, in the Parham Library (from Mount Athos). One of the best cursive MSS. of the Apocalypse.

Apoc. 96 : fourteenth century, in the Parham Library (from Mount Athos).   Akin to 7 and 28.

The remaining cursive MSS. of the Apocalypse, so far as they are known at all, are of minor importance.   Little, too, is known of most of the lectionaries (uncial and minuscule), the only one that need be particularly mentioned being Evl. 259 (A.D. 1319, in the British Museum), which Hort (who cites it as 39) quotes as containing a considerable early element.   The texts of lectionaries may be good ; but as they are comparatively late in date, and also labour under the suspicion that their transcribers might feel themselves less bound to textual accuracy than in the case of copies of the New Testament itself, they have generally been left on one side by textual students. Consequently in a summary of results, such as the present, there is little or nothing to be said of them.

So ends the roll of direct witnesses to the text of the New Testament—of witnesses, that is, which give the text of the sacred books in the language in which they were written.   No doubt the roll is not complete.   There are many copies of the Greek New Testament which have not yet been brought into the recognised lists, because they have not yet found a home in any of the great libraries or in accessible collections of private owners. No doubt, also, the roll as it stands is still largely nominal.   Only a small proportion of the whole number has been fully examined ; many, especially of those which are still in Eastern libraries, have hardly even been cursorily inspected.   It is possible, and even probable, that among these are some of really notable character, fit to be ranked with the best of those which we have described above, such as Evann. 1, 13, 33, 69, 157, 209, or 604 ; and a commission of German scholars is now engaged in a systematic examination of the minuscule MSS. for this purpose.   Yet it may be doubted whether they can contain anything which will add substantially to our knowledge.   The minuscules are in themselves so late, and we have so many authorities reaching back to an age far nearer that of the original autographs, that they can have but little independent value.   Their value lies in the light which they throw on the evidence of the earlier witnesses. They show decisively what type of text was prevalent in the mediaeval church, while in the case of the less common types of text they may supply gaps or explain difficulties which the scantiness of the uncial evidence has left.   But for this purpose the minuscules which we have already are perhaps sufficient.   Something may be accomplished in the way of grouping them, as has been done in the case of the Ferrar MSS., though even this is not of much value unless the archetype can be thrown back to a very early date.   Something, too, may be obtained by the examination of some of these groups, as in the case of the Euthalian MSS.   The most promising outlook, however, in the department of Greek MSS. is the possibility of the discovery of early copies on papyrus in Egypt.   The fragments which have been found show what may yet come to light in that unexhausted field, and hold out to us the hope that we may yet possess copies of the Gospels written in the third, or even in the second century.   Save for such chances as this, it does not seem as if there could be much added to our existing knowledge in the way of the evidence of Greek MSS. to the text of the New Testament.   Some points are settled by it, some are left unsettled.   The exact bearing of this mass of testimony, and the principles upon which it should be treated, will be the subject of consideration in a later chapter.   But first it is necessary to pass in review another body of witnesses, whose evidence may be called for when that of the Greek manuscripts proves doubtful or inadequate.

CHAPTER V

THE ANCIENT VERSIONS

[**Authorities**: Gregory, *Prolegomena*; Scrivener-Miller, *op. cit.*, chapters by H. J. White, G. H. Gwilliam, A. C. Headlam, F. C. Conybeare, etc.; Westcott and Hort, *op. cit.*; Nestle, *op. cit.*—On **Syriac** versions: *Studia Biblica*, i. 39 ff., 151 ff., iii. 47 ff., 105 ff.; J. H. Hill, *The Earliest Life of Christ . . . being the Diatessaron of Tatian* (London, 1893); Rendel Harris, *The Diatessaron of Tatian, a preliminary study* (London, 1890); A. S. Lewis, *The Four Gospels translated from the Sinaitic Palimpsest* (London, 1894); Gwynn, *The Apocalypse of St. John in a Syriac version* (Dublin, 1897); A. S. Lewis and M. D. Gibson, *Studia Sinaitica*, pt. vi. (1897), and *The Palestinian Syriac Lectionary* (1899).—**Armenian**: F. C. Conybeare, art. in Hastings' *Dictionary of the Bible*; J. Armitage Robinson, *Euthaliana* (Cambridge, 1895).—**Coptic**: Hyvernat, *Étude sur les versions coptes de la Bible*, in *Revue Biblique*, 1896-97; Forbes Robinson, art. in Hastings, *op. cit.*; [G. Horner], *The Coptic Version of the New Testament in the northern dialect* (Oxford, 1898); information from Mr. W. E. Crum.—**Latin**: Sabatier, *Bibliorum sacrorum Latinae versiones antiquae* (Paris, 1751); Bianchini, *Evangeliarium quadruplex* (Rome, 1749); Wordsworth, Sanday, and White, *Old Latin Biblical Texts*, parts i.-iv. (Oxford, 1883-97); Westcott, art. "Vulgate" in Smith's *Dictionary of the Bible*; F. C. Burkitt, *The Old Latin and the Itala* (Cambridge, 1896); S. Berger, *Histoire de la Vulgate* (Paris, 1893); Wordsworth and White, *Novum Testamentum Domini nostri Iesu Christi Latine* (vol. i. Oxford, 1889-98); H. A. A. Kennedy, art. in Hastings, *op. cit.*; P. Corssen, *Bericht über die lateinischen Bibelübersetzungen*, in *Jahresbericht über die Fortschritt d. class. Altertumswissenschaft*, bd. 101 (1899); and works on special MSS. mentioned below.]

In the case of most ancient books, the evidence for the establishment of the true text is exhausted when we have come to the end of the manuscripts which contain it in the original language; but with the Bible the situation is wholly different. For both Testaments evidence of the greatest value is to be derived from the early translations which were made of them into other tongues. The cause of this difference has nothing to do with the distinctive character of the sacred Scriptures; it is simply due to the fact that in the case of the Bible we possess copies of translations which were made as early as, or earlier than, the most ancient existing manuscripts in the original language, while of the secular classics we have no such ancient translations.[1] No doubt this evidence has to be used with caution. In the first place, the true text of the version itself has to be recovered, so far as may be possible, from the various manuscripts which contain it; next, the original Hebrew or Greek text represented by the translation has to be determined, due allowance being made for possible liberties taken by the original translator (which, in the case of the Old Testament especially, were often very considerable); then the date of the original translation must be considered, to show at what point in the stream of tradition this branch diverged from the main current; finally, its relation to the other witnesses must be discovered and the value of its testimony estimated. All this requires the exercise of considerable knowledge and judgment; but in spite of all difficulties and deductions the evidence of the versions is of the very greatest importance, and (as will be seen later) questions connected with them are now among the most interesting of those which demand the attention of textual students.

In the present chapter the various ancient versions of the New Testament—all those, namely, which can be held to be of any textual value—will be considered in turn, and an attempt made to summarise the existing state of knowledge with regard to them. The most natural order would seem to be geographical, taking first the versions made in the East, in the countries bordering upon Palestine, and afterwards those which were made

---

[1] There are Latin and Arabic translations of Aristotle which are of some textual importance, and a Greek translation of Ovid's *Heroides*; but these are very trivial exceptions to the general rule.

further afield, in the more distant, but not less important, West.

1. **The Syriac Versions.**—Syriac or Aramaic was the language in common use in Palestine and the surrounding country in the time of our Lord,[1] and was naturally the first language into which a translation of the New Testament was required. It was the language in which our Lord Himself spoke,[2] and in which, according to some very ancient authorities, the Gospel of St. Matthew was originally written. Phrases of it, such as *Talitha cumi* or *Eloi, Eloi, lama sabachthani*, remain imbedded in our Greek texts. As Christianity spread through Syria, and as the canonical Gospels and Epistles were more and more recognised as the authoritative records of our Lord's life and the apostolic teaching, a demand would naturally arise for translations of these books into the vernacular. At first, perhaps, such translations would be merely oral and provisional, but before long they would be written down for greater convenience and security ; and from this first translation or translations the versions now in existence may trace their descent.

Five such versions are at present known, and the questions of their inter-relation with one another are not yet finally settled. Sixty years ago, the priority both in age and in importance would unquestionably have been given to the Peshitto, which may be called the authorised version of the Syrian Church ; and some scholars still claim this position for it. Recent discoveries, however, have thrown fresh light on the problem, and of these it will be convenient to speak first.

a. **The Diatessaron of Tatian.**—Little more than

---

[1] It was in use in Northern Syria from very early times, and was adopted as their vernacular by the Jews after their return from Babylon, where another dialect of the same language (called "Chaldee" in the Old Testament) was spoken. Cf. Neubauer in *Studia Biblica*, i. 39 ff., on "The Dialects of Palestine in the Time of Christ." The Aramaic of Palestine is not identical with the dialect of the versions described below, but it is closely akin to it.

[2] This has been disputed, notably by Dr. A. Roberts, who maintains that our Lord spoke Greek ; but he does not seem to have made out his case.

twenty years ago the name of this work was a battle-cry
for controversialists of opposing schools, and its discovery
is one of the most curious, and also one of the most
important, episodes in the history of modern Biblical
criticism. It belongs, however, rather to the " higher
criticism" of the New Testament, and it will be sufficient
here to indicate briefly its bearings on textual problems.
That Tatian, an Assyrian Christian, compiled about the
year 170 a Gospel narrative, by a process of selection
and harmonisation from the four canonical Gospels, has
long been maintained by Christian apologists, on the
strength of statements by Eusebius and other ancient
writers; but the interpretation of these statements was
disputed, and no vestige of the original work seemed to
have been left to establish its character, much less its
precise text. It is true that in 1836 an Armenian
version of a commentary on the *Diatessaron* by Ephraem
of Syria was published by the monks of the Mechitarist
monastery in Venice; but this was a sealed book to
Western scholars until a Latin translation of it was
produced in 1876 by Dr. G. Moesinger, to which general
attention was called by Dr. Ezra Abbot in 1880. The
discovery of this commentary (in which large parts of
the *Diatessaron* itself are quoted *verbatim*) not only
established finally the general character of the work,
proving that it was really a compilation from the four
canonical Gospels, but also stimulated further research,
as a result of which first one and then another copy of
an Arabic translation of the entire *Diatessaron* was
brought to light (one in Rome and one in Egypt, but
both now in the Vatican Library), the text of which
appeared in print in 1888 under the editorship of Ciasca.[1]

That the original *Diatessaron* was written in Syriac
is now generally accepted, though formerly (chiefly on

[1] The recovery of the *Diatessaron* has shown that the Latin Harmony of
Victor of Capua, preserved in the Codex Fuldensis (see below, p. 194), was in
fact derived from Tatian's work; but as Victor substituted the Vulgate text
for the Old Latin which he found in his exemplar, it does not help us to recon-
stitute the text of the *Diatessaron*.

the ground of its Greek name) it was often supposed
to ·have been in Greek.   Certainly the Arabic version,
which is all we now possess, was made from the Syriac,
and there is no good reason to believe that this was
other than the original language of Tatian's compilation,
which is known to have been generally used in the
churches of Syria, and to have been annotated by the
Syrian father Ephraem ; while there are signs that the
Old Testament quotations in it were in accordance with
the Syriac version of the Scriptures, and (as we shall
see later) its text has strong affinities with that which
is found in other Syriac versions.   If this is so, then we
know that in the third quarter of the second century
there was in existence a Syriac harmony of the four
Gospels.   It is perhaps not admissible to argue that this
implies the existence of a complete Syriac version of the
Gospels at this date, since Tatian may have made his
own translation from the Greek ; but it is highly probable
that before this time the churches of Syria had required
a written translation of the sacred books, and in that
case Tatian would naturally make use of the material
which lay ready to his hand.   In any case the *Diatessaron*, so far as we can recover its original form, provides
us with a text which must go back to Greek MSS.
of at least the middle of the second century, and possibly
much earlier.

The original form of the *Diatessaron* can, of course,
only be approximately known to us, since what we possess
is but two copies of an Arabic version, made early in
the eleventh century from a Syriac MS. written about
the year 900, together with an Armenian version of a
Syriac commentary composed by a writer who died in
378.   But Orientalist scholars tell us that the Arabic
bears signs of being a faithful translation from the Syriac,
and the affinities of the text with other Syriac versions
support this belief.   No doubt the text has suffered
modification since it left the hand of Tatian, and (as is
invariably the case in such matters) has been partially

assimilated to the versions which were popular at a later
date. There are traces in it of the influence of both the
Peshitto and the Philoxenian versions (see below); but
there is also a large proportion of the text which has
a different character from these, and which may fairly
be held to represent the original form of the work. This
belongs to what has been called in the last chapter the
δ-type of the Gospel text. It has affinities with B and
א, but even more with D and its associates, and therefore
tends to support the view that these come nearer than
the α-form to the primitive text of the books of the
New Testament.[1]

b. **The Old Syriac.**—Somewhat fuller, but still very
meagre, is the knowledge that we have of the next Syriac
version which falls to be described; and this knowledge
too is of very recent date. Up to 1842 the Peshitto held
the field as the earliest Syriac version of the Bible; but
in that year a large number of Syriac manuscripts were
acquired by the British Museum, through the instru-
mentality of Archdeacon Tattam and others, from the
monastery of St. Mary Deipara in the Nitrian desert in
Egypt, among which Dr. W. Cureton, then assistant-
keeper in the department of manuscripts, identified one
(now Add. MS. 14451) as containing a hitherto unknown
version of the Gospels. The text of this MS., edited by
Cureton, was printed and privately circulated in 1848,
though not formally published until 1858; and from
him the version has been commonly known as the
Curetonian Syriac, though in view of the discovery to be
mentioned in the next paragraph it will now be more
convenient to assign the term Curetonian to this particular MS. and not to the version of which it is but one
of the representatives. Three additional leaves of the
same version, and probably of the same MS., were

[1] For the *Diatessaron*, see, in addition to the authorities quoted at the head
of this chapter, *The Diatessaron of Tatian*, edited by S. Hemphill (1880). A
good popular account of it is given in *Recent Evidence for the Authenticity of
the Gospels: Tatian's Diatessaron*, by Michael Maher, S.J. (London, Catholic
Truth Society, 1893).

brought from the East by Dr. Sachau to Berlin, and were edited by Roediger in 1872.

Cureton's discovery stood by itself for just fifty years, during which time the problem of its relation to the Peshitto was a subject of active controversy ; but in 1892 another discovery was made which enlarged and at the same time complicated the problem. Two Cambridge ladies, twin-sisters, Mrs. Lewis and Mrs. Gibson, emboldened by the success of Mr. Rendel Harris in finding the Syriac MS. of the *Apology* of Aristides in the monastery of St. Catherine on Mount Sinai, undertook an expedition to the same monastery in search of further treasures. Among the manuscripts which they examined was a palimpsest containing some remarkable lives of female saints, with a lower writing which Mrs. Lewis so far identified as to see that it was a copy of the Gospels ; but it was not until the photographs which she took of it had been brought to Cambridge that it was recognised by Mr. F. C. Burkitt and Professor Bensly as belonging to the same family as the Curetonian MS. On this a second expedition was organised, in 1893, by Messrs. Burkitt, Bensly, and Rendel Harris, with the two original discoverers, in order to make a complete transcript of the MS. ; and as a result of this expedition the text was published in full in 1894. A revised edition of several pages, with many supplementary readings and an English translation, was subsequently published by Mrs. Lewis, after a third visit to Sinai and a re-examination of the original.[1] The Gospel text is assigned to the beginning of the fifth or even to the fourth century, being thus somewhat older than the Curetonian MS., which is placed later in the fifth century. The upper text is dated in the year 778.

The Sinaitic and Curetonian MSS. are far from

---

[1] *The Four Gospels in Syriac transcribed from the Sinaitic Palimpsest*, by the late R. L. Bensly, J. Rendel Harris, and F. C. Burkitt (Cambridge, 1894) ; *Some Pages of the Four Gospels retranscribed*, by A. S. Lewis (London, 1896). An English version, with brief introduction, was published by Mrs. Lewis in 1894 (*The Four Gospels translated from the Sinaitic Palimpsest*).

PLATE XI.

THE CURETONIAN SYRIAC MS.   Fifth Century.

(Scale 3 : 8.   The page shown includes part of the additional passage inserted after
Matt. xx. 28 in this MS., in DΦ, and in many MSS. of the Old Latin version.   It
also contains Matt. xx. 29-xxi. 3.)

To face p. **130.**

containing identical texts, but they agree so far as to
make it certain that they derive from a common original,
and may be treated as representatives of a single version
in different stages of development. Neither is complete,
the Sinaitic containing (with local mutilations) Matthew
i. 1-vi. 9, viii. 2-34, ix.-xvi. 15, xvii. 12-xx. 24, xxi. 20-
xxviii. 7 ; Mark i. 12-44, ii. 21-iv. 17, v. 1-26, vi. 5-xvi.
8 (where the Gospel ends) ; Luke i. 1-16, i. 39-v. 28, vi.
12-xxiv. 53 ; John i. 25-47, ii. 16-iv. 37, v. 6-25, v.
46-xviii. 31, xix. 40-xxi. 25 ; while the Curetonian has
only Matthew i. 1-viii. 22, x. 32-xxiii. 25 ; Mark xvi.
17-20 ; Luke ii. 48-iii. 16, vii. 33-xvi. 12, xvii. 1-xxiv.
44 ; John i. 1-42, iii. 5-viii. 19, xiv. 10-12, 15-19,
21-23, 26-29 (Luke being, however, placed after John).
Both manuscripts differ markedly in text from the
majority of Greek MSS. and from the Peshitto Syriac ; but
this divergence is greater in the Sinaitic than in the
Curetonian, the latter appearing to represent a later stage
in the history of the version, and to be the result of a
revision in which many readings were introduced from
the texts in ordinary use. In both forms the version
belongs to the δ-type of text, often ranging itself with
Codex Bezae and the Old Latin version.

Some of the more notable readings may be mentioned.
That which has aroused most controversy is in Matthew
i. 16, where the Sinaitic has the remarkable reading,
" Joseph, to whom was betrothed Mary the Virgin, begat
Jesus, who is called the Christ," while the Curetonian has,
" Joseph, to whom was betrothed Mary the Virgin, who
bare Jesus Christ." At first sight the Sinaitic text
appears to deny the divine birth of our Lord, and it is
not surprising that it was on the one hand accused of
heretical leanings and on the other claimed as representing the true original version of the passage, which had
been corrupted in all other known copies in all languages.
That this text, *if* it denies the divine birth, cannot be original,
may easily be shown, since the context of the passage proves
the writer's knowledge of the Christian story (" Mary *the*

Virgin," " the Christ," "when Mary his mother was espoused
to Joseph, when they had not come near one to the other,
she was found with child of the Holy Ghost," and the
reference to the fulfilment of Isaiah's prophecy of the
virgin birth); and the difference of the reading from that
of all other authorities [1] makes it highly improbable that
it is the true form of the text. But, in addition, good
reason has been shown for the belief that the words used
in verse 16 were never intended to deny the divine birth
at all, the use of the word "begat" being precisely
analogous to its use throughout the genealogy, in which,
as is well known, it does not always indicate literal
descent, but rather an official line of succession.[2] The
variant reading therefore, though interesting (and possibly
coming near to the text of the original document from
which St. Matthew's genealogy was derived, and in which
our Lord would of course be entered as the son of Joseph),
has no important doctrinal bearings.

Other important readings are as follows.[3]   The Curetonian MS. inserts the names Ahaziah, Joash, and Amaziah
in Matthew i. 8 with some support from D, but the
Sinaitic agrees with the mass of authorities in omitting
them ; both MSS. agree with ℵ and B in omitting "first-
born" in i. 25; "bless them that curse you, do good to
them that hate you" and "despitefully use you" in v. 44 ;
in vi. 13 the Curetonian MS. (against ℵBD) retains the
doxology to the Lord's Prayer, except the words "and
the power" (the Sinaitic is defective here); both omit
xii. 47 with ℵBL; in xiv. 24 Cur. has "was many
furlongs distant from the land" with B and the Ferrar
group (Sin. is defective); xvi. 2, 3 and xvii. 21 are
omitted by both, with ℵB; xviii. 11 is omitted by Sin.

---

[1] Partial agreements with it are found in the Ferrar group of Greek MSS.
(see p. 112 above) and in some copies of the Old Latin.

[2] Cf. Mrs. Lewis' English translation, pp. xxiii.-xxv., and a paper read by
Mr. F. C. Burkitt before the Church Congress of 1895.

[3] Syriac students will find a careful collation of both MSS. with one another
(the readings of the Peshitto being also added where they differ, for purposes
of comparison) in Mr. A. Bonus' *Collatio Cod. Lewisiani evangeliorum
Syriacorum cum Cod. Curetoniano* (Oxford, 1896).

with אBL, but retained by Cur.; in xix. 17 both read "why askest thou me concerning the good" with אBDL; in xx. 22 and 23 both omit "and to be baptized with the baptism that I am baptized with" with אBDL; Cur. agrees with D in inserting a long additional passage after xx. 28, but Sin. is defective here; in xxiv. 36 Sin. omits the words "neither the Son" against אBD (Cur. is defective here and for the rest of this Gospel); in xxvii. 16, 17 Sin. has "Jesus Barabbas" with a few minuscules and some MSS. mentioned by Origen. Mark ix. 44, 46 are omitted by Sin. with אBCL, and the latter half of verse 49 with אBL; also xv. 28 with אABCD. Cur. is defective in the whole of St. Mark, except one small fragment containing xvi. 17-20, which is sufficient to show that it contained the last twelve verses of the Gospel, which Sin., like א and B, omits. In Luke ii. 14 Sin. supports the common reading εὐδοκία, not the εὐδοκίας found in אABD and the Latin versions; in iv. 18 Sin. omits "to heal the broken-hearted" with אBDL; both are defective in vi. 5, where D has its most remarkable addition (see p. 76); in ix. 55 Cur. has the words "and said, Ye know not what manner of spirit ye are of," etc., with D (partially), the minor uncials, minuscules, and Latin versions, while Sin. omits them with אABCL and several other uncials; in x. 41 Sin. omits "thou art careful and troubled about many things" with partial support from the Old Latin version, which has "thou art troubled" only, while Cur. retains the whole; in the Lord's Prayer in xi. 2-4 Sin. omits "Our," "which art in heaven," "thy will be done, as in heaven, so in earth," "but deliver us from evil," with BL and (except in the third passage) א, while Cur. omits only the third passage; both insert xxii. 17, 18 in verse 20, agreeing with no Greek MS.; Sin. omits xxii. 43, 44 (the angel in the garden and the Bloody Sweat) with א*ABRT and the Coptic versions, while Cur. retains them with אD and the great mass of authorities; similarly in xxiii. 34 Sin. omits the word from the Cross, "Father, forgive them," etc., with אᵃBD and the Coptic versions, while Cur. retains it ; in xxiii. 48 both add "saying, Woe to us, what hath befallen us ! woe to us for our sins," with one MS. of the Old Latin ; in xxiv. 6, 12, 36 both retain the words which D and the Old Latin version omit, but both agree with these authorities in omitting verse 40 ; in verse 42 Sin. omits "and of a honey-comb" with אABDL, but Cur. retains it ; in verse 47 Sin. has "in my name" for "in his name," with one cursive (Evan. 33) ; in verse 51 Sin. has "he was lifted up from them," thus agreeing neither with אD (which do not expressly mention the Ascension) nor with the other authorities (Cur. is defective to the end of the Gospel) ; and in verses 52, 53 Sin. omits προσκυνήσαντες αὐτόν with D and αἰνοῦντες with אBCL. In St. John Cur. is very defective (see above) ; in iii. 13 Sin. retains "which is in heaven" against אBL, and in iv. 9 "for the Jews have no dealings with the Samaritans," against אD ; both are defective in v. 3, 4 ; in vi. 69 Sin. has "thou art the Christ, the Son of God" against אBCDL (σὺ εἶ ὁ ἅγιος τοῦ θεοῦ) ; vii. 53-viii. 11 is omitted by both, with all the best authorities ; Sin. also omits the last words of viii. 59, with אBD and the Latin versions ; in xi. 39 Sin. inserts in Martha's speech the words "Why are they lifting away the stone ?" with no other authority ; in xviii. the sequence of the narrative is altered in Sin., verse 24 being inserted between verses 13 and 14, and verses 16-18 being placed after verse 23, thus representing Caiaphas, not Annas, as the questioner of our Lord, and bringing together the whole narrative of Peter's denial. There are also many smaller variants, some peculiar to one or both of these MSS., which can only be realised by a full examination of their texts, either in the original or in the published translations.

The relation of the Sinaitic and Curetonian MSS. to one another is still obscure, and different views have been held by different scholars. The age of the MSS. themselves, and their frequent agreement with the oldest Greek authorities, show at once that their text is an ancient one ; while their divergences indicate that the common original from which they are unquestionably derived must almost certainly be placed at a considerable distance of time from them.   Some scholars have contended that the Curetonian is the earlier form of the text, and that the Sinaitic text has been produced from it by a process of excision ; but this is not the view generally held.   The common tendency in literary history (especially in sacred writings) is in the direction of expansion rather than of reduction ; and most of those scholars who have examined the subject are of opinion that the Sinaitic MS. contains the earlier form of text, and that the Curetonian shows signs of revision and the influence of other authorities.   It does not follow that in every case where they differ the Sinaitic preserves the original form, while the Curetonian is a modification. Neither MS. accurately represents the common archetype ; and if the Curetonian has diverged from it oftener, it still may be, and probably is, the case that sometimes it has remained uncorrupted when the Sinaitic has been altered. The whole question, however, of the relation of the two MSS. to one another still needs further examination,[1] and the conclusions which can be expressed here must be regarded as only provisional.

The wider question of the relation of the version as a whole to the other Syriac versions is best reserved until the Peshitto has been described.

c. **The Peshitto.**—This is the great standard version of the Scriptures in Syriac, which has occupied among the Syrian Churches the place held by the Vulgate in the Roman Church or the Authorised Version in the English.   The name by which it has generally been known since the thirteenth century means " the simple," but its meaning is not clear.   It has been suggested (by Tregelles and Field) that it was originally applied only to the Syriac

---

[1] A new edition of the Old Syriac version is being prepared by Mr. F. C. Burkitt, which should be of great assistance in this respect.

Old Testament, and was intended to distinguish it from the Hexaplar version, of which a translation into Syriac existed and still exists, and was thence extended to the New Testament also; but it is hardly likely that the Hexaplar version was in sufficiently general use to make such a differentiation necessary or popularly known. It might, perhaps, be intended to distinguish it from Tatian's composite Gospel narrative; but at present evidence is wanting to carry back the name to a date at which the *Diatessaron* was still in common use. The point, which after all is not of great importance, must therefore remain unsettled.

The history of the Peshitto version offers a marked contrast to that which has just been described. While the Sinaitic-Curetonian version was unknown before 1842, and now is represented only by two imperfect and divergent manuscripts, the Peshitto has been in public and general use for at least fifteen centuries, and exists in many manuscripts and printed volumes. Further, while the Sinaitic-Curetonian, so far as our present knowledge goes, contains only the four Gospels, no copy of the other books of the New Testament being yet forthcoming,[1] or of any part of the Old Testament, the Peshitto contains the whole of the Old Testament except the Apocrypha, and the whole of the New except the Apocalypse and the four minor Catholic Epistles (2 Peter, 2 and 3 John, and Jude). These books were omitted from the original Peshitto as not being then recognised as canonical by the Syrian Church, but were subsequently supplied from the later versions, the four Epistles from the Philoxenian and the Apocalypse from the Harkleian (see below). The Peshitto (without these additional books) was first edited by A. Widmanstadt at Vienna in 1555, from two MSS., and

---

[1] It is, however, fairly certain that the rest of the New Testament once existed in this form; for Armenian translations of commentaries by St. Ephraem on the Acts and Pauline Epistles, which have lately been published in Venice, show that Ephraem used a Syriac text differing considerably from the Peshitto (cf. J. H. Bernard in the *Guardian* of May 9, 1894, and J. A. Robinson, *Euthaliana*, pp. 83, 91).

this is still the standard text, although later editions were issued by Tremellius in 1569, and by several other editors in the sixteenth and seventeenth centuries, followed by that of Leusden and Schaaf (1708-9), which contains a collation of its predecessors. In the last century a reprint of Widmanstadt was issued among the Bagster Biblical texts in 1828, and a fresh edition (intended primarily for practical use, and therefore without critical apparatus) was published by Professor S. Lee in 1816 for the British and Foreign Bible Society, based upon the collation of three additional MSS. A new critical edition was commenced by Mr. Philip Pusey, son of the great Hebrew professor, and has been continued since his death by the Rev. G. H. Gwilliam. This edition, of which the first part (containing the Gospels) is believed to be approaching completion, is based upon an examination of forty MSS., and will at last provide scholars with a really critical text of the Peshitto. Mr. Gwilliam has, however, stated [1] that his text, founded though it be on authorities much more numerous and more ancient than that of Widmanstadt, does not differ substantially from its predecessors, owing to the accuracy with which the Syrian scribes have preserved the sacred text from corruption.

The number of MSS. in which the Peshitto is preserved, though not approaching that of the Greek or Latin authorities, is still very considerable. The list given by Gregory consists of 125 MSS. of the Gospels, 58 of the Acts and Catholic Epistles, and 67 of the Pauline Epistles (the Apocalypse, as stated above, not being contained in this version); and after making allowance for MSS. which appear in more than one of these groups, the total number of separate copies is 177. Of these almost exactly half (88) are preserved in the British Museum, which owes most of its wealth in Syriac literature to the Nitrian collection, to which we are also indebted for the Curetonian MS.

Many of these MSS. are very ancient, and some have

---

[1] *Studia Biblica*, i. 161.

the advantage over their Greek coevals in being precisely dated. The oldest (Brit. Mus. Add. MS. 14459) is assigned to the fifth century, and another (Brit. Mus. Add. MS. 17117) is nearly contemporary with this. At least a dozen may be referred to the sixth century, four of them being dated in the years 530-539, 534, 548, and 586. The critical materials now available are consequently plentiful in number and good in character ; and it is a strong testimony to the care with which the Syrian Christians copied their sacred books that Widmanstadt's text, based upon two late MSS., is now found to be so correct in all essentials.

With regard to the date of the original composition of this important version, it is clear at once from the age of the most ancient MSS. that it goes back to a very early period. This is made even more certain by the fact that the Peshitto is the version in use among all the branches of the Syrian Church. The secession of the Nestorian Church goes back beyond the middle of the fifth century, and since that date it is certain that neither Nestorian nor Monophysite would have adopted his Bible from the other. The Peshitto must consequently have been not merely in existence before 431 (the date of the Council of Ephesus), but so well established that its position could not be shaken by any schism in the Church. How much further it can be carried back is a matter of controversy, in the determination of which the question of its relation with the Sinaitic-Curetonian version plays an important part. ᛫ Mr. Gwilliam, whose opinion, as editor of the Peshitto, is entitled to all respect, believes it to date back to the second century, and to be the original translation of the Scriptures into Syriac ;[1] and his view is warmly supported by Burgon and those who follow his lead. On the other

---

[1] Cf. his article on the Syriac versions in Scrivener (ed. 4), ii. 6-24, and *Studia Biblica*, i. 151-174, iii. 47-104. Mr. Gwilliam's arguments to prove that the Curetonian shows signs of revision, and therefore is probably later than the Peshitto, are much weakened by the discovery of the Sinaitic MS. The Curetonian may be the result of a revision ; not, however, from the Peshitto, but from the Sinaitic or something similar.

PLATE XII.

THE PESHITTO (Brit. Mus. Add. MS. 14459). A.D. 530-540.

(Scale 7 : 10. The first part of this volume, containing Mt. and Mk., is of the fifth
century ; the second part, here represented, contains Lk. and Jn., and is of the sixth
century. The page shown contains Lk. ix. 46-55, including the doubtful words in
verse 55, "and said, Ye know not what spirit ye are of," which are found in D and a
few other MSS., in the Curetonian, Peshitto, and Harkleian Syriac, and the Latin
versions, but not in ℵABCL etc.)

To face p. 138.

hand, Hort and the majority of modern scholars would not place it (at any rate in its present shape) earlier than the third or fourth century, and believe that the Sinaitic-Curetonian version represents a more ancient stage in the history of the Syriac New Testament.

It would be idle to say that this controversy has been decided, while the relations and early history of these versions remain so obscure as they still are ; but the balance of evidence certainly appears to be in favour of the priority of the Sinaitic-Curetonian. So far back as the days of Griesbach and Hug it had been suspected that the Peshitto was not the original form of the Syriac version, though so long as no rival was forthcoming the belief of these scholars was no more than a hypothesis ; and so long as no very early manuscripts of it were known, the phenomena which suggested it might have been accounted for as the result merely of local corruption and gradual revision, not of a fresh translation. The Nitrian MSS. abolished this latter theory, by showing that the text of the Peshitto has come down to us practically un-changed since the fifth century, if not earlier ; and Cureton's discovery, strengthened as it is by that of Mrs. Lewis, has quite altered the situation, suggesting that this, or something like this, is the pre-Peshitto version which earlier scholars desiderated. If we had any considerable number of early Syriac writers, the question might be decisively solved by an examination of their Scripture quotations ; but the material of this kind is very scanty. Such as it is, how-ever, it points in the direction favoured by Hort and his followers. The text of the *Diatessaron*, so far as it can now be disentangled from the late authorities which pre-serve it, appears to be akin to that of the Sinaitic-Cure-tonian. Dr. Rendel Harris believes the Sinaitic to be the earliest of all, going back to the first half of the second century, and supplying the foundation both for Tatian's text and for that of the Curetonian ; while other authorities (e.g. Dr. Nestle) think that the Sinaitic represents a later stage than the *Diatessaron*. However this may be (and further research, or further discoveries, may be expected to elucidate this point), both would appear to be earlier than the Peshitto.   The Scripture quotations of the Syrian father Aphraates (fl. circ. 340) appear to be taken from a text akin to the Sinaitic-Curetonian text ; while those of Ephraem (ob. 378), though often agreeing with the Peshitto, differ often enough to show that he also had access to another type of text, whether in Greek or Syriac.[1]   Further, the long neglected Armenian version, which was made about 400 from Syriac and Greek codices, and revised in 433 from Greek codices brought from Constantinople, proves to have a considerable element of kinship with the Sinaitic-Curetonian text ;[2] which forcibly suggests that at the end of the fourth century the Peshitto was not the accepted version in the Syrian Church.

It would appear, therefore, that the Sinaitic-Curetonian version may reasonably claim priority over its better-known and more widely used rival, and may fairly be called the Old Syriac.   Its very roughness is in favour of it ; for it is difficult to believe that it would ever have been produced if the Peshitto were already in existence.   To revise the Peshitto into anything like the Sinaitic-Curetonian form would be a very remarkable literary performance ; but the contrary process is quite conceivable.   At the same time it would be going too far to say that the Peshitto is merely a revision of the Old Syriac, as our English Authorised Version is a revision of the Bishops' Bible, or the Revised Version of the Authorised.   A connexion between the two there certainly is, so that the author (or authors) of the Peshitto must have been acquainted with the Old Syriac ;[3] but he must have used

---

[1] Cf. *Studia Biblica*, iii. 105-138, " An Examination of the New Testament Quotations of Ephrem Syrus," by F. H. Woods.   Recently, however, Mr. Burkitt (*Journ. Theol. Studies*, i. 569) has shown, on the authority of Dr. Pohlmann, that in the published edition of Ephraem the N.T. quotations have been altered to suit the Peshitto, so that without further examination it cannot be assumed that Ephraem knew the Peshitto at all.

[2] Cf. Conybeare's article in Scrivener ii. 148-154, and *Euthaliana* (*Text and Studies*, iii. 3), pp. 72-98, by J. Armitage Robinson.

[3] Cf. Gwilliam in Scrivener, ii. 16.

it in an independent manner, rather as an assistance than as the basis of his work. For one thing, he must have used Greek MSS. of a different family from that which is represented by the Old Syriac. This, as we have seen, belongs to the δ-type, agreeing mainly with D and the Old Latin, and often also with אB ; while the Peshitto ranges itself rather with the authorities of the *a*-type. It does not, however, contain the *a*-text pure and simple, as we find it in the great mass of later Greek manuscripts, but has a considerable intermixture of readings characteristic of the β or δ-texts. The explanation of this depends on the general view that we take of the textual history of the New Testament, which will be the subject of a later chapter. If the *a*-text is the more authentic, the Peshitto has been to some extent contaminated by erratic influences ; but if the β-text comes nearer to the original, while the *a*-text is the result of a later revision, then the Peshitto represents an intermediate stage in the process, though nearer to the latter than to the former.

d. **The Philoxenian and Harkleian Syriac.** — The history of the remaining Syriac versions is much plainer and more certain. In the year 508 (as we know from the colophon appended to the Gospels in the MSS. of this version) a fresh translation of the New Testament into Syriac was prepared for Philoxenus, Jacobite bishop of Mabug or Hierapolis in eastern Syria, by one Polycarp, a χωρεπίσκοπος. Of this translation, however, as originally made, very little has come down to us ; a thorough-going revision of it having been made about a century later by Thomas of Harkel, himself subsequently bishop of Mabug. This revision, which involved a double process of collation of the original with Greek MSS. at Alexandria, was completed (as the same colophons inform us) in 616. Until recently the characteristics of these two stages in the development of the version, the Philoxenian and the Harkleian, were little known, and the version as a whole had been little studied ; but within the last few years some of this obscurity has been removed. Before 1892 the only part of the New Testament which could definitely be assigned to the original Philoxenian version was the four minor Catholic Epistles (2 Peter, 2 and 3 John, and Jude), which had been taken from this version to supply the omission in the Peshitto; and these hardly provided sufficient material for a judgment on the version as a whole.   In that year, however, Dr. Gwynn, of Trinity College, Dublin, published an account of a twelfth century manuscript belonging to Lord Crawford, containing a hitherto unknown version of the Apocalypse, which he showed conclusively to be Philoxenian.[1]   From this it is clear that the Philoxenian version was written in free and idiomatic Syriac, being the most literary in form of all the translations of the New Testament into this language. The Greek text underlying it was that of the great mass of later MSS., which (as is abundantly clear from other evidence also) was firmly established as the standard type of text in the Greek-speaking Church at the time when Polycarp prepared this version of the Scriptures for Philoxenus.

Possibly it was this very freedom of treatment that led to the revision of the translation after little more than a century.   At any rate it is certain that when Thomas of Harkel put his hand to the task, he did so in a spirit wholly opposed to that of his predecessor.   The free rendering of Polycarp was converted into extreme literalness, the Syriac being forced, even to the extent of doing violence to the language, into precise accordance with the Greek.   The Harkleian version of the New Testament may, in fact, be compared with that made by Aquila of the Greek Old Testament.   One advantage there is in this method of treatment, from the textual critic's point of view, that it is usually easy to determine what the exact form of Greek was that the translator meant to represent.   From this it appears that Thomas modified

[1] The text of this MS. was published by Dr. Gwynn in 1897 (*The Apocalypse of St. John in a Syriac Version*, Dublin), with an introductory dissertation on the various Syriac versions.

the work of his predecessor, not only in fidelity but in text, having evidently used Greek MSS. of a type akin to Codex Bezae (D) and its fellows. Additional readings of the same type are noted in the margin of this version, which may perhaps be the result of the second stage of Thomas' revision.

With regard to the Gospels and Pauline Epistles little attempt has yet been made to distinguish the Philoxenian and Harkleian elements in the text which has come down to us. Dr. Gwynn's discovery should stimulate further inquiry into the matter; but at present it appears that all the known MSS. contain the version in its final form after the Harkleian revision. Thirty-five distinct MSS. are enumerated in Gregory's list,[1] half of them (as in the case of the Peshitto) being in England. The oldest, however, are at Rome, one copy (in the Vatican) being assigned to the seventh century, and another to the eighth, while one, which is at Florence, bears a date in the year 757. Two important copies in the British Museum belong to the ninth or tenth century. The Italian copies have not been fully examined, but at present the best text is believed to be contained in a MS. at Cambridge, written in 1170, which, in spite of its comparatively late date, appears to have been very carefully and correctly written.

The Philoxenian-Harkleian version, though the four minor Catholic Epistles were published from the Philoxenian, by Pococke in 1630, and the Apocalypse from the Harkleian revision by De Dieu in 1627, was practically unknown to scholars until the eighteenth century. In 1730 two copies of it were sent from the East to Dr. Ridley, of Oxford, who wrote a dissertation on them; and after his death a text derived from them was published by Professor J. White (1778-1803). This remains the only printed edition of the version to the present day. Preparations for a new edition were made by the Rev. H. Deane, of

---

[1] Evan. 29, Act. 10, Paul. 5, Apoc. 6; but nearly all in the three last groups also contain the Gospels. In some MSS. one or more groups of books contain the Peshitto text, while the rest are Harkleian.

St. John's College, Oxford, who examined fifteen of the MSS. preserved in England ; but the failure of his eyesight unfortunately stopped his work.   If some scholar could be found to continue his labours, he might do much to elucidate the history of what Dr. Hort described as "one of the most confused texts preserved."[1]

   e. **The Palestinian Syriac.**—Yet another version of the New Testament in Syriac remains to be mentioned, which holds a somewhat peculiar position.   In 1789 the German scholar Adler, in a treatise on the Syriac versions of the New Testament, gave a description and collation of a Gospel lectionary in the Vatican (first observed by Assemani in 1758), containing a text entirely different from any other that was then known.   The difference was not merely in text but in dialect.   Both in vocabulary and in grammatical forms it resembled the " Chaldee " found in certain books of the Old Testament, or the dialect of the Palestinian Targum, rather than the Syriac employed in the Peshitto or Harkleian ; and from its resemblance to this Targum it has received the name of the Palestinian, or Jerusalem, Syriac.   The lectionary discovered by Adler (an imperfect MS., written at Antioch in 1030) was edited in full by Count Miniscalchi-Erizzo in 1861-4, and re-edited by Lagarde in a' posthumous volume published in 1892.   It is not now, however, the sole authority for this version.   Some fragments of it (also from Gospel lectionaries) came to the British Museum among the Nitrian MSS. ; the Imperial Library at St. Petersburg possesses some fragments of the Gospels and Acts ;[2] the Bodleian has four small fragments from the Pauline Epistles ;[3] and still more recently the monastery of St. Catherine on Mount Sinai has made some important contributions to our knowledge of this version. A single leaf from this monastery, containing portions of the Epistle to the Galatians, was published by Mr.

---

[1] *Introduction*, p. 156.
[2] Edited by Dr. Land, of Leyden, in 1875.
[3] Published by Mr. Gwilliam in *Anecdota Oxoniensia* (1893).

Rendel Harris in 1890 ;[1] but this was completely over-shadowed by Mrs. Lewis' discovery in 1892 of a complete Gospel lectionary, while another, equally complete, was identified by Mr. Rendel Harris in the following year. Both lectionaries (the first of which is dated 1104, and the second 1118) were published by Mrs. Lewis and her sister, Mrs. Gibson, in 1899.[2] Meanwhile yet another MS., containing lessons from the Acts and Epistles, besides parts of the Old Testament, was acquired by Mrs. Lewis in Cairo in 1895, and published two years later.[3] To complete the list up to the present time, it may be added that a few leaves from another Palestinian lectionary had been used in the bindings of the Sinai volumes, and are included in the above-mentioned edition of them ; and four fragments of this version, from a MS. recently acquired by the British Museum, have been edited by Mr. G. Margoliouth.[4] Thus, though only a few leaves which can have belonged to copies of the New Testament Scriptures in their ordinary consecutive form have come to light, we now have considerable materials on which to found an opinion as to the character of this version. The earlier editors referred it to the neighbour-hood of Jerusalem, and to a relatively ancient date, Miniscalchi-Erizzo placing it as high as the second century; but Mr. Burkitt[5] has recently demonstrated that it is of Antiochian origin, that it probably originated in the sixth century as a part of the efforts of Justinian and Heraclius to abolish Judaism from Judaea and Samaria, and that it revived with a renaissance of Palestinian Christianity about the eleventh century. Its text is of good quality, though somewhat mixed in character, sometimes associating itself with the β-type, and sometimes with the δ-type. Hort regarded it as "not altogether unaffected by the

---

[1] *Biblical Fragments from Mount Sinai* (1890).

[2] *The Palestinian Syriac Lectionary*, re-edited by A. S. Lewis and M. D. Gibson (1899).

[3] *Studia Sinaitica*, vol. vi. (1897).

[4] *The Palestinian Syriac Version of the Holy Scriptures, four recently discovered portions*, edited with a translation by the Rev. G. Margoliouth (1897).

[5] *Journal of Theological Studies*, ii. 174-183 (1901).

Syrian Vulgate [the Peshitto], but more closely related to the Old Syriac";[1] while on this Old Syriac (or δ-type) base some β-type readings have been engrafted in the course of tradition. The later date now assigned to it, however, lessens the importance of its evidence.

One other version sometimes figures in the list of Syriac authorities, under the name of the *Karkaphensian* version, to which allusion was supposed to be made by an ancient writer, Gregory Bar-Hebraeus, and which Cardinal Wiseman believed himself to have discovered in a Vatican MS. in 1828. Other MSS. of the same type have since been brought to light, and it is now universally recognised that it is not a continuous version at all, but a collection of texts accompanied by annotations on their spelling or pronunciation. It corresponds, in fact, to the Massorah of the Hebrew Old Testament, and only those passages are quoted on which some annotation is supposed to be required. It may, therefore, incidentally furnish us with evidence as to the text of the Syriac Scriptures used by the commentators, but it is not a version itself; and as no copy of it appears to be earlier than the later part of the ninth century, its value for textual purposes is not great. Seven MSS. of this Syriac Massorah are known, six of which emanate from the Jacobite branch of the Church, and only one from the Nestorian. The name *Karkaphensian* is believed to be derived from the monastery in which the Jacobite commentary was compiled, meaning [the Convent of] the Skull.

2. **The Armenian Version.**—Adjoining Syria to the north and north-west lay the territory of Armenia, the debatable land between the Roman and Parthian Empires; and as the circle of Christianity widened outwards from Jerusalem, it was naturally through Syria that Armenia received the Christian teaching and the Christian Scriptures. Until recently little was known of the Armenian version, and little interest taken in it; but, thanks especially to the labours of Mr. F. C. Conybeare, its

[1] *Introduction*, p. 157.

general character is now known, and proves to be un-expectedly interesting. With respect to its origin, the evidence is unusually explicit. Three Armenian writers of the fifth century (whose statements, though not identical, are reasonably reconcilable) record that the Scriptures were translated into Armenian partly by St. Mesrop, with the assistance of a Greek scribe named Hrofanos (pre-sumably = Rufinus), and partly by St. Sahak (Isaac). The date of these first translations would appear to be about A.D. 395-400. Subsequently, however, after the Council of Ephesus (A.D. 431), Sahak and Mesrop received "correct" copies of the Greek Bible from Constantinople, whereupon they revised their previous work in accordance with this new evidence. With regard to the language from which the original translations were made, the evidence is conflicting, both Greek and Syriac being men-tioned ; and since both languages were current in Armenia it is very probable that authorities of both kinds were employed. That Syriac formed the basis of it is not only *a priori* probable, but is made almost certain by Dr. Armitage Robinson's examination of the Armenian New Testament, in which he establishes a clear connection between its text and that of the Old Syriac, not only in the Gospels, but also in the Pauline Epistles. In the latter the Armenian version appears to have been made from a Syriac text substantially identical with that used by St. Ephraem. These conclusions are confirmed and extended by the information derivable from an Armenian writer of the seventh century, named Theodore, who in the course of a treatise against heretics refers to an ancient Armenian version of the New Testament as containing Luke xxii. 43, 44, and also the apocryphal third Epistle to the Corinthians, which he says was quoted by St. Gregory the Illuminator, the Apostle of the Armenians at the beginning of the fourth century. From this it appears that Mesrop and Sahak were not the first translators of the Bible into Armenian, but that there was an Armenian version as early as the beginning of the fourth century, including the Pauline Epistles as well as the Gospels (since 3 Corinthians was contained in it), and taken from the Syriac (since 3 Corinthians occurred in the Syriac canon and in no other).[1]

The earliest known MS. of the Armenian Gospels (now at Moscow) is dated in the year 887. Copies written in the years 966, 986, and 989 are still in Armenia (where the most important library is that of Edschmiadzin); one of 960 is at Constantinople, and two of 902 and 1006 at Venice. Two more of those described by Mr. Conybeare[2] probably fall into the ninth century. The other books of the New Testament rarely appear in MSS. before the thirteenth century, and never apart from the Gospels. These late MSS. are much less trustworthy than the earlier ones, their texts having been affected by the introduction of the Vulgate into the East during the Crusades. The fullest collation hitherto of the Armenian version was published by Tregelles and repeated by Tischendorf; but this is based on a few MSS. and those not the oldest. The text was first printed at Amsterdam in 1666, while the first critical edition appeared in 1805 from the Mechitarist convent in Venice, to which we are also indebted for the discovery of the commentary of Ephraem on the Diatessaron, and so indirectly of the Diatessaron itself.

The Armenian version contains some interesting features, apart from its bearing on the question of the priority of the Old Syriac over the Peshitto, which has been mentioned already. The last twelve verses of St. Mark are omitted from three out of the four very early MSS. collated by Mr. Conybeare, while the fourth (the earliest MS. at Edschmiadzin), which has them, adds a note stating that they are "of the elder Ariston." This has naturally been taken to refer to Aristion,[3] whom Papias

---

[1] See F. C. Conybeare in the *Academy*, Feb. 1, 1896 (in a review of Robinson's *Euthaliana*).

[2] In his article on the Armenian version in Scrivener, ii. 148-154.

[3] The slight discrepancy in the name is unimportant. By a curious coincidence, exactly the same discrepancy occurs between Aristotle ('Aθ.

mentions as one of the disciples of the Lord to whom he had recourse for information with regard to our Lord's life and teaching. The statement of the Armenian codex lacks confirmation, but in itself it supplies a very plausible explanation of the difficulty connected with these verses. The original ending of the Gospel having been lost (or never written), a brief summary was added, to round off the narrative, by Aristion, one of the disciples of Jesus, and therefore in a position to know the facts ; but this conclusion, not being by St. Mark, was sometimes omitted, and consequently does not appear in some of our earliest extant authorities. On this hypothesis we can accept the passage as true and authentic narrative, though not an original portion of St. Mark's Gospel.

Two other notable passages may be mentioned. Luke xxii. 43, 44 is omitted in three out of Mr. Conybeare's four collated MSS., but appears in the oldest of them (the Venice MS. of 902) ; and this agrees with the statement referred to above, that in the "first translation" or "ancient edition" these verses were found, but were omitted in the "newly issued translations." The same statement is made with reference to the apocryphal third epistle to the Corinthians. On the other hand the testimony of the earliest Armenian codices is entirely against the authenticity of the episode of the woman taken in adultery. The first which has it is the Edschmiadzin MS. of 989, and this has it in a very different form from that in which it generally appears, adding the curious detail that what our Lord wrote on the ground was the sins of the several self-constituted judges, so that each slunk away as he saw his own fault written down before him.

Further examination of the Armenian version may yield additional fruit, especially in respect of its connection with the Old Syriac ; but for this we must await the

τολ.) and Plutarch with regard to the name of the adherent of Pisistratus, who proposed that he should be provided with a body-guard ; the former calling him Aristion, the latter Ariston.

pleasure of the few scholars capable of informing us. Meanwhile we have good reason to be grateful for the work which has been done and for the results which have already been obtained.

3. **The Georgian Version.**—The Iberian Church in the Caucasus, on account of its geographical position, would naturally receive Christianity and the Christian Scriptures by way of Armenia, and the Armenian tradition is to the effect that St. Mesrop was the author of the Georgian version as well as of that in his own language. This, however, is denied by the Georgians, who looked to Constantinople as the source from which Christianity had been brought to them, and whose associations were rather with the Greeks than with the Armenians. The version itself, according to Mr. Conybeare,[1] shows signs of both influences. On the one hand it has many parallels with the Old Syriac, which seems to indicate that this is the text on which it was originally based ; while on the other, it has evidently been revised from the Greek. This revision, according to tradition, was made as late as the tenth century, to which date the earliest MSS. appear to belong. If, however, a somewhat earlier MS. should come to light, as may easily happen, it may be found to contain the original version, based on the Old Syriac. In the Pauline Epistles the Georgian version, like the Armenian, seems to have been made from a Syriac text of the same type as that used by Ephraem, often agreeing with Ephraem against the Peshitto when the two differ. At present, however, so little is known of either the history or the text of this version that it does not need more detailed description here.

4. **The Persian Versions.**—Another kinsman of the Syriac New Testament is to be found in the earliest of the two Persian versions of the Gospels at present known, which was evidently taken from the Peshitto, though at

---

[1] *Academy*, Feb. 1, 1896. In his article in Scrivener (ii. 156) Mr. Conybeare speaks of the Georgian version as certainly made from the Greek ; but the article in the *Academy* is his latest utterance, and presumably represents the results of maturer study.

what precise date is doubtful. It was printed in Walton's Polyglot from a single MS., which appears to be dated 1341. A later version from the Greek was edited by A. Wheelocke, professor of Arabic at Cambridge, and published posthumously in 1657. Neither would seem to be of much value for critical purposes, on account of their late date. Portions of earlier versions are said to exist in Persia, but they are still unpublished.

5. **The Coptic Versions.**—Turning southwards from Jerusalem we reach a new group of versions, of which the first and the most important are those which were made in the adjoining country of Egypt. Here, and especially at Alexandria, a flourishing colony of Jews had been established since the days of the earliest Ptolemies ; and here the great Greek translation of the Hebrew Scriptures, known as the Septuagint, had been prepared. Here, therefore, there was ground on which Christian preaching might work at once, and there is evidence that it did so work. The story of Apollos (Acts xviii. 24-28), the Jew of Alexandria, suggests that some imperfect exposition of Christianity had reached Egypt within a few years after our Lord's ministry, though it is possible that his knowledge on the subject had only been acquired since his arrival in Asia Minor ;[1] but, whether St. Mark (as tradition tells) preached there or not, it may be taken as certain that the generation of the Apostles did not pass away without the Gospel having been carried into Egypt. At first, however, this would not imply a translation of the Scriptures into the Egyptian tongue, since the community first addressed would be the Greek-speaking Jews of Alexandria, next to whom would come the considerable Greek colonies in that town and in Egypt generally, the existence of which is amply established, not only by the statements of historians, but by the Greek papyri of the Ptolemaic and Roman periods which have come to light in such great numbers of late years. These documents,

---

[1] The reading of the δ-text would exclude this possibility, since it has ὃς ἦν κατηχημένος ἐν τῇ πατρίδι τὸν λόγον τοῦ κυρίου.

indeed, show that not only Greeks and Romans but even native Egyptians not infrequently used the Greek language for business purposes, although in many instances the parties were too illiterate to write with their own hands. For some time, therefore, the Scriptures in the Greek tongue would have been sufficient for the purpose of the missionaries; the more so as they would hardly have been able to use any other. The hieroglyphic script of ancient Egypt was by this time obsolete for practical purposes, while it is not likely that the Christian missionaries would have been able to use the demotic characters, as they are called, which were then the form of writing in everyday use among the native Egyptians.

In the course of the second century, however, a new kind of writing came into existence, which formed a sort of bridge between Greek and Egyptian. It was, in fact, the Egyptian language (somewhat modified by its contact with Greek) written in Greek characters, with the addition of six other letters borrowed with modifications from the demotic alphabet for the representation of special Egyptian sounds. To this the name *Coptic* was subsequently given; and it is in the Coptic dialects that the native Egyptian versions of the Scriptures were written. The date of the adoption of the Coptic script is somewhat uncertain, and it is a matter of some importance with regard to the probable date of the original Coptic versions. The earliest known specimen of it occurs in a horoscope, written on papyrus and now in the British Museum. Astronomical calculations show that this horoscope (the bulk of which is in Greek) was calculated for a nativity in either 95 or 155 A.D., the former being the more probable of the two; and the palaeographical indications also suit the earlier date best. The Coptic in this document is of a very primitive type;[1] but it is sufficient to make it practically certain that this form of Egyptian writing

---

[1] Mr. C. W. Goodwin calls it "the first effort of the system from which Coptic was shortly afterwards developed."

established itself in general use in the second century, and was therefore available for the translation of the Scriptures before A.D. 200.

Whether advantage was immediately taken of it is uncertain. It has usually been supposed that it was, and that the principal Coptic versions date back to the second century.[1] In favour of this view a passage is cited from a Life of St. Anthony, the authorship of which is attributed to St. Athanasius, and in which St. Anthony, when about twenty years of age (i.e. about A.D. 270), is said to have been greatly affected by hearing the Gospel read in church. Since he is known to have been unacquainted with Greek, this passage is taken to imply that the Bible which he heard read was in Coptic, which would prove that a Coptic version was in existence soon after the middle of the third century, and would make it very possible that it was made at the beginning of that century, or perhaps somewhat earlier. Mr. Forbes Robinson, however, argues that what St. Anthony heard may have been only an oral paraphrase from a Greek Bible ; just as in the early days of Christianity in England, the Vulgate was paraphrased into English for the benefit of the uninstructed converts. But even if this be admitted as a possible (though by no means a certain) explanation of the passage, clear evidence of the existence of a Coptic Bible not much later is provided by the life of St. Pachomius (the great organiser of Egyptian monachism), whose monks (common Egyptians, without knowledge of Greek) were required to be zealous in the study of the Scriptures. This was at the beginning of the fourth century, and affords a fair presumption that the original Coptic version was made not later than the middle of the third century, while it is of course consistent with an even earlier date. There is therefore not much disagreement between the best authorities, whose estimates only range between the latter part of the second century and the middle of the third. In favour of the earlier view it may

---

[1] See Lightfoot (*ap.* Scrivener), Headlam (*ibid.* ed. 4), Hort, Hyvernat, etc.

be noted that (as will be shown below) the types of text contained in the Coptic versions are unmistakably early, the Sahidic New Testament in particular being of a type which we know to have been prevalent in the second century, while it can hardly have flourished much later than the middle of the third. Similarly the original Sahidic Old Testament was evidently pre-Origenian in character, not containing those insertions from the Hebrew which Origen made in his Hexapla, and which thenceforth appear in all editions of the Septuagint; from which it may fairly be inferred that this version was not made substantially later than the death of Origen, while it may be decidedly earlier. If therefore we put the origin of the Coptic versions about A.D. 200, we shall be consistent with all the extant evidence, and probably shall not be very far wrong.

Different dialects of Coptic were spoken in different parts of the country, but their number and their divergences have only lately begun to be made known to us. Two of them stand out in importance above the rest, and until recently were the only two of which scholars had any knowledge. They belonged to Lower and Upper Egypt respectively, and the former used to be entitled the *Memphitic* version, and the latter the *Thebaic*, from the most important towns in the two districts. Fuller information, however, has shown that the district of Memphis had its own dialect, which is not that of the principal Lower Egyptian version; hence this is now generally termed *Bohairic*, from Bohairah, the Arabic name of the coast district of Lower Egypt, while its rival is called *Sahidic*, from Es-sa'id, the Arabic name of Upper Egypt. These are the names assigned to them by Athanasius, Bishop of Kos in the Thebaid in the eleventh century, and they are now generally adopted by scholars. The Bohairic dialect was that of the sea-coast, including Alexandria, the literary capital of Egypt; it was the most literary of all the dialects, and ultimately it superseded them all and became the accepted language of the Coptic Church, as it remains to this day, when the language is otherwise dead. The Sahidic dialect had its home in the district about Thebes. Athanasius of Kos mentions the former existence of a third dialect, which he calls Bashmuric, from the district of Bashmur, which appears to have lain in the marshes of the Delta; but of this no remains now exist. On the other hand, at least three additional dialects have been found among the papyri which have come to light of recent years. The first of these, when only a few fragments of it had been discovered (about a century ago), was provisionally named Bashmuric, but is now shown to have belonged to the province of the Fayyum, which, lying by itself away from the Nile, not unnaturally had a dialect of its own, and in which most of the discoveries of papyri in the last thirty years have been made. This dialect is consequently now known as *Fayyumic.* Another dialect, found in documents from the neighbourhood of Memphis, is generally termed *Memphitic,*[1] or *Middle Egyptian*; while in Upper Egypt, apart from the Sahidic, a distinct dialect has been found in papyri from Akhmîm (Panopolis), which is provisionally entitled *Akhmîmic.* This last is marked by the possession of a new letter, which is not found in the other dialects.

It is not to be supposed, however, that these dialects cover the whole field, or that they all occupy clearly defined provinces. On the contrary, the more papyri come to light, the more is it clear that the greatest amount of intermixture of neighbouring dialects prevailed, especially with regard to Middle Egypt. Future discoveries will no doubt enable Coptic scholars to reduce their subject-matter to greater order, and especially to show how far the intermixture of dialects, which is natural in colloquial correspondence and the business documents of daily life, extended into works of literature. For the

---

[1] The only objection to this name is its former use to denote the version which we now call Bohairic; but this is an objection which becomes daily of less importance, as the term Bohairic establishes itself in all text-books. *Middle Egyptian* is wanted for a wider use, covering all the (as yet) ill-defined dialects which range between Bohairic and Sahidic.

present it is probably most convenient to group all the dialects of Central Egypt together as Middle Egyptian, while provisionally classifying them into sub-species [as Fayyumic, Memphitic, Akhmimic, and other local names, as may be found necessary.

a. **The Bohairic Version.**—The Bohairic dialect, as stated above, ultimately superseded all the others, and consequently the remains of it now extant are the most plentiful.   In it alone are there MSS. containing complete books of the New Testament ; and although no single MS. contains the New Testament in its entirety, yet there is fairly plentiful evidence for each book of it.   The first scholar to make it known was T. Marshall, Rector of Lincoln College, Oxford, from whose papers many readings were drawn for the New Testaments of Fell in 1675 and Mill in 1707.   In 1716 the text of the whole version was published at Oxford by the Prussian, David Wilkins ; but the execution of the task left much to be desired. The Gospels were re-edited by Schwartze in 1846-47, but with a very inadequate critical apparatus ; and the Acts and Epistles by Lagarde (then known as Boetticher) in 1852.   All these editions, however, are in course of supersession by that now being issued from the Oxford University Press by the Rev. G. Horner.   Of this the Gospels have already appeared,[1] and the remainder is in course of preparation.   Mr. Horner prints the text of the best MS. (Huntington MS. 17 in the Bodleian Library), and gives a very full critical apparatus.   Thirty - four MSS. were collated for St. Matthew, and six more examined ; for the other Gospels it was found sufficient to collate about twenty MSS. and to examine about ten. In all, the character of forty-six MSS. (sought out from all the principal collections in Europe and Egypt) was ascertained with adequate certainty, and a thoroughly broad and solid foundation laid for our knowledge of the Bohairic version.

---

[1] *The Coptic Version of the New Testament in the northern dialect, otherwise called Memphitic and Bohairic*, vols. i. and ii. (1898).

THE BOHAIRIC VERSION (Curzon Catena).   A.D. 889.
(Scale 1 : 3.   The page shown is the first of St. Mark's Gospel.)

To face p. 157.

The MSS. of the Bohairic version, though fairly numerous (Mr. Horner's list,[1] which does not claim to be complete, gives thirty-six copies of the Gospels, eighteen of the Acts and Epistles, and ten of the Apocalypse, besides Lectionaries), are all late in date. The earliest is that known as the Curzon Catena, in the Parham Library (at present located in the British Museum), which is dated in the year 889; but in this MS. text and commentary (derived from various sources) are intermixed, often indistinguishably, so that its value as an authority is impaired. Of the MSS. of the Gospels, the oldest and best is the Huntington MS. 17, already mentioned, of the year 1174 (Horner's A); and closely akin to this are a MS. in the Bibliothèque Nationale at Paris of 1196 (Horner's C) and one in the Institut Catholique at Paris of 1250 (Horner's H). These three embody the purest text of the Bohairic version; but there are also MSS. of 1179 (Paris), 1184 (Cairo), 1205 (Rome), 1208 (British Museum), 1216, 1229, and 1250 (Paris), 1257, 1272, and 1291 (Cairo), besides others which, though not precisely dated, may be as early as these.[2] Late though all these MSS. are, there is good reason to suppose that they contain a substantially pure text. There are no such wide variations as we find among Greek MSS.; rather the Copts seem to have resembled the Jews, who have not preserved the early copies of their Scriptures, but have copied them with the greatest fidelity, so that their MSS. of the tenth century and later contain a text which has come down substantially unaltered from at least the second century. Indeed many of the Bohairic MSS. which contain corrections have notes affirming that the variants are Greek, not Coptic, thus implying, as Mr. Horner points out, that the Copts jealously preserved their own textual tradition. The later MSS. have, it is true, suffered some corruption by the insertion of words and passages which

[1] In Scrivener, ii. 110-123; Gregory gives a somewhat longer list, but his additional MSS. are almost all of the eighteenth and nineteenth centuries.
[2] A few scattered leaves of earlier date have recently been found, but not many.

bring them into closer conformity with the Textus
Receptus ; but these insertions can for the most part
be recognised by reference to the earlier copies. The
Huntington MS. 17, indeed, supplies an instructive
example of this process of corruption ; for while the main
text is pure, most of the passages which we find inserted
in the later copies are here written in the margin. It is
easy to understand that these would, before long, find
their way into the body of the text.

Taking, then, the earlier MSS. as substantially representing the Bohairic version in its integrity, it will be
found that no such difficulties present themselves as in
the case of the Old Syriac or (as will be shown below) the
Old Latin. It is an example of the β-text of the New
Testament in its purer form, of which the leading representative is the Codex Vaticanus. It is not marked by
the numerous erratic variants which are characteristic of
the Codex Bezae and its friends. Further, the translation
is careful and obviously adheres closely to the Greek, so
that it can be used with confidence as evidence for the
Greek text. Its general agreement with the text of אB
is shown by the fact that out of twenty-one passages
enumerated on pp. 57, 58, where those two MSS. agree
as against the Textus Receptus, the earlier MSS. of the
Bohairic support them in fifteen and oppose them in six ;
while in two more cases where א joins the Textus
Receptus, the Bohairic adheres to B. The last twelve
verses of St. Mark are contained in all Bohairic MSS. ;
but two copies (Hunt. 17 and Brit. Mus. Or. 1315)
give in their margins a short alternative ending which
is practically identical with that found in L. The
passage Luke xxii. 43, 44 is omitted in nearly all the
better Bohairic MSS. ; John v. 3, 4 (the angel at the
pool of Bethesda) is omitted by most of the better MSS.,
but appears in the best of all (Hunt. 17); John vii. 53-
viii. 11 is omitted by all the better MSS. The Apocalypse apparently did not form part of the original
version. In nearly all cases it is found in a separate

MS.; when otherwise, it is markedly distinguished from the other contents of the MS.; and it is not noticed in the Copto-Arabic Bible vocabularies. It is therefore probable that the version was made at a time when the Apocalypse was not universally recognised as a canonical book. From the end of the third century it seems to have been accepted; but in the middle of that century doubts were expressed about it. To this period, therefore, the origin of the version is ascribed by Lightfoot[1]; though the possibility remains that the version may have come into existence earlier, and have dropped the Apocalypse at that date. On the other hand, the fact that the Bohairic version (unlike the Sahidic) contains Origen's insertions in the text of the Old Testament (see above, p. 154) points rather to the end of the third century or to some part of the fourth. The point must remain at present somewhat uncertain; but the type of text contained in this version is distinctly in favour of as early a date as is compatible with the other evidence.

b. **The Sahidic Version.**—Very little notice was taken of this version until about a century and a quarter ago, when (in 1778) Tuki published a grammar of the dialect, with quotations from both Testaments, and Woide simultaneously announced a forthcoming edition of the fragments of the New Testament, which did not appear until 1799, nine years after his death. Since that date the number of extant fragments has increased enormously, and it would probably now be possible to piece together an almost entire New Testament; though it would be a very patchwork production, being compiled from innumerable scraps of different MSS., the relative worth of which we are hardly in a condition to test. No complete copy of any book of the New Testament exists in the Sahidic dialect,[2] though seven MSS. contain books which

---

[1] Scrivener, ii. 123.

[2] Until lately the same might have been said of the Old Testament, with the exception of the book of Job; but Dr. E. A. W. Budge has recently acquired for the British Museum a complete Sahidic Psalter, the text of which he has edited (1898). This MS. is also almost unique as an example of a complete papyrus MS. in book-form, and of very large size.

approach completeness ; but fragments are very numerous. In 1810 Zoega published a large number from the Borgian Library, which have since found their way to the library of the Propaganda at Rome, where they are in course of re-publication by, Ciasca (the Old Testament fragments having already appeared, 1885-89). A still larger collection was acquired by the Bibliothèque Nationale at Paris in 1883 from the great White Monastery near Sohag in Upper Egypt ; and these are being edited by Amélineau.[1] The Apocalypse was edited in 1895 by H. Goussen from a MS. partly in London and partly in Berlin (Plate XIV.). The British Museum also possesses many fragments, a catalogue of which is being prepared by Mr. Crum. Before long, therefore, it will be possible for some one to take in hand a formal edition of the Sahidic New Testament, which, though in some respects it could only be provisional, would yet be of great service to Biblical students.

The manuscripts of the Sahidic version are much earlier than those of the Bohairic ; and the reason of this is simple. In the earlier centuries of Coptic Christianity, manuscripts of both versions no doubt existed in considerable numbers ; but since no special effort was made to preserve them, they went the way of all books, to the rubbish heap, and their places were taken by later copies. But as the Bohairic dialect ultimately became the literary and religious language of the country, Sahidic manuscripts ceased to be written, and the volumes which we possess, nearly all of which (as we have seen) are later than the eleventh century, are all Bohairic. On the other hand, the fragments of earlier date which have been unearthed by explorers and excavators of modern times are almost all Sahidic, because the climate of Upper Egypt is far more favourable for their preservation than the moister air and soil of Lower Egypt. To what precise age they

---

[1] For a catalogue of these fragments see Scrivener, ii. 134-36. Some other fragments from the White Monastery have been edited by Maspero (*Mémoires de la Mission française au Caire*, vol. vi. 1892).

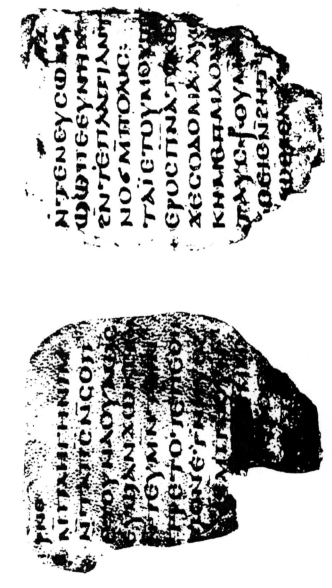

THE SAHIDIC VERSION (Brit. Mus. MS. Or. 3518). Fifth Century (?).

should be referred is a matter of considerable doubt. Very few indeed are dated, or even approximately datable, and consequently there is no firm basis for early Coptic palaeography. The only clue is to be found in its resemblance to Greek writing ; and this would lead us to suppose that the most ancient Sahidic fragments may be referred to the fifth century, or perhaps slightly earlier. Since, however, Coptic never attained the position of a literary and fashionable language, it was not usually written by scribes of the first class. The Coptic MSS. which remain will seldom bear comparison with the Greek uncial MSS., and the roughness of style which nearly always characterises them makes any attempt to fix their date extremely precarious.

It might be thought that light would be thrown on this problem from two sources, namely, the bilingual Greek and Coptic MSS., of which there are several extant,[1] and the Coptic papyri which have been discovered in large numbers of late years, and which might be expected, like the similarly discovered Greek papyri, to contain a considerable amount of dated ⸱material. But in the case of the bilingual MSS., it is generally the Coptic which regulates the style rather than the Greek. The Greek is written with all the peculiarities and roughnesses of the Coptic, and therefore takes no assured place in the development of Greek palaeography. Some approximation to ordinary Greek writing there is, and the clue is a valuable one ; but it is only imperfectly and uncertainly applicable. With regard to the papyri, it so happens that nearly all the extant business documents (in which dates may naturally be looked for) belong to that late Byzantine period, from the seventh or eighth century onwards, when dating was done by the fifteen-year indiction-cycle, which is wholly useless after the lapse of a few years, since there are no means of knowing which is the

---

[1] See above, p. 95. A description of the Graeco-Sahidic fragments in the Bibliothèque Nationale has been given by Amélineau, in *Notices et extraits des manuscrits de la Bibl. Nat.* vol. xxxiv. pp. 363 ff. (1895), with some facsimiles.

indiction spoken of. One large group of Sahidic papyri, from the neighbourhood of Thebes, can be shown to belong to the eighth century ; others, from the Fayyum, are said to belong to the sixth and seventh centuries, but since these are unpublished it is impossible to say what light they may throw on the palaeographical question. At present the evidence derivable from papyri is practically *nil.*

Taking, then, the fifth century as the most probable starting point, a considerable number of the extant Sahidic Biblical fragments may be assigned to the period between A.D. 400 and 800; but they are generally so small in extent that no detailed description of them can be given, and none can be singled out as pre-eminently valuable above the rest. Among the largest and most noticeable is the bilingual fragment at Rome, which has already been described under the letter T (p. 95), and which contains an almost unadulterated sample of the β-type of text, such as we find in the best Bohairic MSS., though of considerably earlier date than those. On the whole, however, the Sahidic version shows a large admixture of those aberrant readings which we associate with D and its allies, the Old Syriac and Old Latin. It must have been made independently of the Bohairic version, and from Greek MSS. of a different type. Whether it was made earlier or later is a point upon which experts have differed. On the one hand there is the probability that Lower Egypt, from its greater proximity to Palestine and to the Jewish-Christian colony of Alexandria, would be first evangelised and would first require a Bible in the vernacular ; to which it is added (1) that some of the commonest abbreviations in Coptic MSS. could only have been derived from the Bohairic, which suggests that it was in this dialect that the Coptic writing was first used, and (2) that the greater purity of the Bohairic text is a sign of its greater antiquity.[1] On the other hand it may be argued that Greek would probably suffice for the purposes of Christianity for a longer period in the neigh-

---

[1] So Headlam in Scrivener, 126, 127, following Krall.

bourhood of Alexandria than in Upper Egypt; that the abbreviations of which mention has been made cannot be shown to go back to a pre-Sahidic period, since there are no Bohairic MSS. of earlier date than the Sahidic, and at most they only prove that these abbreviations were first adopted by Bohairic scribes[1]; and that the type of text found in the Sahidic version is shown by the evidence of the Old Syriac and Old Latin versions and all the early Fathers (including Clement of Alexandria) to go back to quite primitive times, certainly to a period earlier than the production of any Coptic version, so that its non-appearance in the Bohairic MSS. (even admitting their text to be intrinsically purer) is not due to its non-existence when that translation was first made. The Sahidic text may be less pure, and yet more ancient; indeed, since that type of text is only found in very early authorities, and evidently perished when the growth of Christianity brought with it greater care for accurate copies of the Scriptures, its occurrence in the Sahidic version is rather to be taken as an indication of a very early date for the origin of that version. To this it may be added that in the Old Testament the Sahidic version shows strong signs of being older than the Bohairic. The original Sahidic text was certainly pre-Origenian in some books (notably in Job), and probably in all (though modified later); while the Bohairic version appears to represent the Hesychian edition of the Septuagint, which was produced about the beginning of the fourth century, at least half a century after the epoch-making labours of Origen in his Hexapla. On the whole, therefore, the balance of evidence, though not decisive, appears to be in favour of the priority of the Sahidic version, and of its assignment to a date not later than the middle of the third century,[2] and probably appreciably earlier. In any

[1] Mr. Forbes Robinson also denies the applicability of this argument of Krall's, affirming that the abbreviations are equally derivable from Middle Egyptian.

[2] If the original absence of the Apocalypse from the Bohairic version may be taken as a fairly close indication of date (see above, p. 159), the two versions must be nearly contemporary, since it seems equally to have been absent from the Sahidic. But the omission cannot really be dated with any certainty.

case it may be said with confidence that both versions are ancient, in origin if not in extant representatives ; both are valuable, and the more so because of their independence ; and if the greater roughness and even the more erratic readings of the Sahidic are indications of an age when such licenses had not been pruned away, the Bohairic probably comes nearer to the original purity of the sacred text, as preserved in the more literary atmosphere of Alexandria.

c. **The Middle Egyptian Versions.**—Doubtful as many points are with regard to the Bohairic and Sahidic versions, they are as clear as day compared with what we know of the remaining dialects of Egypt. Though the existence of a third dialect was known so long ago as 1789, when Giorgi published a small fragment from the Borgian Library, it is only of late years that any considerable body of materials relating to it has been brought to light. The excavations in search of manuscripts, which have been made at various points in Egypt within the present generation, have led to the discovery of many fragments which cannot be ranged as either Bohairic or Sahidic. As has been indicated above, manuscripts have been found in the neighbourhood of Memphis, the Fayyum, and Akhmim, presenting dialects which, though akin to one another, have distinctive differences ; and these have been tentatively classified as separate species. The greatest obscurity, however, still rests over their relationships. In the first place, the evidence of locality is not always satisfactory. Many of the fragments have been acquired from dealers' shops ; and the statements of native dealers as to the *provenance* of their wares are ordinarily valueless. Nor is it always safe to argue from the MSS. in company of which they are found ; for the collocation may be only that of the dealers' box, not of actual discovery. Further, the intermixture of dialects is great. All are more associated with Sahidic than with Bohairic, but the degree of affinity with Sahidic varies indefinitely.

Some points, however, seem fairly established.   In the first place, the Middle Egyptian versions are independent of both Bohairic and Sahidic in substance, being derived from a different Greek text.   Next, traces have been found of more than one Middle Egyptian text,[1] so that more than one translation must have been made.   Thirdly, though the extant fragments are not precisely datable, they plainly go back to a very early date, to the sixth and fifth centuries at least, if not the fourth.   More than this it is impossible to say at present, for want of evidence. Of the Memphitic version only a very few fragments are extant, published by Bouriant, Krall, and Crum.   The Fayyumic, which was the first to be published, the fragment found by Giorgi being of this type, is more fully represented, the Fayyum having hitherto been the most prolific field for papyri of all kinds.   Some were published by Zoega in 1810, others more recently by Maspero and Krall, while many still remain unpublished.[2] All, however, are small, rarely reaching the extent of a chapter ; the largest being a bilingual palimpsest of the sixth century in the British Museum, containing John iii. 5-iv. 18, iv. 23-35, 45-49, in a dialect which Mr. Crum hesitates to characterise definitely as Fayyumic or Memphitic, and with a very pure text.[3]

Finally, of the Akhmimic version the only extant fragments were published by Mr. Crum (1893), but at present the remains are extremely scanty, and the character of the text quite obscure.   Time will, no doubt, add much to our acquaintance with all the Middle Egyptian dialects, and with the versions of the Bible current in them ; but meanwhile it cannot be said that they yet contribute much of value to the criticism of the sacred texts.

6. The Ethiopic Version.—Abyssinia might have

[1] Mr. Crum has found two fragments of Romans (one in the British Museum and one at Vienna), both in the Middle-Egyptian dialect, but markedly different in text.

[2] Several will be included in Mr. Crum's forthcoming catalogue of Coptic MSS. in the British Museum.

[3] Published by Mr. Crum and myself in *Journal of Theological Studies*, i. 415 ff.

received Christianity either through its immediate neighbour, Egypt, or more directly from Palestine, by travellers voyaging down the Red Sea; but records on the point are wanting. About the end of the fifth century Christianity became the national religion, and to this date, or somewhat later, the Ethiopic version of the Scriptures is assigned.[1] Little, however, is known of it; for, in the first place, the manuscripts, though fairly plentiful, are very late in date, and secondly, the text has never been critically edited. The New Testament was first printed at Rome in 1548-49, whence it was included (with a Latin translation) in Walton's Polyglott; and another text was issued by the Bible Society in 1830; but neither of these editions was based on a critical study of manuscripts, comparatively few of which were then known. The Abyssinian war led to the discovery of many more, and over a hundred copies are now extant in the libraries of Europe. The oldest is believed to be a manuscript in the Bibliothèque Nationale (MS. aeth. 32) written in the thirteenth century, while another is dated in the year 1378; but most are of the seventeenth century or later. According to the latest statement on the subject (by L. Hackspill, see note below), the oldest MS. stands alone for comparative purity of text, all the others representing a text revised in the fourteenth century from the Arabic version then current in Egypt. It is not at all impossible that this and other points will be cleared up in the future by the discovery of earlier MSS.; but at present our knowledge of the Ethiopic version is too slight for much use to be made of it.

7. **The Arabic Versions.**—Translations of the Bible into Arabic are plentiful, but are useless for critical purposes, on account of their late date and of the

[1] So Guidi (quoted by Margoliouth in Scrivener, ii. 154) and Hackspill (*Zeitschrift für Assyriologie*, xi. 117, 1897). Dillmann, however, assigns the Ethiopic Old Testament to the fourth century, and the New Testament would certainly be translated as soon as, or sooner than, the Old Testament.

extremely mixed character of their texts.[1] Some are translated from the Greek, others from Syriac, others from Coptic ; others have been translated from one language and corrected from another. There is a tradition that a version was made from the Syriac in the seventh century, and the earliest extant MS. is one in the Vatican, which is assigned to the eighth century, and appears to contain a translation from the Peshitto. This comes from the monastery of Mar Saba, where there are also MSS. of the ninth century containing a version from the Greek, probably ultimately from the bilingual MS. of which the few surviving leaves have been described above as Θ^b. Other MSS. belong to the tenth and subsequent centuries ; the predominant version being perhaps one due to a revision undertaken in the Patriarchate of Alexandria in the thirteenth century. This is the only version which has found its way into print, several editions of various parts of the Bible having appeared since 1591. Recently some early Arabic MSS. have been found at Mount Sinai, which may be derived from an older translation than those hitherto known. Mr. Rendel Harris first published a fragment of a Greek and Arabic MS. of the ninth century from this source, containing a few verses of St. Matthew.[2] Since then Mrs. Gibson has published a large part of the Pauline Epistles (Romans, 1 and 2 Corinthians, Galatians, and part of Ephesians) from a MS. of equal date,[3] and more recently the Acts and Catholic Epistles from a MS. of the eighth or ninth century.[4] Both of these MSS. contain texts different from any hitherto known, and no doubt earlier. The former is said to have been made from the Greek, the latter from the Syriac,—the Acts and the three longer Epistles from the Peshitto, the four shorter and more

---

[1] See Burkitt's article on the Arabic versions in Hastings' *Dictionary of the Bible.*

[2] *Biblical Fragments from Mount Sinai* (1896), No. 9 ; reprinted with additions in *Studia Sinaitica*, i. App. 1.

[3] *Studia Sinaitica*, ii. (1894).

[4] *Ibid.* vii. (1899).

disputed Epistles (2 and 3 John, 2 Peter, and Jude) from the Philoxenian. In connexion with the text of the Philoxenian version, the Arabic has some value; but with this exception the textual importance of all the Arabic versions hitherto known is infinitesimal.

We pass now from the East to the West, where the ground is almost wholly occupied by the Latin versions.

8. **The Latin Versions.**—The history of the Latin Bible divides itself into two well marked portions, namely, the history of the Vulgate, the great translation which has been the Bible of Roman Christendom for fifteen hundred years, and the history of the texts which preceded it. Historically the former is infinitely the more important, by reason of its commanding position in the Christianity of the West; but textually its predecessor is the more interesting, by reason of its early date and its remarkable characteristics. Of this version it is now our duty to speak.

a. **The Old Latin Version** (or **Versions**).—Difficulties confront us at the outset. It is doubtful whether one should speak of it in the singular or in the plural; for the extant MSS. differ so greatly from one another that it is questionable whether they could have originated from a single archetype. Nor is it easy to determine the locality in which it (or the earliest form of it) had its birth.

A priori it would seem natural to look to Rome for the origin of the Latin Bible. Christianity, as we know from the Acts of the Apostles, was carried thither ·by the middle of the first century, and it was a leading Church by the end of that century. It is clear, however, that the early Roman Church was more Greek than Latin. The earlier bishops of Rome, with few exceptions, have Greek names; and Clement, the most notable exception, wrote his epistle in Greek. The first clearly Latin bishop of Rome is Victor (189-199). The early literature of the Roman Church, the Epistle of Clement, the "Shepherd" of Hermas, the Apologies of Justin Martyr, and the works of Hippolytus, are in Greek. The first Roman liturgy was in Greek, as is still indicated by the "Kyrie" which survives from it. Nor is this apparent anomaly difficult to explain. The educated inhabitants of Italy used Greek as freely as their own tongue; the private meditations of a Roman emperor (Marcus Aurelius) were written in Greek. On the other hand, the trading and slave population of the towns, in which Christianity was probably preached most in the early days, was largely recruited from the Greek-speaking nations. Certain it is, in any case, that the earliest Latin Bible shows every sign of having been produced far from the literary influences of the capital.

The roughness of the more primitive forms of the Old Latin text, and the characteristic peculiarities of its dialect and vocabulary, have commonly been held [1] to point to Africa as its home, since they are also found in the African Latin authors, such as Tertullian, Apuleius, Cyprian, Arnobius, etc. Nor is this hypothesis improbable on general grounds. Greek would be little known in Northern Africa, which has always been parted by a great gulf from Egypt, and easily remains unaffected by its influence. On the other hand, it was conspicuously flourishing in intellectual activity during the second century, and the writings of Tertullian (flor. 195-225) show that Christianity must have been preached there at a very early date. Here, then, a Latin version of the Scriptures would be required earlier than at Rome, and as the linguistic peculiarities of what appears to be the earliest Latin Bible suit this hypothesis, it may be admitted that a strong case has been made out, while contradictory arguments are few. It must be noticed, however, that the linguistic argument is not so strong as it looks; for it so happens that there are hardly any extant Latin authors of this period who were not Africans, so that, while we can say that the characteristics

[1] Since Wiseman's letters on the controversy concerning 1 John v. 7 (1832-33).

of the Old Latin vocabulary existed in Africa, we cannot certainly say that they existed nowhere else in the Roman Empire. Still, the roughness and vigour of the language suit some such energetic province as this, and the agreement in text between the quotations in the African Fathers and what appears to be the earliest form of the Latin Bible is a strong confirmation of this hypothesis. Hence at present, at any rate, the theory of an African origin of the Latin Bible must be said to hold the field, and to hold it with increasing strength.[1]

The date of it cannot be fixed with precision, nor is it likely that all the books of the Bible were translated at one time or by one person. Later than the end of the second century it cannot be, since Tertullian clearly knew of a complete Latin Bible; and corroborative evidence may be found in the fact that in the Old Testament the primitive Latin translation (which was made from the Septuagint) has none of those insertions from the Hebrew which were made by Origen in his Hexapla. On the other hand, we have no evidence which will carry us back to the beginning of that century. Early though the type of text found in the Old Latin MSS. unquestionably is, some interval of time must be allowed for the dissemination of its peculiar vagaries. Probably if we assign it to the middle of the second century we shall not be very far wrong.

The Old Latin version having eventually been superseded by the Vulgate, it is not surprising that the extant manuscript authorities for it are neither numerous nor perfect. On the other hand, they are almost all of very early date. They differ so greatly from one another that it is necessary to describe them separately. The several MSS. (or fragments) are indicated by the small letters of the Latin alphabet. The authorities for the

---

[1] Sanday (*Guardian*, May 25, 1892; cf. Kennedy, in Hastings' *Dict. of the Bible*) suggests Antioch as the original centre whence the Latin and Syriac versions alike took their origin. In any case, as will be shown below, the earliest form in which we now have the version appears to be closely connected with Africa.

Gospels (which are almost wholly distinct from those for the other books) are given first.

a. **Codex Vercellensis**, at Vercelli : probably of the fourth century. Traditionally written by Eusebius, Bishop of Vercelli (ob. 371). Contains the four Gospels (in the usual Latin order, Matthew, John, Luke, Mark), somewhat mutilated, and in a much damaged condition.[1] Collated by Bianchini in 1727, published by Irico in 1748 and Bianchini in 1749 (with *b* and *f*, in his *Evangelium Quadruplex*, reprinted in Migne, *Patrologia*, vol. xii.) ; finally by Belsheim (a prolific editor of Old Latin texts) in 1894.

a[2] : see *n*.

b. **Codex Veronensis**, at Verona: fifth century. Written in silver letters on purple vellum. Contains the Gospels with mutilations. Edited by Bianchini (and Migne) with *a.* Facsimile in the Turin *Monumenta palaeographica sacra*, pl. ii.

c. **Codex Colbertinus**, at Paris : twelfth century. An extraordinarily late copy of the Old Latin, due to its having been written in Languedoc, where the use of this version lingered late. Contains the four Gospels complete, with the rest of the New Testament added later from the Vulgate. Edited by Sabatier in his great edition of the Old Latin Bible (1751), and Belsheim (1888).

d. **Codex Bezae**, the Latin text: see p. 73. The four Gospels and Acts, with 3 John 11-15.

e. **Codex Palatinus**, formerly at Trent, now at Vienna, with one leaf at Dublin : fifth century. Written in silver letters on purple vellum. Contains the Gospels (Matthew, John, Luke, Mark), considerably mutilated. Borrowed from Trent and copied by Bianchini in 1762, but not published until 1847, when Tischendorf edited it ; and almost simultaneously the Dublin leaf was acquired and edited by J. H. Todd. In 1879 this was identified by T. G. Law as belonging to *e* (*Academy*, 1879, March 1), subsequently being re-edited by T. K. Abbott (1880).

---

[1] White's statement (in Scrivener) that this MS. is written in silver letters on purple vellum appears to be erroneous.

The text of *e* is akin to that of *k*, but represents a later stage of it.

f. **Codex Brixianus**, at Brescia: sixth century. Written in silver letters on purple vellum. Contains the Gospels, nearly complete. Edited with *a* and *b* by Bianchini (and Migne); and thence printed by Wordsworth and White in their great edition of the Vulgate, as representing, in their opinion, the type of Old Latin text on which Jerome's revision was based.

ff[1]. **Codex Corbeiensis I.**, originally at Corbey in Picardy, then (circ. 1638) at St. Germain des Prés in Paris, which was plundered during the Revolution, now in the Imperial Library at St. Petersburg. Variously assigned to the eighth, ninth, or tenth century, the latter being probably the true date. Edited by Martianay in 1695, and (being the first Old Latin MS. published) used by subsequent editors of the version. Republished by Belsheim in 1881. Contains only St. Matthew. Its text is a mixture of Old Latin and Vulgate readings, and it is quoted by Hort (*Introduction*, p. 82), among examples of the process by which Old Latin readings found their way into texts fundamentally Hieronymic.

ff[2]. **Codex Corbeiensis II.**, formerly at Corbey, now at Paris: sixth or seventh century. Quoted by Calmet (1787) and subsequent editors; edited by Belsheim (1887). Contains the Gospels, with mutilations, especially in Matthew, the first eleven and a half chapters of which are lost.

g[1]. **Codex Sangermanensis I.**, formerly at St. Germain des Prés, now in the Bibliothèque Nationale: eighth or ninth century. Quoted by Martianay and others, and collated for Bentley; St. Matthew edited by Wordsworth (*Old Latin Biblical Texts*, i. 1883). The second volume of a complete Bible. Contains the Gospels, but only Matthew is Old Latin, the rest being Vulgate with some Old Latin readings. Hort reckons the whole with *ff*[1] as a modified Vulgate, but Wordsworth concludes with regard to Matthew that its basis was not Hieronymian, but a

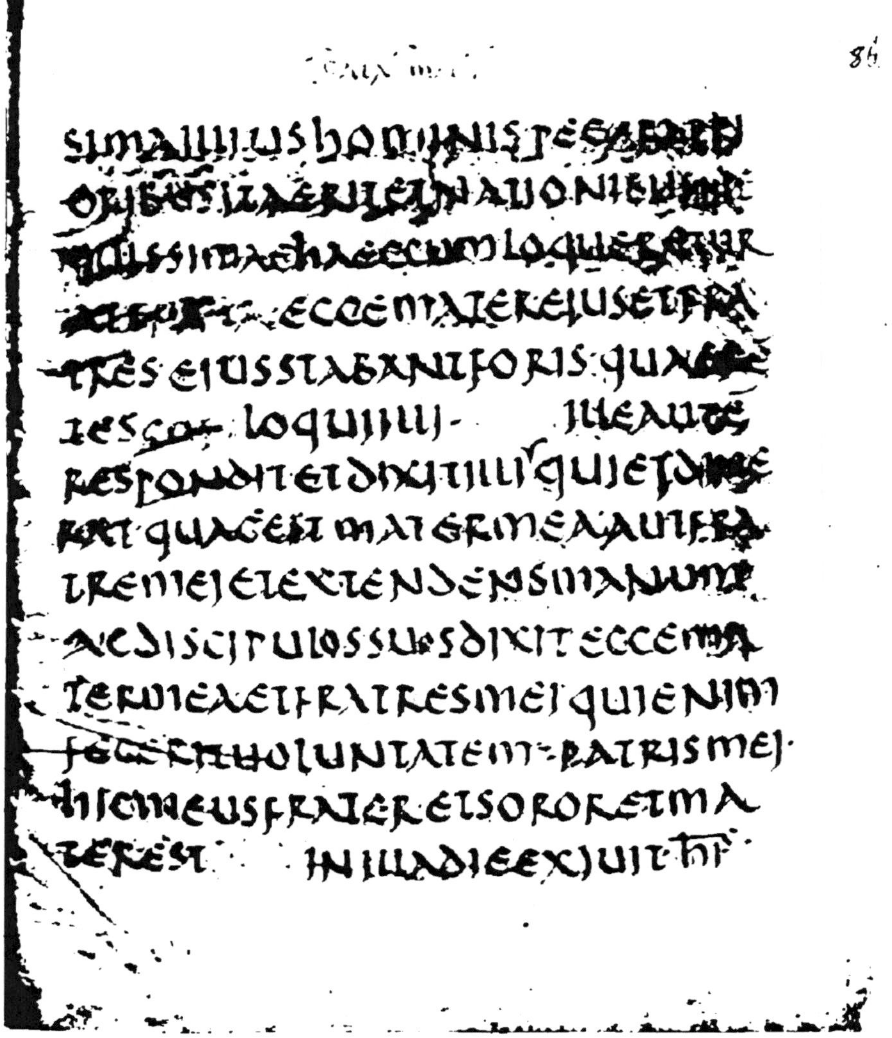

PLATE XV.

SIMAIIIIUSHOMINISPESSERS
ORIBESIIAERIIEINAUONIEUEM
MIISSIMAEHAECUMLOQUEREIUR
ECCEMATEREIUSETFRA
TRES EIUSSTABANTFORIS·QUAE
TESCQT·LOQUIIIIIJ-   IIIEAUTE
RESPONDITETDIXITIIII·QUIETAE
EST QUAEEST MATERMEAAUTFA
TREMIEIETEXTENSENSMANUM
AEDISCIPULOSSUSDIXITECCEMA
TERMEAETFRATRESMEIQUIENIM
FECERITUOLUNTATEM·PATRISMEI
IIISEMEUSFRAIERETSOROKETMA
TERESI·   INILLADIEEXIUITIHS

CODEX BOBIENSIS (*k*).   Fifth Century (?).

(Scale 4 : 5.   The page shown contains Matt. xii. 45-xiii. 1, verse 47 being omitted, as in ℵBLΓ, the Old Syriac, and *ff*¹.)

mixture of different types of Old Latin texts, occasionally corrected to the Vulgate, and containing a large peculiar element.

g². **Codex Sangermanensis II.**, formerly at St. Germain des Prés, now in the Bibliothèque Nationale: tenth century. Used by Sabatier, but not published. Contains the Gospels, written in an Irish hand. The text is a mixture of Old Latin and Vulgate.

h. **Codex Claromontanus**, formerly at Clermont, now in the Vatican: fourth or fifth century. Contains Matthew (mutilated) of the Old Latin, the other Gospels of the Vulgate text. Quoted by Sabatier; Matthew edited by Mai (1828) and Belsheim (1892).

i. **Codex Vindobonensis**, formerly at Naples, now at Vienna: variously assigned to the fifth, sixth, or seventh century. Written in silver letters on purple vellum. Contains fragments of Luke and Mark. Quoted by Bianchini, edited (in periodicals) by Alter (1791-95), re-edited by Belsheim (1885).

j. **Codex Saretianus**, at Sarezzano: fifth century. Written in silver letters on purple vellum. Contains only fragments of John. Discovered in 1872, and not yet published. Its text is said by White to agree much with *abde*.

k. **Codex Bobiensis**, formerly at Bobbio, now at Turin: fifth or sixth century.[1] Written in rather rough uncials, with many blunders. Traditionally said to have belonged to St. Columban (543-615), who founded Bobbio in 613. Originally contained the four Gospels, but now has Mark viii.-xvi. (ending at xvi. 8), Matthew i.-xv., with some mutilations. Edited by Fleck (1837), by Tischendorf (in several numbers of a periodical, 1847-49), and finally by Wordsworth (*Old Latin Biblical Texts*, ii. 1886), with facsimile and elaborate introductions by himself and Sanday. One of the most im-

[1] Mr. Burkitt has recently sought to establish a fourth century date for this MS. The hand is peculiar (see Plate XV.), but at present palaeographical evidence for so early a date is wanting. The internal character of the MS. certainly favours an early period.

portant Old Latin MSS., containing the version in what is probably its oldest form, which Sanday shows to be near akin to the Bible used by St. Cyprian. The Greek text underlying it has a large element in common with D, but one almost equally large in common with אB; while in having the shorter alternative ending to Mark it agrees with L, Ψ, Evan. 274, etc.

l. **Codex Rehdigeranus**, at Breslau : seventh century. Contains the Gospels, nearly complete, except the last five chapters of John. Edited in part (Matthew and Mark) by Scheibel (1763), and in full by Haase (1865-66).

m. This letter is assigned to the treatise entitled **Speculum**, falsely assigned to St. Augustine, which contains extracts from all books of the New Testament, except Philemon, Hebrews, and 3 John, in an Old Latin text. Attention was first called to it by Mai, who edited it from a single MS. at Rome of the eighth or ninth century (1852); re-edited from six MSS. by Weihrich (in the Vienna *Corpus script. eccles. Lat.* xii. 1887). Its text is probably of Spanish origin. It is notable as containing the famous passage on the Three Heavenly Witnesses (1 John v. 7), for which there is practically no Greek evidence, though the Latin evidence goes back to Priscillian, in the fourth century.

n. **Fragmenta Sangallensia**, at St. Gall : fifth or sixth century. Fragments of the four Gospels, mainly Matthew and Mark. Mentioned by Lachmann (1842), and independently edited by Batiffol (1885) and White (*Old Latin Biblical Texts*, ii. 1886), the latter with the help of a transcript made by Tischendorf. Two leaves are separated from the rest, being in the town library of St. Gall, while another is at Coire, where it was seen and edited by E. Ranke (1872), and identified as belonging to *n* by Batiffol. This leaf is separately numbered as a^2 by White (*op. cit.*), who formerly disputed the identification with *n*, and Gregory, who would transfer the whole MS. to that letter; but *n* has the prior claim, and it is also undesirable to multiply sub-tenants of a single letter (as

a^1, a^2, etc.), if it can be avoided. The text of these fragments is closely akin to that of a.

o. A single leaf at St. Gall, of the seventh or eighth century, containing the last seven verses of Mark, and perhaps written to supply a lost leaf in n, which leaves off exactly at this place. Edited by Batiffol and White, *ubi supra*.

p. Two leaves at St. Gall : seventh or eighth century. Written in an Irish hand, as are many other MSS. in this monastery. Contains part of John xi., and is believed to have formed part of a service-book, not a copy of the whole Gospels. Edited by Forbes (1864), Haddan and Stubbs (1869), and White (*ubi supra*).

q. **Codex Monacensis,** formerly at Freising, now at Munich : sixth or seventh century. Written by a scribe named Valerianus, probably in Germany. Contains the Gospels, somewhat mutilated. Transcribed by Tischendorf, and edited by White (*Old Latin Biblical Texts*, iii. 1888). In text it holds a middle position between b and f.

r^1. **Codex Usserianus I.,** at Dublin : sixth or seventh century. Contains the Gospels (Matthew, John, Luke, Mark), but mutilated, especially in Matthew. Edited by T. K. Abbott (1884). Its text is akin to that of p, which appears to indicate the existence of an Irish type of Old Latin text.

r^2. **Codex Usserianus II.,** also at Dublin : ninth century. Contains the Gospels, but only Matthew is Old Latin, the rest being Vulgate. Collated by Abbott in his edition of r^1.

s. **Fragmenta Ambrosiana,** formerly at Bobbio, now at Milan : sixth century. Consists of four leaves from Luke. Edited by Ceriani (1861) and Wordsworth (*Old Latin Biblical Texts*, ii. 1886). Its text is very much mixed.

t. **Fragmenta Bernensia,** at Berne : fifth or sixth century. Palimpsest fragments of Mark i.-iii., very difficult to decipher. Edited by Hagen (1884) and Wordsworth (*ubi supra*). The text is somewhat akin to that of d, and in a rather less degree to b and f.

v. **Fragmentum Vindobonense,** at Vienna : seventh century. A single leaf of John. Edited by Wordsworth and White (*op. cit.* iii. 1888).

δ. **Codex Sangallensis :** the interlinear Latin text of Δ, q.v. Chiefly notable for giving many alternative renderings of the Greek words.

For the Acts the authorities are as follows :—

d = d of the Gospels.

e. **Codex Laudianus :** the Latin text of E$_2$. Edited by Belsheim, 1893.

g. **Codex Gigas,** formerly in Prague, now at Stockholm : thirteenth century. This MS. receives its name from its huge size. Contains the whole Bible, but only the Acts and Apocalypse are Old Latin. These books were edited by Belsheim (1879). The survival of an Old Latin text in so late a MS. may be explained, as in the case of *c,* by the secluded character of the country (Bohemia) in which it was written.

g^2. **Fragmentum Mediolanense,** at Milan : tenth or eleventh century. A portion of a lectionary, containing some verses of Acts vi.-viii., in a text akin to that of *g.* Edited by Ceriani (1866).

h. **Palimpsestus Floriacensis,** formerly at Fleury, now at Paris : sixth or seventh century. Contains fragments of the Apocalypse, Acts, 1 and 2 Peter, and 1 John. Quoted by Sabatier, edited by Belsheim (1887) and Berger (1889, with facsimile). Gregory assigns it the name *reg* instead of *h.* Like *k* its text is closely akin to that used by St. Cyprian.

m = m of the Gospels.

p. This letter is given by Nestle, and by Sanday and Turner in their forthcoming edition of the New Testament of Irenaeus, to a manuscript recently discovered by M. Samuel Berger,[1] the great French authority on the Latin Bible, whose recent death is a severe loss to Biblical scholarship.

---

[1] *Un ancien texte latin des Actes des Apôtres decouvert* . . . par M. Samuel Berger (*Notices et Extraits des Manuscrits de la Bibliothèque Nationale,* xxxv. 169, 1896).

It is a MS. now in the Bibliothèque Nationale at Paris, but is shown by an inscription in it to have belonged, at or soon after its origin, to a monastery at Perpignan. It is a thirteenth-century copy of the New Testament, containing a Vulgate text throughout, except in Acts i. 1-xiii. 6, xxviii. 16-30, which is Old Latin. It thus resembles *c* as an example of a late survival of the ancient version in a remote district.

s. **Codex Bobiensis**, formerly at Bobbio, then at Naples, now at Vienna : fifth or sixth century. Palimpsest fragments of last six chapters of Acts, James, and 1 Peter, in one volume, with portions of Lucan and other works. First noticed by J. von Eichenfeld (1824), partly deciphered and published by Tischendorf (1847), more fully but less accurately by Belsheim (1886) ; finally, with further additions, by White (*Old Latin Biblical Texts*, iv. 1897). Agrees mainly with *g*.

x[1]. **Codex Bodleianus**, at Oxford : seventh or eighth century. Contains Acts, nearly perfect. Berger, however, reckons this among the Anglo-Saxon MSS. of the Vulgate. Described, with specimen facsimile, by Westcott (Smith's *Dict. of Bible*, art. "Vulgate"), who says that it is a most valuable MS.

For the Catholic Epistles :—

ff. **Codex Corbeiensis**, formerly at Corbey, now (like *ff*[1]) at St. Petersburg : probably of the tenth century. Contains the Epistle of James, together with the unique Latin text of the Epistle of Barnabas, and two other treatises. Published by Martianay (1695) with *ff*[1]; subsequently by Sabatier and Belsheim, and finally by Wordsworth (*Studia Biblica*, i. 1885). The text is predominantly Old Latin, but has many agreements with the Vulgate, and therefore probably represents a comparatively late stage in the development of the Old Latin text. The Epistle of James does not seem to have been recognised in the Latin Church before about the end of the fourth century, and it will be observed that in this MS. it is associated with uncanonical writers.

$h = h$ of Acts.

$m = m$ of the Gospels.

q. **Fragmenta Monacensia,** at Munich: sixth or seventh century. Contains fragments of 1 John, 1 and 2 Peter (including 1 John v. 7, which is placed after verse 8). Extracted from the bindings of books by Ziegler, and edited by him (1877).

$s = s$ of Acts. Its text here agrees generally with the Vulgate (which in the Epistles was not greatly altered from the Old Latin), with perhaps a strain of late African text.

For the Pauline Epistles :—

d. **Codex Claromontanus,** the Latin text of D_2.

e. **Codex Sangermanensis,** the Latin text of E_3.

f. **Codex Augiensis,** the Latin text of F_2. The text is said to be largely Vulgate.

g. **Codex Boernerianus,** the Latin text of G_8, but with a purer form of Old Latin text than its kinsman *f.*

gue. **Codex Guelferbytanus,** at Wolfenbüttel: sixth century. Fragments of Romans found in the palimpsest MS. containing PQ of the Greek Gospels. Edited by Knittel (1772) and Tischendorf (1855).

$m = m$ of the Gospels.

r. **Codex Frisingensis,** at Munich: fifth or sixth century. Contains twenty-six leaves from Romans, 1 and 2 Corinthians, Galatians, Ephesians, Philippians, 1 Timothy, Hebrews. Noticed by Tischendorf, and published by Ziegler in 1876. Two leaves subsequently identified by C. Schnorr were edited by Wölfflin in 1893.

r^2. A single leaf, also at Munich, of the seventh century, containing a few verses from Philippians and 1 Thessalonians. Published by Ziegler with *r.*

r^3. **Codex Gottvicensis,** at Göttweig on the Danube: sixth or seventh century. Contains small fragments of Romans and Galatians. Edited by Rönsch (1879).

x^2. **Codex Bodleianus,** at Oxford: ninth century. Contains the Pauline Epistles, nearly complete. The text often agrees with that of *d.*   Described by Westcott, with *x* of the Acts.

Finally, for the Apocalypse:—

g = *g* of the Acts.

h = *h* of the Acts.

m = *m* of the Gospels.

In addition to these MSS. the Old Latin text of the Apocalypse is to be found almost complete in the commentary of Primasius, an African father of the sixth century, and considerable portions of it in the writings of Cyprian (third century) and Tyconius (late fourth century). Indeed, for all parts of the Old Latin version the evidence of patristic quotations is especially important, on account of the fragmentary and divergent character of the manuscript authorities. The consideration of these, however, belongs rather to the next chapter.

Such, then, being the roll of witnesses to the Old Latin text, what do they tell us of the history of the version? At first sight the differences among them are so great as to appear to confirm the complaint of Jerome, when he undertook the revision of the Latin Bible: "si enim Latinis exemplaribus fides est adhibenda, respondeant quibus ; tot enim sunt exemplaria paene quam codices." [1]   Augustine also complains of the "infinita varietas" of the Latin translators, and asserts that in the early days of Christianity any one who possessed a Greek MS., and some degree of familiarity with both languages, would take upon himself the office of a translator.

Closer examination, however, has shown the possibility of grouping and classifying the authorities, at least to some extent. On the one hand, the evidence that the version originated in Africa suggested the possibility that some of the MSS. might be associated with that country, especially as Augustine specifically mentions "codices Afros" (*Retr.* i. 21, 3). On the other hand, a well-known passage in Augustine appears expressly to name an Italian type of text as superior to all the multitude of others : " In ipsis

---

[1] *Ep. ad Damasum*, prefixed to the Vulgate.

autem interpretationibus Itala ceteris praeferatur ; nam est verborum tenacior cum perspicuitate sententiae " (*De Doct. Christ.* ii. 22).[1] Starting from these indications, Hort, followed by the great majority of modern scholars, divided the Old Latin version into three types—(1) African, the most primitive ; (2) European, including the greater number of extant MS. authorities ; (3) Italian, the type praised by Augustine, and representing the text which formed the basis of Jerome's revision. Whether the African and European families spring from a single origin, or are the products of two distinct translations, was then and still remains an undetermined point. On the one hand the differences, both in readings and in renderings, are so very marked as almost to preclude the possibility of a common origin ; on the other, there occur here and there resemblances of a kind which can hardly be otherwise accounted for. The most careful and competent investigators, such as Hort and Sanday, express themselves as uncertain ; and lesser students can but accept their verdict. In any case there has been a considerable amount of intermixture of texts ; and in any case it is possible to distinguish broadly between characteristically African and characteristically European readings. With regard to the Italian family, no such question arises. Some scholars, indeed, deny its existence in the sense in which the passage of Augustine is usually interpreted, as will be shown more fully below ; but if it exists, it is the result of a revision of the European text, carried out in North Italy early in the fourth century.

When we come to apply this classification to our extant authorities, the African family can be tested and identified by reference to the Biblical quotations in the African Fathers; not so much Tertullian, who seems habitually to have made his own translations direct from the Greek,

---

[1] Bentley, who did not believe in an Italian recension of the Old Latin, proposed to read *et illa* for *Itala ;* but this is condemned (1) by the fact that it involves the further alteration of *nam* into *quae* before it will make any sense at all, and (2) by the exceedingly commonplace character of the remark which is the result of these emendations.

as Cyprian, who quotes copiously and textually. The MS. *k* (Codex Bobiensis) comes closest of all to this standard ; next to it, though at some little distance, stands *e* (Codex Palatinus) ; and a somewhat later stage is represented by *m*. In the Acts we have, besides *m*, only the fragments of *h* ; in the Epistles, only *m*, and the quotations of Priscillian, which are most frequent here, and mainly agree with *m* ; in the Apocalypse, *h* and Primasius, and the quotations in Tyconius, whose commentary on this book is to a considerable extent preserved in the works of other writers. The European family is much more fully represented, though it must not be understood that all the MSS. here mentioned form a homogeneous group. On the contrary, they are full of diversities among themselves ; but in spite of these diversities, the MSS. *a* (with its close ally *n*), *b* (perhaps the most typical representative of the family, the other MSS., however much they differ among themselves, all seeming to show kinship with this), *c* (a more mixed text), *ff*^{2}, *h*, *i*, the fragments *n*, *o*, *s*, *t* (*p* and *r* giving an Irish sub-species of the same family), and *s*, all appear to belong to the European family in the Gospels. To these may be added the Latin version of Irenaeus. In the Acts the European text is represented by *g*, *g*^{2}, *p*, *s*, and the quotations of Lucifer of Cagliari ; in the Catholic Epistles by *ff* (?) ; in the Pauline Epistles by nothing that can be certainly established ; in the Apocalypse by *g* (though Gregory regards this as rather Italian). Finally, the Italian family is especially to be looked for in *f*, and somewhat less in *q*, of the Gospels ; in *q* of the Catholic Epistles ; and in *r*, *r*^{2}, *r*^{3} of the Pauline. Of the MSS. not accounted for in this classification, *d* of the Gospels and Acts, and *d*, *e*, *f*, *g* of the Pauline Epistles are the Latin texts of bilingual MSS., and have suffered by their collocation with the Greek ; while the characters of the remainder are mixed or uncertain.

Such is the view of the Old Latin version which holds the field to-day, giving us the picture of a translation originally free in text and rough in rendering in its African home, and progressively toned down in both respects in Europe, having its readings brought more into conformity with the Greek copies and its Latinity smoothed down into more conventional forms, until the process reached its consummation in an Italian revision, which itself paved the way for the further revision by Jerome, to which the Vulgate owes its origin. Recently, however, Bentley's disbelief in the very existence of the " Itala " has been revived by Mr. F. C. Burkitt of Cambridge. Mr. Burkitt's main position [1] is that by his " Itala interpretatio " Augustine meant nothing more nor less than the Vulgate, the New Testament portion of which had been published for some ten years at the time when he wrote ; in support of which view he appeals to Augustine's own works. In short quotations, such as a writer would naturally make from memory, he often quotes the Old Latin, even to the end of his life ; but in longer passages, requiring reference to a manuscript, he appears in his later works to have used the Vulgate. Mr. Burkitt refers especially to the *De Consensu Evangelistarum*, written about A.D. 400, in which precise textual quotations are constantly required ; and to the *Acta contra Felicem*, a report of a trial for heresy at Hippo in 404, in which Augustine is said to have read a long passage from a copy of the Gospels and another from a copy of the Acts. These passages are quoted in full, and while that from the Acts is undoubtedly of the African Old Latin type, that from the Gospels is pure Vulgate. If this were due to subsequent corruption in the MS. it is unlikely that the other passage would have escaped similar alteration ; hence Mr. Burkitt is fully entitled to argue that the Church at Hippo in 404 read the Gospels in the Vulgate text, though it had not cared to adopt the revised version of the Acts.

These are the two most striking testimonies to

[1] See *The Old Latin and the Itala* (Cambridge *Texts and Studies*, iv. 3, 1896).

Augustine's use of the Vulgate (in the New Testament; in the Old Testament we know that he approved less of Jerome's more extensive alterations); but in his later works in general Mr. Burkitt holds that his Gospel quotations exhibit a Vulgate base with occasional Old Latin readings. Hence he may naturally have been referring to Jerome's work when he commended the "Itala interpretatio" as "verborum tenacior cum perspicuitate sententiae." And if it be asked, by way of answer, "But have we not concrete evidence of the existence of the Itala in such MSS., as *f* and *q*?" Mr. Burkitt is apparently prepared to deny to *f*, at any rate, the character of an Old Latin MS. at all, regarding it as a post-Vulgate text which owes its peculiarities to the corrupting influence of the Gothic;[1] while *q* would no doubt be classified as merely a variety of the European family.

Mr. Burkitt's theory has not as yet met with either acceptance or rejection, and indeed neither is possible without a detailed examination of the Biblical quotations in Augustine's later works; but the case in its favour appears strong. It may be observed, however, that even if Augustine's testimony to the existence of a specially Italian pre-Vulgate text be thus disposed of, the facts with regard to the Old Latin version established by the manuscripts themselves remain unaltered. We have on the one hand a group of texts which is shown by the evidence of the African Fathers to be closely connected with Africa, and on the other we have a number of texts in a somewhat later stage of development, and showing among themselves signs of progressive revision, until at last we reach texts which may have furnished a basis for Jerome's work. The classification of our MSS. consequently remains the same, whether the final stage is entitled Italian or not. Whether *f* represents the final stage is a further question, on which the verdict of Bishop Wordsworth and Mr. White, the editors of the Vulgate,

---

[1] See *Journal of Theological Studies*, i. 129-134 (in a review of Wordsworth and White's Vulgate).

who have selected it as the nearest extant representative of the text upon which Jerome worked, will rightly have great weight. Mr. Burkitt's suggestion of corruption from the Gothic is not, *prima facie*, attractive. It does not seem likely that the owner or transcriber of a Latin MS. would introduce corrections from what he would consider as the less authoritative Gothic text, and it would seem most natural to explain any coincidences between *f* and the Gothic as due rather to the influence of the Latin text on the Gothic during the occupation of Italy by the Goths, than to the reverse process.

Looking now finally at the Old Latin version as a whole, its text is found to be of a very early character. It belongs to, and is a principal member of, that class of authorities (the δ-type, as we have called it) which is distinguished by the boldest and most striking departures from the received text. It is found in company with the Codex Bezae and its attendant group of minuscules, and with the Old Syriac. It shares with these the additions to, and (at the end of St. Luke) the omissions from, the received text, of which some mention has been made on p. 76. It shares also their constant verbal divergences, suggestive of a time when strict accuracy in the transmission of the sacred texts was not much regarded. The history of this type of text, and its position in modern textual criticism, will have to be considered in the final chapter; at present we are only concerned in pointing out the witnesses to its existence. It is, naturally, in the earlier or African family of the Old Latin that these characteristics are most marked. Successive revisions gradually toned them down or removed them, until in the last days of the existence of this version it approximates to the type of text which we know to-day as the Vulgate.

b. **The Vulgate.**——The chaotic character of the Old Latin texts, still evident to us in the scanty remnants which have survived to our time, led at the close of the fourth century to the production of the great version which supplied all Western Christendom with its Bible for over a thousand years, and still is the Bible of that great branch of the Church which owns allegiance to Rome. It is to Damasus, Pope from 366 to 384, that the credit of its origin is due. Impressed with the uncertainty as to the true text which the variations in the manuscripts of the day made so evident, he applied to Eusebius Hieronymus (better known to us as Jerome) to undertake an authoritative revision of the Latin Bible. No living scholar was equally competent for the task. Born about 345 at Stridon in Pannonia, in the region of modern Trieste, he had devoted himself before everything to Biblical studies. After many years at Rome and in Gaul, in 372 he visited the East, spending ten years there, mainly in the study of Hebrew, before returning to Italy. It was on his return, about the year 382, that the request of Damasus laid upon him the great work of his life, the production of an authoritative Latin Bible. In its beginnings the undertaking was not so great as it subsequently became. The Pope's invitation to him was that he should revise the existing text by reference to the original Greek in the New Testament, and to the Septuagint in the Old Testament, and in the part of the work first taken in hand, the New Testament and the Psalter, this was all he did. It was only later that, becoming dissatisfied with the process of revision, he laid aside all that he had done with regard to the Old Testament, and undertook a new translation of it from the Hebrew. With this we have nothing to do here ; and in the New Testament he was emphatically a reviser, not a new translator.

The revised version of the Gospels, which (with the Psalter) were Jerome's first care, appeared in 383 ; and his preface tells us something of his principles and methods of work. Only in passages of some importance did he think himself entitled to introduce alterations ; smaller blunders and inexactnesses remained uncorrected, in order that the familiar language of the Bible should be left untouched, so far as possible. For the purpose of comparison and correction he used several Greek MSS., the character of which will be considered later. In the other books of the New Testament, a revision of which followed very shortly on that of the Gospels, his work was more perfunctory. Some, indeed, have doubted whether he revised any part of the New Testament except the Gospels, and point to the fact that, contrary to his habit, he wrote no preface to these books; but his own statement that he revised them all is express.

So far, then, as the New Testament is concerned, the Vulgate is merely a revision of the Old Latin, fairly thorough, though not pedantically exact, in the Gospels, but only superficial in the remaining books. One result of this conservative treatment was that the new version met with general acceptance—far more so than was the case with Jerome's wholly new translation of the Old Testament. It did not supersede the older version at once, as is shown by the fact that all the extant copies of the Old Latin, except possibly the Codex Vercellensis, were written subsequently to the publication of Jerome's work; but it was adopted, no doubt by the order of Pope Damasus, as the official Bible of the Church of Rome, and gradually won its way to universal acceptance among the Latin-speaking peoples of the West. It would be going outside the scope of this book to trace the fortunes of the Vulgate throughout the Middle Ages.[1] With success and general adoption came, as was natural, extensive corruption of the text through the carelessness or rashness of scribes and editors. From time to time attempts were made to purify it. Bede and his contemporaries and successors in northern England reached a high level of Biblical scholarship. The great revival of France under Charlemagne led to two revisions of the Vulgate text: one the private undertaking of Theodulf, Bishop of Orleans, about 800; the other the work of the

---

[1] For this the reader cannot do better than consult M. Berger's *Histoire de la Vulgate pendant les premiers siècles du moyen age* (Paris, 1893), an admirable and fascinating study of a most intricate subject.

English scholar Alcuin, whom Charlemagne invited to France to superintend the education of his people. But even Alcuin's official edition had but a temporary effect in staying the progress of corruption, and it was not until four hundred years later that any vigorous effort was made for a reform. In the thirteenth century great activity prevailed in the production of copies of the Bible, as the numbers of manuscripts of this date in our public libraries to-day amply testify; and this activity was largely stimulated and directed by the doctors of the recently founded University of Paris. To one of them, Stephen Langton, afterwards Archbishop of Canterbury and leader of the barons in their contest with King John, we owe our modern division of the Bible into chapters; to others, known or unknown, we owe the redaction of the Vulgate text, not indeed into a scientifically accurate form, but substantially into that form in which it now circulates in the printed copies officially sanctioned by the heads of the Roman Church.

With the invention of printing came naturally the demand for a printed Bible; or rather we may say that the supply preceded the demand. The first book committed to the press in Europe was the Latin Bible, which appeared in 1456 in the splendid edition of Gutenberg, now commonly known as the Mazarin Bible. For the purposes of this edition, however, no critical examination of texts had been undertaken. It was merely an example of the current text of the fifteenth century. The editors employed by Cardinal Ximenes in the preparation of his great Complutensian Polyglott (New Testament printed in 1514, published in 1522) devoted considerable labour to the Latin portion of their text, and Erasmus quotes readings from various Vulgate MSS. examined by himself; but the first really critical editions of the Latin Bible are those published by Stephanus at Paris between 1528 and 1546, of which the best is said to be the fourth, issued in 1540. This, in which seventeen MSS. are quoted, is taken by Wordsworth and White as the

typical representative of Stephanus' editions. In 1546
the Council of Trent passed a decree, prescribing the
Vulgate as the standard text of the Bible to be used in
the services of the Church, and desiring that an accurate
edition of it should be printed ; and it may have been in
consequence of this pronouncement that John Hentenius
in 1547 published a new edition at Louvain, in which he
made use of no less than thirty-one MSS. This edition
was very commonly used in church services, but was never
officially adopted to the exclusion of others ; and it was
not until the accession of Sixtus V. in 1585 that steps
were taken for the preparation of an authorised text.
This Pope took up the matter vigorously, both by
appointing a committee of scholars to undertake the work,
and by devoting himself strenuously to the task of revision. In 1590, accordingly, the Sixtine Vulgate issued
from the Vatican press, accompanied by a papal bull
declaring it to be the "true, legitimate, authentic, and
indubitable" text of the Holy Scriptures, which alone was
to be regarded as authoritative.

Unfortunately for the success of this edition, Sixtus
died in the year of its issue ; and Clement VIII., who was
elected Pope in 1592, promptly decreed its recall and
suppression. The pretext for this action was the in-
accuracy of its printing ; and in justification of this plea
it has been pointed out that many corrections were made
in it, after the sheets were printed off, by means of hand-
stamped type. Mr. H. J. White, however, who has
recently examined the Sixtine Vulgate minutely in the
Gospels, declares that in these books, at any rate, the
charge of inaccurate printing cannot be sustained, and
that the corrections are almost wholly in the introductory
prefaces, the text itself being in fact printed with unusual care and accuracy. It therefore appears that the
other reason which has been suggested is the real one,
namely, that the Jesuits had not forgiven Sixtus for
placing one of Bellarmin's books on the *Index*, and took
this method of revenging themselves. Certain it is that

the alternative edition issued by Clement's authority in
1592 was accompanied by a preface by Bellarmin himself,
in which the allegation of inaccurate printing is made, and
it is even asserted that Sixtus himself had intended to
recall his own edition, but was prevented by death. The
Clementine edition is estimated to differ from the Sixtine
in about 3000 places, approximating rather to the text of
Hentenius, while the Sixtine is nearer to that of
Stephanus ; nevertheless, in order to disguise the conflict
of popes, it was sometimes issued under the name of
Sixtus instead of, or as well as, that of Clement.

Under one name or the other, the edition of 1592
became the standard text of the Roman Church, and has
so continued from that day to this. Not only so, but, in
order the more to ensure its authority, the bull with
which Clement accompanied its issue forbade the slightest
alteration in it, or any insertion of various readings in the
margins. By this measure the textual study of the Latin
Bible was effectually killed in the Church of its home,[1]
although increasing knowledge has shown beyond the
possibility of doubt that the text issued by Clement is by
no means an accurate representation of the version as it
left the hands of Jerome. It has been left to scholars of
other countries, and of other branches of the Christian
Church, to do the work which would have been most
fittingly encouraged and patronised by the Vatican.
Perhaps the more liberal tradition which has been established by the present pontiff may bear good fruit in this
direction also, as in others.

For the present, however, we have to look especially
to England and Germany for attempts to recover the
true text of the Vulgate. Bentley, with the assistance
of his colleague John Walker, made great preparations
for a critical edition, making or procuring collations of a

---

[1] An exception must be made to this statement in the case of the editors of
Jerome, Martianay in 1693 and Vallarsi in 1734, who were able to treat the
Vulgate as part of the saint's literary works, and give something like a critical
edition of it. Vercellone in 1860 published a collection of *Variae Lectiones*,
but without a continuous text.

large number of MSS. ; but he rashly committed himself beforehand to the assertion that the Greek and Latin texts of the Bible could be shown to be identical down to their smallest details, and it is supposed that the discovery of the fallacy of this assertion, forced upon him by increasing knowledge, was a main cause of his failure to bring his work to any conclusion. Nothing was printed by him, and since Walker had died shortly before his master and colleague, the work came to nothing, and the collations which they had accumulated have since remained in the library of Trinity College, Cambridge, almost unused from that day until, in this present generation, the work has been resumed by another pair of scholars from the sister university.

Before reaching, however, this final stage in the history of the Vulgate text, mention is due of the labours of Lachmann, who, carrying out the principles of Bentley to a happier result, issued in 1842-50 a critical edition of the Latin and Greek New Testament which was far in advance of anything that had previously been done. The two texts are printed together, the upper part of the page containing the Greek and the lower the Latin, with the authorities between them ; the Latin text being based upon two excellent authorities, the Codex Fuldensis and the Codex Amiatinus (see below), though the latter, unfortunately, was only accessible to him in an imperfect collation.

Lachmann's authorities, though good, were few, and his text could not be considered a fully critical edition of the Vulgate. Such an edition, however, was at last undertaken by the Rev. John Wordsworth of Brasenose College, Oxford, now Bishop of Salisbury, with whom has been associated during the greater part of the work the Rev. H. J. White of Merton College, Oxford. The first part of this, which will long remain for critical purposes the definitive edition of the Vulgate, appeared in 1889, after twelve years of preparation ; while another nine years have seen the completion of the text of the four Gospels, together with elaborate *prolegomena* and *epilogus*. The edition, so far as the Gospels are concerned, is based upon a collation of thirty selected manuscripts, accompanied by the full text of the Codex Brixianus, as best representing (in the opinion of the editors) the type of Old Latin text upon which Jerome's revision was based. A description of these manuscripts, and of the general conclusions to which the editors have come with regard to Jerome's work, will be given below ; but first, for completeness' sake, it is right to mention that while Wordsworth and White have been labouring mainly at the Gospels, Dr. P. Corssen has been doing similar work with especial reference to the Epistles. The text of the Epistle to the Galatians was published in 1885 ; but it is said that other books also are approaching completion.[1] There is good ground, therefore, to hope that within a reasonable length of time we may possess a complete critical edition of the New Testament, at least, in the Latin Vulgate version.

The task of producing such an edition is, however, no light one. The number of extant MSS. of the Vulgate is immense. No complete catalogue of them exists, and the precise total is unknown ; but it must greatly exceed the 3000 (approximately) of the Greek New Testament. Gregory gives (in addition to the 46 MSS. quoted by Tischendorf) a catalogue of 2228 copies, which he calls merely " pauca ex innumera multitudine codicum " ; while White estimates that there are at least 8000 scattered throughout the various libraries of Europe, out of which he gives a select list of 181, with brief descriptions. For the ordinary purposes of a student, however, it will be sufficient to give some account of the forty copies comprised in the list of Wordsworth and White, using the notation which they have adopted in their edition.

[1] So White in Scrivener, ed. 4, published in 1894; but seven years have elapsed since that date without any further publication. In 1892 Dr. Corssen published a text of the Acts, as it appears in the works of Cyprian ; but this belongs to the history of the Old Latin version.

A. **Codex Amiatinus**, in the Laurentian Library at Florence. The history of this magnificent MS. has recently been made clear by the ingenuity of De Rossi and Hort.[1] The former observed (as others had done before him without carrying the matter further) that in some dedicatory lines at the beginning, which purported to state that the volume was the gift of Peter the Lombard to the monastery of Monte Amiata, these names were written over erasures and spoilt the metre of the verses ; and by a brilliant conjecture he substituted for them the names of Ceolfrid of England and the See of Rome respectively. These conjectures commanded confidence in themselves, being suitable to the context and to the known history of Ceolfrid, but were converted (with slight alterations) into certainties by Professor Hort, who showed that the verses themselves were already extant in an anonymous life of Ceolfrid, used by Bede, where they are expressly stated to have been prefixed to a copy of the Vulgate written at Ceolfrid's order for a gift to the Pope. The history of the MS. was then clear. It was written in the north of England, at either Wearmouth or Jarrow, of both of which monasteries Ceolfrid was abbot, and was copied from MSS. brought from Italy either by Ceolfrid himself or his master, Benedict Biscop, or, perhaps more probably (see description of Y below), by Theodore of Tarsus when he came to England to be Archbishop of Canterbury in 669. It must have been written quite early in the eighth century, and was taken by Ceolfrid as a present to Pope Gregory in 716. Ceolfrid himself died on the way, but the manuscript was carried on to Rome by some of his companions, was subsequently given to Monte Amiata, was recalled temporarily to Rome to be consulted for the Sixtine edition of the Vulgate, and finally found a home at Florence, where the inquiring visitor may now see it. It is a huge and splendid volume, measuring 1 ft. $7\frac{1}{2}$ in. in height by 1 ft. $1\frac{1}{2}$ in. in width, written in double columns in a large

---

[1] For the fullest account see White in *Studia Biblica*, ii. 273 ff.

and beautiful uncial hand. The text is not written continuously, but in short clauses corresponding to breaks in the sense (technically known as *cola* and *commata*, i.e. clauses and sub-clauses). This system of division goes back at least to the middle of the fifth century. The text is also divided into paragraphs, the Gospels having the Ammonian sections (see p. 56, note), while in the Acts a section-numeration is found which occurs also in the Codex Fuldensis (F, see below) and in the Greek MSS. א and B (see p. 66). The MS. contains the whole Bible in an excellent form, and is generally regarded as the best authority extant for the Vulgate text. It was collated by Fleck in 1834 (published in 1840), by Tischendorf in 1843, by Tregelles in 1846, and the New Testament published in full by Tischendorf in 1850. Finally it was re-collated by Mr. H. J. White in 1887 for the Oxford edition, in which it heads the most important and trustworthy group of MSS. Specimen facsimiles of it are given by the Palaeographical Society (ii. 65, 66).

B. **Codex Bigotianus**, formerly at Fécamp, now at Paris : eighth or ninth century. Collated by Walker and Wordsworth. Contains the four Gospels. Its text shows a mixture of Irish and French influences.

Ɛ. **Codex Beneventanus**, formerly at Beneventum, now in the British Museum ; written for an abbot Atto, who has generally been supposed to be identical with an Atto who was abbot of St. Vincent, near Beneventum, from 739 to 760. Berger, however, states that the text is French rather than Italian, and believes that it was written in France, probably in the ninth century. Collated by Bentley, and in Luke and John by White. It contains the four Gospels.

C. **Codex Cavensis**, at La Cava in South Italy : ninth century. Written in Spain, in a small Visigothic hand, and contains the whole Bible. It is a typical representative of the Spanish type of text, in which respect it is associated with T. A transcript of it, made about the beginning of this century, is in the Vatican. Collated by Wordsworth.

D. **Codex Dublinensis**, at Trinity College, Dublin, known as the Book of Armagh : eighth or ninth century. Contains the New Testament (including the apocryphal Epistle to the Laodiceans). Transcribed by G. M. Youngman for the Oxford edition. It belongs to the Irish type of Vulgate text, which is characterised by small additions and insertions, but is based upon a good and ancient tradition. It shows signs of having been corrected from Greek MSS. akin to the Ferrar group (see p. 112).

Δ. **Codex Dunelmensis**, in the Cathedral Library at Durham : seventh or eighth century. Traditionally said to have been written by Bede. Contains the Gospels. Its text is akin to that of A, and, like that MS., it may very probably have been written at Wearmouth or Jarrow. Collated by Bentley. Used by Wordsworth for John only.

E. **Codex Egertonensis**, formerly at Tours, now in the British Museum : ninth century. Contains the Gospels, considerably mutilated, written in Caroline minuscules, but with ornamentation in the Irish style ; its text also is of the Irish type, akin to that of D. Collated by Youngman.

ℱ. **Codex Epternacensis**, formerly at Echternach, now at Paris : ninth century, although it contains a note (no doubt copied from its ancestor) affirming that it was corrected in A.D. 558 from a MS. attributed to St. Jerome's own hand. It contains the Gospels, in a very mixed text. Berger classes it with the Irish family, but Wordsworth considers this as true mainly in such matters as orthography, its readings approaching rather to those of B and Z. The marginal readings are oftener Irish than those of the main text. Collated by White.

F. **Codex Fuldensis**, at Fulda in Germany : written A.D. 541-546 at the order of Bishop Victor of Capua. Contains the whole New Testament, the Gospels being

arranged in a continuous narrative, according to the plan
of Tatian's *Diatessaron*, a copy of which, in a Latin
translation, had fallen into the Bishop's hands. The
author's name was wanting, but Victor rightly (as we
now know) guessed it to be Tatian's, and took it as his
model, substituting, however, the Vulgate text for the
Old Latin of his original. Among the Epistles that to
the Laodiceans is inserted. Its text is very good, being
akin to that of A. It was the principal authority used
by Lachmann for his Latin text, and was published in
full by E. Ranke in 1868 (with facsimiles).

G. **Codex Sangermanensis**, formerly at St. Germain
des Prés : eighth or ninth century. Described above as
*g*¹ of the Old Latin version. In the Old Testament the
text is wholly of the Spanish type ; but in the New
Testament (where it is not Old Latin) it presents a
mixture of French and Irish readings. Berger (who gives
a minute description of it, *Hist. de la Vulgate*, pp. 65-72)
thinks it was written in the region of Lyons ; and it is
noticeable that it contains a curious collection of *sortes*
for purposes of divination, written in the margin of St.
John's Gospel, which also occur, in Greek, in Codex Bezae.
Collated by Walker, and again by Wordsworth and
Youngman.

H. **Codex Hubertianus**, formerly at the monastery of
St. Hubert in the Ardennes, now in the British Museum :
ninth century. It contains the whole Bible, written in
a small Caroline minuscule, with three columns to the
page. Berger and Wordsworth differ somewhat in their
description of its text, the former treating it as a representative of the edition of Theodulf (see above, p. 186),
though somewhat negligently written, while the latter
describes it as closely akin to A and Y, though with
occasional affinities to the Theodulfian Bible, and in its
corrections being thoroughly Theodulfian. This divergence
may be explained by the fact that Theodulf's text in the
Gospels is of the Anglo-Saxon type, though elsewhere
it is predominantly Spanish. Collated by Wordsworth.

Facsimile in *Facsimiles of Biblical MSS. in the British Museum*, pl. xv.

Θ. **Codex Theodulfianus**, the property successively of the Cathedral of Orleans (eleventh century), the family of Mesmes, and the Bibliothèque Nationale at Paris: ninth century. Contains the whole Bible, written in a small hand much resembling that of H, and, like it, is of the edition of Theodulf. Indeed Berger believes it to have been actually prepared under Theodulf's directions, the many corrections which are made in the margins and between the lines being due to his own editorial work. It may be doubted, however, whether the writing is as early as the time of Theodulf. Collated by C. Wordsworth and H. J. White. Facsimile in Delisle's *Album Palœographique*, pl. 18 (1887).

I. **Codex Ingolstadiensis**, formerly at Ingolstadt, now at Munich; ninth century. Contains the Gospels, St. Matthew being much mutilated. Tischendorf (who assigned it to the seventh century) made a collation, which, having been purchased by the Oxford University Press, was used by Wordsworth, with the result that his representation of its readings is not infrequently inaccurate (see Wordsworth and White, i. 673).

J. **Codex Forojuliensis**, mainly at Cividale in Friuli, partly at Venice and Prague; sixth or seventh century. Contains the Gospels, with a text of the class which is headed by Z. The Friuli portion (Matthew, Luke, and John) was edited by Bianchini (1749), the Prague portion by Dobrowski (1778), while the Venice fragment is almost wholly illegible.

K. **Codex Karolinus**, in the British Museum; ninth century. A huge MS., containing the whole Bible according to the edition of Alcuin (see above, p. 187). Consequently it agrees generally with V, which is also Alcuinian, though of the two V is the better; and both have affinities to A and Y, since Alcuin made use of MSS. from Northumbria. Collated by Youngman and White for the Oxford Vulgate. Facsimile in

Facsimiles of Biblical MSS. in the British Museum,
pl. xiv.

L. **Codex Lichfeldensis,** formerly at Llandaff, now in
the Chapter Library at Lichfield, known as the Gospels
of St. Chad ; seventh or eighth century. Contains
Matthew and Mark and Luke i.-iii. 9, with illuminations
in the Celtic-Saxon style. Its text also belongs to the
Celtic family, like that of D. Collated by Scrivener
(1887).

M. **Codex Mediolanensis,** in the Ambrosian Library
at Milan ; sixth century. Contains the Gospels, in a
somewhat independent type of text, agreeing now with
one group, now with another. It appears to have been
corrected from the Greek. Transcribed by Padre F.
Villa for the Oxford Vulgate.

M. **Codex Martini-Turonensis,** formerly in the monastery of St. Martin at Tours, now in the Public Library ;
eighth or ninth century. Contains the Gospels, written
in golden letters, in a text akin to that of Alcuin, but
with more of an Irish element in it. Used by Sabatier,
and from him by Tischendorf. Collated by Walker and
Youngman.

O. **Codex Oxoniensis,** formerly in the monastery of
St. Augustine, Canterbury, now in the Bodleian Library,
Oxford, and known as St. Augustine's Gospels ; seventh
century. Contains the Gospels, in a mixed text, showing
Irish influence, akin to that of X. Collated by Words-
worth, Madan, and Youngman.

P. **Codex Perusinus,** in the Chapter Library at Peru-
gia ; sixth or seventh century. A fragment of a MS.
on purple vellum, containing only Luke i. 26-xii. 7, with
many mutilations. In spite of its age, its text, according
to Wordsworth, is not very good. Edited by Bianchini
(1749).

Q. **Codex Kenanensis,** the famous Book of Kells, at
Trinity College, Dublin ; seventh or eighth century.
Contains the Gospels, in an Irish hand, and with the
most elaborate and beautiful Celtic decorations. The text

is, naturally, of the Irish type, with a peculiar tendency to duplicate renderings. Collated by Dr. T. K. Abbott (1884). Facsimiles in *Pal. Soc.* i. 55-58, 88, 89.

R. **Codex Rushworthianus**, in the Bodleian Library, known also as the Gospels of Mac Regol, from the name of the scribe, who died in A.D. 820. Contains the Gospels, with an interlinear English gloss (as in Y); Matthew in the Mercian dialect, the other Gospels in Northumbrian. Written by an Irish scribe, and has an Irish text, with corrections apparently from the Greek. Collated by Stevenson and Waring (1854-65) and Skeat (1887).

S. **Codex Stonyhurstensis**, formerly at Durham, now at Stonyhurst College; seventh century. Traditionally said to have belonged to St. Cuthbert and to have been preserved with (or in) his coffin. A beautiful little copy of the Gospel of St. John, with an excellent text, akin to that of AΔY, which likewise belong to the north of England. Collated by Wordsworth.

T. **Codex Toletanus**, formerly at Seville, then Toledo, now in the National Library at Madrid; eighth century (cf. Berger, *Hist. de la Vulgate*, pp. 13, 14). Contains the whole Bible, in the Spanish type of text, so that it is an ally of C. A collation was made by C. Palomares for the Sixtine edition of the Vulgate, but was received too late to be used. This collation was printed by Bianchini in 1740. Re-collated for the New Testament by·Wordsworth.

U. **Fragmenta Ultratraiectina,** at Utrecht; seventh or eighth century. Fragments, containing only Mt. i. 1-iii. 4, Jn. i. 1-21, bound up with the well-known Utrecht Psalter; written in a hand closely resembling that of the Amiatinus, and evidently produced in the same scriptorium. Published in facsimile with the Utrecht Psalter (1873).

V. **Codex Vallicellianus**, formerly in the Oratory of S. Maria in Vallicella in Rome, now in the Biblioteca Vittorio-Emanuele; ninth century. Contains the whole Bible written in three columns to the page. The text is

THE LINDISFARNE GOSPELS. Circ. A.D. 700.

(Scale 2 : 5. The page shown contains Luke xxii. 37-47. It includes verses 43 and 44, which are omitted in אABRT and several versions. The small interlinear writing is an Anglo-Saxon gloss,—the earliest form of the Gospels in English.

To face p. 199.

that of the edition of Alcuin ; see description of K, above. Collated by Wordsworth.

W. **Codex Willelmi de Hales,** formerly at Salisbury (having been written for T. de la Wile, master of the schools there), now among the Royal MSS. in the British Museum ; written in 1254. Contains the whole Bible. Employed by Wordsworth and White in their edition as an average representative of the thirteenth-century Vulgate (see p. 187), which is closely related to the printed Vulgates of the sixteenth century. Collated by White and Youngman.

X. **Codex Corporis Christi Cantabrigiensis,** formerly at St. Augustine's, Canterbury, now among Archbishop Parker's MSS. at Corpus Christi College, Cambridge ; seventh century. Contains the Gospels. Its original text is closely akin to that of O, formerly its companion at Canterbury ; but it has been corrected into close agreement with AY. Collated by A. W. Streane for the Oxford Vulgate.

Y. **Codex Lindisfarnensis,** the celebrated Lindisfarne Gospels, formerly at Lindisfarne and Durham, now in the British Museum ; late seventh or early eighth century, being written in honour of St. Cuthbert, who died in 687, and preserved with his body. Written in a splendid uncial hand, and adorned with beautiful decorations in the Celtic-Saxon style. A table of festivals on which special lessons were read shows that it must have been copied from a Bible used in a church at Naples, no doubt one brought to England by the Neapolitan abbot Hadrian, the companion of Archbishop Theodore. Its text is closely akin to that of A. Edited by Stevenson and Waring (1854-65) and Skeat (1887). Facsimiles in *Pal. Soc.* (ii. 65, 66) and *Facsimiles of Biblical MSS. in the British Museum*, pl. xi.

Z. **Codex Harleianus,** formerly in the Bibliothèque du Roi in Paris, now among the Harley MSS. in the British Museum ; sixth or seventh century. A beautifully written little copy of the Gospels, standing at the head of the group of MSS. opposed to AY, and therefore tracing its origin to a different archetype. Collated by Griesbach and others, finally by White. Facsimiles in *Pal. Soc.* (i. 16) and *Facsimiles of Biblical MSS. in the British Museum*, pl. ix.

For the Acts, Epistles, and Apocalypse eleven MSS. out of the preceding list are available, viz. ACDFGH ΘKTVW, and ten more have already been selected by Bishop Wordsworth and Mr. White. As their edition of these books has not yet begun to appear, it is impossible to say whether they regard this selection as final. The additional MSS. are the following:

B_2. **Codex Bambergensis,** originally written in the monastery of St. Martin at Tours, now in the Royal Library at Bamberg; ninth century. A beautiful copy of the entire Bible, wanting the Apocalypse, with elaborate ornamentation of the Carolingian type. The text is Alcuinian. Collated by White.

L_2. **Codex Lombardicus,** in the Bibliothèque Nationale at Paris; eighth century. Contains the Pauline Epistles, written in Lombardic characters. The text is said to be valuable, but apparently it has not yet been fully collated.

L_3. **Codex Lemovicensis,** also in the Bibliothèque Nationale, formerly in the monastery of St. Martial at Limoges; eighth-ninth century. Contains the Catholic Epistles, in a mixed text akin to those of the southern MSS. generally.

M_2. **Codex Monacensis,** formerly at Freising, now at Munich; ninth or tenth century. Contains the Acts, Catholic Epistles, and Apocalypse, in a good but mixed text. Collated by White.

O_2. **Codex Oxoniensis II.,** in the Bodleian Library at Oxford, known as the Selden Acts; seventh or eighth century. Contains the Acts, written in an Anglo-Saxon hand, and in an excellent text of the Irish type. Collated by Wordsworth.

O_3. **Codex Oxoniensis III.,** also in the Bodleian; ninth century. Contains the Pauline Epistles, in a text

originally Old Latin, but corrected into conformity with
the Irish type of Vulgate text. White notes that it often
agrees with the Latin text of the Codex Claromontanus.

R₂. **Codex Regius,** in the Vatican Library at Rome :
seventh century. Contains the Pauline Epistles in a
fairly good text. Used by Corssen in his edition of
Galatians, and collated by Dr. Meyncke for the Oxford
Vulgate.

S₂. **Codex Sangallensis,** written at St. Gall by the
monk Winithar, and still preserved there ; eighth century.
Contains Acts and Apocalypse, with a quantity of non-
biblical matter, bound up with another MS., containing
the books of Numbers and Deuteronomy. The text of
Acts is akin to that of F (Codex Fuldensis), but with
admixture of other elements. Collated by White.

U₂. **Codex Ulmensis;** written for Hartmut, abbot of
St. Gall in 872-883, the Epistle to the Laodiceans being
added (after Hebrews) in his own hand ; subsequently
at Ulm, now in the British Museum. Contains Acts,
Epistles, and Apocalypse. The text, as usual in the St.
Gall MSS., is of a mixed character, but with the southern
type predominating. Collated by White. Facsimile in
Facsimiles of Biblical MSS. in the British Museum, pl. xvi.

Z₂. **Codex Harleianus II. ;** like Z of the Gospels,
formerly at Paris, now among the Harleian MSS. in the
British Museum ; eighth century. Contains the Epistles
(without 3 John and Jude) and Apocalypse (to xiv. 16),
written probably in France, but with decorations in the
Irish style. The text is peculiar. Westcott regards it
as Old Latin, and it certainly has an admixture of old
readings ; Berger notes that Heb. x., xi., especially have
a text quite different from the Vulgate. Collated by
White.

From the above descriptions it will be seen that Bishop
Wordsworth and Mr. White have not only been able to
select and examine a large number of early and important
MSS. of the Vulgate (indeed we may assume that no MS.
of first-rate importance, at present known, has been over-

looked by them), but also to classify them in groups. With regard to the later books of the New Testament, this work is not yet complete ; but for the Gospels their results have been stated, and are not likely to be disputed. The first place is given by them to what may be called the Northumbrian group of MSS., whose origin can be traced to the great schools of Wearmouth and Jarrow, founded about 674 by Benedict Biscop, and promoted by his successor, Ceolfrid. The text of this group (as appears from the history of the Codex Amiatinus and the Lindisfarne Gospels) goes back to MSS. brought from Italy in the seventh century. The group includes the manuscripts AΔSY, with the first hand of H ; while F, though not Northumbrian, is closely akin to this family, and M, though its text is mixed, belongs more to it than to any other. U also, which is Northumbrian, would no doubt have to be reckoned here, if there were more of it. The whole group, therefore, may be said to consist of AΔFHMSUY ; but Δ and S are only available for St. John, and U is hardly available at all. The best text of all, it can hardly be doubted, is that of A, with Y in close attendance.

Over against this group may be set another, consisting of manuscripts which are good, but less good than those which have just been enumerated. It is headed by Z, and composed primarily of BJPZ, with not infrequent assistance from the mixed texts of 𝔉ℑPGM, and the Canterbury books OX. These last have, however, an Irish element in them, and consequently stand half-way between the B-Z group and the thoroughly Irish MSS., DELQR. Another distinct local family is found in CT, the two Spanish MSS. ; while the influence of both the Anglo-Irish and the Spanish families is to be seen in the two special editions of Alcuin (KV, with affinities in M) and Theodulf (Θ and the second hand of H). Finally W stands apart from all (though nearer to the group of Z than to that of A), as the representative of a later stage in the history of the Latin Bible.

The original text of the Vulgate being thus more perfectly restored than ever before, it becomes possible to estimate Jerome's work more adequately. An examination of the corrections introduced by him into the Old Latin version [1] shows that while he must sometimes have used Greek MSS. unlike any which we now possess, his Greek authorities on the whole were of the type represented by our אBL and their associates; א standing out above all as the most constant supporter of his readings. In spite of this, it must be remembered that the Vulgate cannot as a whole be reckoned as a witness on this side. Jerome's revision of the New Testament was very partial, and the basis of his text remains Old Latin, which belongs to a somewhat different type and family. Still less is it possible to use the current Clementine Vulgate as a witness of this early class; for that is a Vulgate corrupted by much use, and by long centuries of alternate neglect and revision, which have approximated it to the late Greek MSS. from which our Textus Receptus is derived. It is the great service of Bishop Wordsworth and Mr. White to have given us back the Vulgate, so far as the Gospels are concerned, much as it left the hands of Jerome, and to have enabled us to estimate alike the materials with which he worked, and the deterioration which his work underwent in the course of the Middle Ages.

9. **The Gothic Version.**—One more version remains to be briefly noticed, namely, that which was made in the fourth century for the Goths who were then settled in Moesia. Its author was Ulfilas, a Cappadocian by descent, who became bishop of the Goths in 348, and died about 380. The Gothic language being wholly unliterary up to that time, he had to devise an alphabet for its expression. The translation was made from the Greek, both in the New Testament and in the Old; and the Greek is followed with great fidelity. The type of text represented in it is for the most part that which is found in the

---

[1] Wordsworth and White, pp. 655-672.

majority of Greek MSS. (the *a*-family), but it also contains readings of the β and δ-types. It has perhaps also been modified by the influence of the Latin versions, as was not unlikely to happen when the Goths occupied Italy. For textual purposes, therefore, its evidence must be used with care.

The version only exists in fragments. The most important MS. of it is a beautiful volume preserved in the University Library at Upsala, known as the **Codex Argenteus.** It contains rather more than half the Gospels (in the Western order, Matthew, John, Luke, Mark), written in silver letters upon purple vellum. The writing is uncial, of the fifth or sixth century. It is supposed to have been written in Northern Italy, and in the sixteenth century it was in Germany. In 1648 it was secured by the Swedes at the capture of Prague, and after having been presented to Isaac Voss, was bought back in 1662. It was edited in 1665 by Patrick Young, and in 1854 by A. Uppström.

In addition to this beautiful manuscript, the Gothic version is also represented by a small fragment from the Epistle to the Romans (sixth century) in the palimpsest MS. at Wolfenbüttel, which also contains the Greek MSS. P and Q; and in five palimpsest fragments (from two MSS. of the sixth century) at Milan, containing considerable portions of the Pauline Epistles, and a few verses of the Gospels. All these fragments appear to have come originally from Bobbio. The Wolfenbüttel fragment was published by F. A. Knittel in 1762, those at Milan by Mai (the discoverer) and Castiglione in 1819-39. Some quotations from the Gospels, occurring in a commentary, were published from a Vatican MS. by J. F. Massmann in 1834, and a few leaves of the Pauline Epistles from a Turin MS. by the same editor in 1868. The best edition of the version as a whole is said to be that of Gabelentz and Loebe (1836-43); the latest is by G. H. Balg, published in America in 1891.

CHAPTER VI

PATRISTIC QUOTATIONS

[**Authorities**: Gregory, *op. cit.*; Harnack, *Geschichte der altchristlichen Litteratur bis Eusebius* (Part i. 1893, Part ii. vol. i. 1897); Smith and Wace, *Dictionary of Christian Biography.*]

TWO of the three classes into which the authorities for the sacred text may be divided have now been passed in review. The third remains, namely, the quotations from it which are found in the works of early ecclesiastical writers. That these may provide useful evidence is obvious. If we know how Clement of Alexandria, or Origen, or Athanasius, or Jerome, quoted certain passages of the Scriptures in their writings, we know (subject to limitations which will be mentioned below) how those passages stood in manuscripts of the second, third, or fourth century—that is, in manuscripts as early as, or earlier than, the most ancient which we now possess. The limits and value of this class of evidence must consequently be investigated. In doing so, the term " patristic quotations," which is commonly used to describe it, must be given the widest possible interpretation. It is not only the writings of those who are specially regarded as the Fathers of the Church that are useful for this purpose. The writings of any author who quotes the Scriptures at all must be taken into consideration. So far as we possess them, the quotations of heretics or of non-Christians are evidence, as truly as those of orthodox Christians. All we have to ask is, Do the quotations which we find in any given author enable us to know how these passages stood in the manuscripts of the Bible current in his day?

The question is not so easy to answer as it perhaps appears. Before we can accept the Scriptural quotations which stand in our texts of the early ecclesiastical writers as faithfully representing the manuscripts which these writers used, there are several deductions to be made. In the first place, the true text of the writer in question has to be ascertained, just as the text of the Bible or of the classical authors has to be ascertained, by the comparison of authorities. The texts of the Fathers, as they have generally been read until recently in the editions of the Benedictines or Migne's *Patrologia*, were based (like the received text of the New Testament itself) upon comparatively few and late manuscripts. It has been the work of modern scholars to lay the foundation for this department of textual criticism by 'producing editions of the principal ecclesiastical writers, accompanied by a sufficient *apparatus criticus*. The work is by no means complete yet, but much has been done. The Imperial Academy of Vienna has made considerable progress with a *Corpus* of Latin ecclesiastical writers; and the Academy of Berlin has embarked on a similar undertaking with respect to the Greek Fathers. When these two great enterprises are completed, it will be possible to handle the raw material of patristic quotations with far more confidence than hitherto.[1]

Secondly, even when the earliest manuscripts of an author have been consulted, we cannot always be sure that we have his Scriptural quotations in their original form. In no part of his text is corruption so likely to creep in as here. A scribe who recognised a quotation

---

[1] A gigantic work was undertaken by the late Dean Burgon, with a view to making the evidence of patristic quotations more accessible; namely, an index of all Biblical quotations in the principal ecclesiastical writers, which is now preserved in manuscript in the British Museum in sixteen huge volumes (Add. MSS. 33421–33436). The references are to comparatively uncritical texts of the Fathers (generally those in Migne), but they could of course be used also in connexion with later editions, where such exist. Considerable use is made of this work in Miller's edition of the Gospels, now in course of issue (see below, p. 262).

from its first words would be only too likely to write it down from memory, without looking too closely at the MS. before him, and so would give it in the form in which it was current in his own day, instead of in that which his author actually used. Or, supposing he noticed that the form of the quotation was unfamiliar, he might very probably alter it into what he believed to be the true form. In either case, it will be seen, this class of corruption consists in the substitution of the familiar Textus Receptus in the place of an earlier type of text; therefore, without any prejudice against the received text, it must be recognised that, where two alternatives are open, the one which diverges from the received text is more likely to be the one originally used by the Father in question. Voluntarily or involuntarily, the scribe is more likely to alter from an unfamiliar form to a familiar form than *vice versa*. The only cases in which we can ascertain without doubt the form in which an ecclesiastical writer made a quotation are when the context points decisively to one reading or another; when this is not the case, we are reduced to a balance of probabilities.

But, thirdly, even when we can ascertain, beyond reasonable doubt, the form in which a quotation was made, we may still doubt whether this form was actually derived from a manuscript lying before the author. Authors at all times and in all countries have been apt to quote from memory, and memory plays strange tricks. Dr. Salmon produces a remarkable instance of this in no less a person than Jeremy Taylor, who quotes the text " Except a man be born again he cannot see the kingdom of God " nine times, yet only twice in the same form, and never once correctly. How often, too, does one see the misquotations " Whatsoever thy hand findeth to do, do it with *all* thy might," or " to give a reason for the *faith* that is in you "? And if this is the case nowadays, when books are plentiful and verification of references easy, how must it have been in the earliest centuries of our era, when a copy of the Bible would not always be at a writer's elbow, and when (in the absence of divisions into chapters and verses, and even of separation of words) it can have been by no means easy to turn up a given passage quickly? Quotations (especially short ones) must often have been made from memory, and sometimes without any intention of giving more than the general sense. An especial source of error was present in the case of quotations from the Synoptic Gospels. An author might very easily amalgamate parallel passages in two or more Gospels, and so produce his quotation in a form which correctly represented none of them. Therefore, just as the second class of considerations tells against indiscriminate acceptance of quotations which agree with the Textus Receptus, so this third class tells against quotations which differ from it.

Under these circumstances, it may fairly be asked whether it is worth while paying any attention to patristic quotations at all. And the answer would be that their testimony is strictly limited in scope, but that within these limits it is not only real but of very great importance. Where a patristic quotation stands alone as evidence for a particular reading, its testimony must be regarded with the gravest suspicion, unless the context renders it quite explicit; but where there is other evidence for the reading, the quotation is of great value in fixing the time and the place at which this reading was current. Thus five cursive MSS., from the tenth to the fourteenth century, have the remarkable reading Ἰησοῦν τὸν Βαραββᾶν in Mt. xxvii. 16; but we could know nothing about the age or locality of this reading were it not mentioned by Origen, which proves that it existed in MSS. accessible in either Egypt or Palestine in the first half of the third century. As will be seen later, the localisation of certain types of text in different periods and districts is a matter of the greatest importance when we come to try to reconstruct the history of the Biblical text, and to see which type of text has the strongest claims on our acceptance; and here the evidence of patristic quotations is indispensable. It will be found that the ascertainment of their precise nature is quite worth the trouble which it involves ; and a short indication of the principal sources of this evidence will not be out of place here.

Quotations from the New Testament are found in the earliest writers of the sub-apostolic age, but they are so scanty as to be of little service for our present purpose. Their importance lies in another direction, namely, as evidence of the existence of the New Testament books at a period earlier than that which some critics have sought to assign to them. The **Epistle of Clement to the Corinthians** (written about A.D. 93-95 [1]) contains two passages which appear to be quotations from memory of Luke vi. 36-38 and of Luke xvii. 1, 2, combined with Matthew xxvi. 24 ; but they are too inexact to be used for textual purposes. The so-called **Second Epistle of Clement** (a homily written about the middle of the second century) contains several quotations from Matthew and Luke, as well as passages which must have come from a lost Gospel ; and though these are useful as far as they go, the amount of evidence which they contribute is not large. The **Epistle of Barnabas** (written early in the second century) contains what is apparently a direct citation of Matthew xxii. 14, and several reminiscences of New Testament language ; but again precision in quotation is wanting. The **Shepherd of Hermas** (about A.D. 140, but embodying writings of rather earlier date) contributes nothing to our purpose. The **Epistles of Ignatius** (about A.D. 110-117) contribute only a few quotations from the Pauline Epistles, the references to the Gospels being in no case verbally exact ; and much the same may be said of the **Epistle of Polycarp** (same date). The **Teaching of the Twelve Apostles** offers more plentiful material, including a considerable extract from the Sermon on the Mount, but its evidence is discounted

---

[1] The dates assigned in this chapter (so far as the first two centuries after Christ are concerned) are generally those given by Harnack (*Geschichte der altchristlichen Litteratur bis Eusebius*, Part ii. vol. i. 1897).

by the doubt attaching to its date; for while the prevalent view assigns it to the beginning of the second century, some critics have put it as early as A.D. 70, and its latest editor (Dr. Bigg) carries it down to the fourth century.

A fuller stream of tradition is reached with **Justin Martyr,** in the middle of the second century, from whose writings a very complete outline of the Gospel narrative can be put together; but it is rather with the facts than the words of the Gospels that he is concerned, so that the total amount of properly textual material to be derived from him is not great. It is, however, enough to enable us to come to some conclusions as to the type of text used by him, and it is noteworthy that the readings given by Justin agree predominantly with those which are characteristic of the Old Syriac and Old Latin versions; that is, they belong to the δ-type of text. This is a fact which will be useful presently. Probably somewhat later than Justin are the **Clementine Homilies,** an Ebionite (or Jewish-Christian) work which falsely claimed the authorship of Clement of Rome; but they do not provide so much material, and for textual purposes fall into the same category as Ignatius or Barnabas. More important are the writings of Justin's pupil **Tatian,** not so much, however, his Apology for Christianity as his Diatessaron, which has been described and discussed in the preceding chapter. Akin to Tatian, as providing a continuous Gospel text rather than isolated quotations, is the work of the heretic **Marcion,** who produced an edition of St. Luke's Gospel and the Pauline Epistles (about the middle of the second century) in accordance with his own peculiar doctrines. Marcion's writings, as separate literary entities, are lost; but much of them can be restored from the references and quotations in the works of the orthodox controversialists who opposed him, notably Tertullian and Epiphanius. The contents of Marcion's Gospel are in this way known with practical certainty, and in many cases the actual text adopted by him. This as a rule resembles that of Tatian and Justin in belonging to the same group as the Old Syriac and Old Latin versions ; but as Marcion's original home was in Pontus, while his principal work was done in Rome, it is difficult to say from what locality he derived his Gospel text. Justin's evidence is equally hard to locate, since by birth he was a Samaritan, but after his conversion resided first in Ephesus, whence he proceeded to Rome, where he ultimately suffered martyrdom. Tatian's activity, as we have seen, lay in Syriac-speaking regions, and his Diatessaron is believed to have been composed in that language.

So far, then, the results arrived at may be thus summarised. Up to A.D. 150 the quotations in extant ecclesiastical writers, though important in their bearing on the questions of the date and acceptation of the New Testament Scriptures, are of little value for purely textual purposes. From 150 to 175 textual evidence of value is forthcoming, but either in a somewhat fragmentary condition, or (in the case of Tatian and Marcion) in a form which can hardly be described as quotation. At the same time the evidence, so far as it goes, tends to show that the δ-type of text was prevalent in this early period. With the last quarter of the second century the position changes ; and henceforth we have a succession of ecclesiastical writers whose works are preserved with substantial completeness, and who quote the New Testament Scriptures, not tacitly or in paraphrase, but fully and explicitly. It is from this point that the evidence of patristic quotations in the full sense may be said to begin ; and the father of it is Irenaeus. It is impossible within the limits of this chapter to examine the evidence, even of the more important Fathers, at any length ; but a brief indication of their date and country, with references to the more important modern works dealing with this aspect of their writings, will serve to show the general bearing of their testimony.

Irenaeus was probably born about A.D. 135 - 140 (according to some, as early as 115), and the home of his youth was in Asia Minor, where as a boy he saw and heard Polycarp. From Asia he is believed to have gone to Rome, and thence (probably after only a brief stay) to Lyons, to join the Church already founded there by missionaries from Asia Minor. After the great persecution in Gaul in 177 he was commissioned to carry the letters of the Church of Lyons to Rome, and shortly afterwards he was made Bishop of Lyons in succession to his martyred countryman, Pothinus. This office he held until his death about 202. Irenaeus' early training consequently belongs to the East, his literary activity to the West; and these facts are of importance in estimating his testimony on textual subjects. His principal work, the Ἔλεγχος καὶ ἀνατροπὴ τῆς ψευδωνύμου γνώσεως, was written between 181 and 189; only fragments of it exist in the original Greek, but the whole is preserved in a Latin translation, which is believed to be nearly contemporary with Irenaeus himself.[1] It abounds with citations from the New Testament; a full examination of them has been taken in hand by Professor Sanday, with the assistance of Mr. C. H. Turner, but this long-announced book has not yet appeared. Until the results of such an examination are published, it must be sufficient to say that Irenaeus (as might be expected from his personal history) is to be reckoned among the authorities that fall into the same group as the Old Syriac and Old Latin versions.

A different quarter of the Roman Empire is represented by **Clement of Alexandria,** a contemporary of Irenaeus, though somewhat junior to him. The dates of his birth and death are unknown, but the former probably occurred between 150 and 160, the latter between 212 and 220. Of Greek nationality (his Roman name, Titus Flavius Clemens, indicates that he was a freedman of a Roman family), and born either in Athens or in Alexandria, he studied philosophy in Greece, Italy, and the East, and

---

[1] Hort placed it as late as the fourth century, but his view has not been generally adopted. The issue depends mainly on the question whether the Latin version of Irenaeus was or was not used by Tertullian in his treatise *adv. Valentinianos.*

ultimately was led from Stoicism into Christianity. He
became a presbyter in the Alexandrian Church, and
about 190 succeeded his last and best teacher, Pantaenus,
as head of the Catechetical School in that city, but was
compelled to retire thence by the persecution in 202-203.
Of the remainder of his life little is known. Of his
works a considerable portion has been preserved, notably
his Στρωματεῖς, or Miscellanies, in eight books, written in
the last years of the second century. He had a wide
acquaintance with Greek literature, and quotes from innumerable authors, pagan, Jewish, and Christian ; hence
he must have had the use of a large library, and must
have been accustomed to look up quotations in it. For
the New Testament, his quotations must be taken as
representing a class of text which was at any rate current,
and perhaps predominant, in the great literary capital of
Egypt at the end of the second century. An examination
of them in the Gospels has quite recently been made by
Mr. P. M. Barnard of Christ's College, Cambridge, which
shows that the text used by Clement was of the δ-type,
akin to the Old Latin and Old Syriac.[1] This is an
important piece of evidence for the early history of the
New Testament text, which will have to be referred to
again in a subsequent chapter.

Important as Clement- is, he is followed in his own
country by a scholar and divine of far greater importance.
In textual scholarship, indeed, **Origen** has no rival among
ancient writers, and no single individual has exercised so
wide an influence upon the Biblical text as he. It is
with regard to the Greek text of the Old Testament that
the precise character of his work is most fully known ;
but there can be little doubt that his critical labours on
the New Testament were almost equally epoch-making.
Born about 185, he was educated from the first as a
Christian, and trained by his father in the study of the
Scriptures. His father perished in the persecution of
202-203, which also created a vacancy in the headship of

---

[1] *Texts and Studies*, v. 5 (Cambridge, 1899). See below, p. 290.

the Catechetical School, through the retirement of Clement; and to this Origen, though barely eighteen, was appointed. Here he laboured, learning and teaching, for many years. About 213 he visited Rome; about 215 he was compelled to leave Egypt, and lived for four years at Caesarea in Palestine. He returned to Alexandria in 219; but the following years were full of difficulties with his ecclesiastical superiors, and in 231 he left Alexandria finally. For the remainder of his life, which lasted till 253, his home was at Caesarea; and here the greater part of his literary work was done. With his philosophical and exegetical writings we are not here concerned. His textual labours on the Old Testament were embodied in the Hexapla, a colossal undertaking which coloured the whole subsequent history of the Septuagint. For the New Testament we know of no such formal edition of the whole text; but he wrote commentaries on most, if not all, of the books of which it is composed, and numerous passages in his writings show that he had examined and compared manuscripts, and considered the weight of the evidence for various readings. He is, indeed, the first textual critic of the New Testament, and when we consider the age of the manuscripts he must have used, the value of his evidence is obvious. In many cases he mentions various readings, and states which is found "in most MSS." or "in the oldest MSS." or "in the best MSS." No doubt we are not always bound to accept his opinion as to what were the best MSS., but at least we learn what readings were extant in Egypt and Palestine in his lifetime, and what readings were preferred by a trained scholar and textual student of unusual ability. The character of the New Testament text used by him differs in different works. In some it is of the δ-type, but as a rule his preference is for the β-type, of which he is the most eminent ally among the Greek Fathers. Whether his connexion with the β-type of text goes even further than this, so that he may be regarded as largely responsible for its preservation, or even for its existence in its present form, is a point which will have to be considered more at length in the final chapter.   It should be added that Origen's services to criticism did not end with his life ; for copies of his writings formed the nucleus of the library collected by Pamphilus at Caesarea, which was thenceforth a recognised centre of textual research.[1]   Many of Origen's works are now lost ; but some are still extant in the original Greek, and many more in Latin translations (largely the work of Rufinus).   Critical texts of nearly all the Greek remains have been produced in modern times, as of the Hexapla by Field, the Philocalia (a volume of selections from Origen, prepared by Basil and Gregory Nazianzen) by Armitage Robinson, and the remains of the Commentary on St. John by A. E. Brooke ; while all, except the Commentary on St. Matthew, have already made their appearance in the Berlin *Corpus* of Greek ecclesiastical writers.

We have a little departed from strict chronological order, in taking Origen in connexion with his fellow-Egyptian Clement, and must return to consider the great African writer whose life overlaps those of both of them, **Tertullian**.   Born about 150, and trained probably as an advocate, he became after his conversion the great controversialist of the early Latin Church.   He was probably a presbyter, in spite of the fact that he was undoubtedly married.   About 203 he seceded from the orthodox church, joining the ascetic and enthusiastic sect of the Montanists.   He died at some uncertain date after 220.   His writings are vehement, rhetorical, unrestrained in style and language ; and though several

---

[1] See above, pp. 52, 87, for records of MSS. copied from, or collated with, MSS. in the library of Caesarea   The description which Jerome gives of the founding of the library of Pamphilus is as follows (*Ep.* cxli. [xxxiv. in Migne], written A.D. 384) : "Beatus Pamphilus martyr, cuius vitam Eusebius Caesariensis episcopus tribus ferme voluminibus explicavit, cum Demetrium Phalereum et Pisistratum in sacrae Bibliothecae studio vellet aequare, imaginesque ingeniorum, quae vera sunt et aeterna monumenta, toto orbe perquireret, tunc vel maxime Origenis libros impensius prosecutus, Caesariensi ecclesiae dedicavit ; quam ex parte corruptam Acacius [successor of Eusebius in the see of Caesarea about 340] dehinc et Euzoius, eiusdem ecclesiae sacerdotes, in membranis instaurare conati sunt."

are lost, many still remain. He quotes freely from the Scriptures; but for textual purposes his evidence is impaired by the doubt whether he is (1) quoting from memory, (2) translating direct from the Greek for himself, or (3) using an early Latin version of the New Testament. Not being a scholar, such as Clement and Origen were, he has not the scholar's accuracy; and his evidence must consequently be used with caution. An examination of it has been made by H. Rönsch (*Das Neue Testament Tertullians*, 1871), while the new edition of his works by Reifferscheid and Wissowa in the Vienna *Corpus Scriptorum Ecclesiasticorum Latinorum* sets out the available textual material for the future use of students.

For the outlying portions of the Roman Empire— for Asia Minor, Egypt, North Africa, and Southern Gaul — we have, as has now been shown, excellent witnesses for the period 175-250; but for Rome itself we are very scantily supplied with material. The principal author whose works remain to us is **Hippolytus,** a writer almost as prolific as Origen, and unquestionably the most prominent theologian in the Roman Church during this period. The details of his life are obscure. So much is known, that he flourished about 220, that he was a presbyter of the Church of Rome, and that he appears to claim for himself the position of a bishop; according to some he was bishop of Portus, according to others a schismatic bishop of Rome, in opposition to Pope Callistus; while others have doubted whether he is correctly described as bishop at all.[1] In any case, he was the last and greatest Greek-writing divine of the Roman Church; and his writings included commentaries upon many books of the Old Testament, and on St. Matthew and the Gospel and Apocalypse of St. John in the New. By far the greater part of his voluminous works has perished. Perhaps the most interesting of all (his *Refutation of all the Heresies*) has been in large measure recovered from a late MS.,

[1] See Dr. Salmon's article in *Dict. of Christian Biography.*

brought to Paris from Mt. Athos in 1842, but not published or identified till 1851; but his commentaries exist only in fragments. All that remains is in course of publication in the Berlin *Corpus*. His quotations from the New Testament, which are fairly numerous, have not been specially investigated; but they are often too inexact to be useful for textual purposes.

The only important writer of the third century who remains to be discussed is **Cyprian**, the great bishop of Carthage, who must be coupled with Tertullian as the main source of our knowledge of the early African Church. Born about 200 in a pagan family, and trained in law and rhetoric, he was converted to Christianity about 245, and was almost immediately elected, much against his will, Bishop of Carthage. This position he held from about 248 until his martyrdom in 258, during Valerian's persecution. Cyprian's importance lies more in his greatness as a bishop and an administrator than in his literary ability, and his writings deal with matters of Church discipline and morals rather than with textual or exegetical questions; but his quotations from Scripture are plentiful, and since he had more of the scholar's instincts than Tertullian, he is the most important patristic witness to the text of the Latin Bible in use in Northern Africa during the third century. For the conclusions to which a study of his Biblical quotations leads, see above, p. 181. His writings have lately been edited by Hartel in the Vienna *Corpus* (1868-71); but in the work of most importance for textual purposes (the *Testimonia*, a classified selection of Biblical passages) Hartel unfortunately followed the least trustworthy of the extant MSS.[1]

Of the other ecclesiastical writers of the third century, brief mention need only be made of a few. **Gregory Thaumaturgus**, Bishop of Neocaesarea in Cappadocia

---

[1] See Sanday in *Old Latin Biblical Texts*, ii. p. xliii. A new edition of the *Testimonia*, and also of the *Ad Fortunatum*, is contemplated by Professor Sanday and Mr. C. H. Turner.

from about 240 to his death in 265, wrote a panegyric on Origen, a paraphrase of Ecclesiastes, and some dogmatic treatises. Contemporary with him is **Dionysius Alexandrinus**, a pupil of Origen, and like him head of the Catechetical School in Alexandria (from 233), and subsequently bishop of that see (247-265). Unfortunately of all his many writings only fragments and a few letters now remain ; for most of these we are indebted to Eusebius. **Methodius**, Bishop of Olympus in Lycia or of Patara (or of both in succession) towards the end of the third century, martyred under Diocletian in 311, wrote many treatises (including polemical criticisms of Origen's theology), some of which survive in a Slavonic version ; in Greek nothing remains but a single dialogue and some fragments. Finally, **Pamphilus** of Caesarea (ob. 309) deserves mention less on account of his literary labours (a defence of Origen, and an edition of the Septuagint extracted from Origen's Hexapla, which he prepared with the assistance of Eusebius) than for the theological library which he established in Caesarea, and which, as we have already seen, played an important part in the textual history of the New (as well as of the Old) Testament.

Passing to the fourth century, the sphere of patristic quotations widens. As the Church became recognised by the State, the number of ecclesiastical writers naturally increased, and their works were less exposed to destruction. Only the more prominent among them can be mentioned here. Few of them have been critically edited in modern times ; but as the Bible text in current use approximates more to the Textus Receptus, it is less liable to corruption. **Eusebius** of Caesarea, the great historian of the early Church, carries on the sequence with those whom we have named above, since he was the friend and colleague of Pamphilus. His life extends from about 270 to about 340, and for the last twenty-seven years he was Bishop of Caesarea. With Pamphilus he prepared for separate publication Origen's text of the

Septuagint; and in the library of Pamphilus he found most of the material for his works. These (so far as they are still extant) fill six volumes in Migne's *Patrologia*, the most important being the *Chronicle* (though this contains nothing to our present purpose), the *Historia Ecclesiastica*, *Praeparatio Evangelica*, and *Demonstratio Evangelica*. Some commentaries on certain books of the New Testament are lost. The fact that Eusebius certainly had a great library at hand, and was accustomed to the use of it, adds much weight to his evidence on textual matters. He had, moreover, a direct influence on the dissemination of the Scriptures in the Roman Empire, since it was to him that Constantine, after his conversion, applied to furnish fifty copies of the Bible for use in the churches of his new capital. See above, p. 41.

Nearly contemporary with Eusebius, and a member of the neighbouring Syriac Church, was **Aphraates**, bishop in the monastery of Mar Matthaeus near ancient Nineveh about the year 340. Twenty-two homilies by him are extant in Syriac, most of them also in an Armenian version, in which their author's name appears in the form of "Jacob of Nisibis." The importance of Aphraates' evidence with regard to the Biblical text current in the Church of Syria has been indicated above, in connexion with the Syriac versions (p. 140). Mention has also been made there of **Ephraem**, a later contemporary of Aphraates, who died in 378. His sermons and theological treatises contain many quotations from the Scriptures; but of more importance are his commentaries on various books of the New Testament, and (as has been shown above, p. 127) on Tatian's Diatessaron. The most recent examinations of his quotations go to show that the text used by him was some form of the Old Syriac.

The Churches of Asia Minor during the fourth century produced several notable writers, among whom may be named **Basil** (329-379), Bishop of Caesarea in Cappadocia, author of sermons, epistles, and ecclesiastical treatises ; his brother, **Gregory of Nyssa**, who wrote commentaries and apologetic works, besides other theological treatises ; and his namesake and contemporary, **Gregory of Nazianzus,** the great preacher, for a short time bishop of Constantinople. In Palestine and Syria, besides Eusebius, we have **Euthalius**, whose work has been described above (p. 67), **Cyril of Jerusalem**, bishop of that see from 351 to 386, and especially **Chrysostom**. Born at Antioch about 347, it was in Antioch that he lived and laboured until 398, when he was removed to become Patriarch of Constantinople, and to enter on that career of struggles with principalities and powers which only ended with his death in exile in 407. His voluminous works (filling thirteen volumes in Migne's *Patrologia*) furnish ample evidence of the New Testament text which he used ; especially his commentaries, from which the complete text of the book commented on could in some cases be restored. He marks a distinct epoch in the history of the New Testament text, since we find in him the *a*-type of text already firmly established. Mention should also be made of another Antiochene writer, **Theodore of Mopsuestia**, a presbyter in the Church of Antioch contemporary with Chrysostom, and like him removed (about 392) to a see in a different country, in this case Mopsuestia in Cilicia. He wrote commentaries on the Pauline Epistles, which survive in fragments and in a Latin version ; but he is of far greater importance from a doctrinal than from a textual point of view.

Egypt contributes during the fourth century no such important authors (for the purpose of textual criticism) as Clement and Origen ; but in **Athanasius**, Bishop of Alexandria from 328 to 373, it has a theologian of the first rank, many of whose works survive. Slightly later than him is **Macarius Magnus**, an Egyptian presbyter, and author of theological treatises and homilies. Finally, to conclude the evidence of the Eastern Churches, mention must be made of **Epiphanius**, Bishop of Salamis in

Cyprus from about 368 to 402. His great work is his treatises against heresies. Previous to his appointment to the see of Salamis, his home was in Palestine, so that his evidence with regard to the Scriptural text is probably to be credited to that locality.

In the Latin Churches during the same period, the earliest name that need be mentioned is that of **Lactantius** (about 260 to 326), an African by birth, but resident in Gaul during the latter part of his life. His Biblical quotations have been examined by Rönsch,[1] but as all but three of them are from the Old Testament, they do not concern us here.

Gaul is also represented by **Hilary**, Bishop of Poitiers from 354 to 368, and author (among other works) of a commentary on St. Matthew. His quotations must be taken as evidence of the Old Latin text current in Gaul about the middle of the fourth century. **Lucifer** (ob. 371), bishop of Cagliari in Sardinia, is a writer of some textual importance, whose works have been recently (1886) edited from the only extant MS. by Hartel in the Vienna *Corpus*. As has been stated in the preceding chapter, his quotations represent the European type of the Old Latin version. **Ambrose**, the great bishop of Milan from 374 to 397, wrote many theological treatises, which likewise witness to the pre-Vulgate text of the Scriptures. The two greatest representatives of the Latin Churches in this century and the beginning of the next are, however, Jerome and Augustine. The life of **Jerome** (circ. 345-420) has been sketched above (p. 185) in connexion with his great work, the production of the Latin Vulgate. Like Origen, he was a textual scholar by profession ; and his travels and his acquaintance with Greek manuscripts give his evidence special weight as that of a trained student of textual criticism, while they deprive him of the character of representative of any local type of text. His great contemporary **Augustine** (354-430), on the other hand, was a theologian rather than a scholar ;

---

[1] *Zeitschrift für die historische Theologie*, 1871, pp. 531 ff.

but his very numerous works provide plentiful evidence for textual purposes. The first twenty-nine years of his life were passed in Africa, where he received the ordinary training of the best schools, and entered on the profession of teacher of rhetoric. In 383 he visited Rome, and shortly afterwards was appointed professor of rhetoric at Milan. Here he came under the influence of Ambrose, and here it was, in 386, that the long period of moral and intellectual disturbance through which he had been passing culminated in his conversion to Christianity. Having been baptized by Ambrose at Easter 387, he returned to Africa, where the rest of his life was spent. At Hippo in Numidia he was ordained priest in 390, and in 395 was consecrated bishop of the see, which he held until the close of his life. His writings, controversial, dogmatic, and devotional, are too many to enumerate, the *Confessions* and the *City of God* being the most famous. The Biblical quotations which occur plentifully throughout his works still need scientific examination. In his earlier books he must necessarily have used the Old Latin Bible, and it has been usual to suppose that he continued to do so even after the publication of the Vulgate. This belief is strengthened by the fact that he expressed strong disapproval of Jerome's revised text ; but this disapproval was confined to the thorough-going revision of the Old Testament, and does not apply to the more conservative treatment of the New, with which, on the contrary, he expressly said that he had no fault to find. Hence there is nothing *a priori* improbable in the opinion lately maintained by Mr. Burkitt,[1] that while Augustine habitually used the Old Latin to the end of his life in short phrases which he would naturally quote from memory, in longer citations, at any rate from the Gospels, he used (after about 400) the revised version of Jerome. Mr. Burkitt has made this clear in the case of two treatises (the

---

[1] *The Old Latin and the Itala* (*Texts and Studies*, iv. 3), pp. 57-59 ; and see p. 182, above.

Contra Felicem and the *De Consensu Evangelistarum*—the latter a work of especial value for textual purposes), and it is probable that a full examination of his later works would show the same result.

An African contemporary of Augustine of some importance is **Tyconius**, whose period of activity belongs to the latter part of the fourth century. He was a member of the sect of the Donatists, whose stern views on the treatment of those who had given up the sacred books or vessels under persecution led them to hold aloof from the rest of the Church. Refusing all association with those who held the more lenient views adopted by the heads of the Church, they adhered to the Old Latin version of the Bible long after the Vulgate had been generally accepted elsewhere. Tyconius was the author of a commentary on the Apocalypse, which is known to us only in fragments ; and of a Book of Rules (i.e. rules of interpretation of the Old Testament prophets), which has survived and has recently been edited with a most interesting introduction by Mr. Burkitt.[1] Mr. Burkitt's conclusion is that the text used by Tyconius was substantially the same as that of Cyprian, slightly altered in Latinity, but not revised from the Greek.

Finally, mention must be made of **Priscillian**, a wealthy Spanish layman who adopted a species of Gnostic-Manichean heresy, which he propagated with great ardour from about 380 till his execution by Maximus in 385. Until recently his writings were supposed to be lost ; but in 1885 a manuscript (probably of the sixth century) was discovered by G. Schepss at Würzburg, containing eleven treatises from his pen.[2] He was also the author of a system of canons of the Pauline Epistles, somewhat similar to those of Eusebius for the Gospels, the text of the Epistles being divided into numbered sections, and the numbers classified under ninety heads in accordance with their subjects. This

[1] *Texts and Studies*, iv. 1 (Cambridge, 1895).
[2] Edited by their discoverer in the Vienna *Corpus*, vol. xviii. (1889).

system is found in some of the Spanish MSS. of the Vulgate.[1]

Beyond the end of the fourth century it is not necessary to pursue the subject. By this time a substantially uniform type of text had been adopted throughout the Christian world, and the vast majority of later patristic quotations are of the same type as our Textus Receptus. Here and there exceptions may be found, just as they are found in the case of manuscripts, where a divergent text has survived into a later age. Of these it must be sufficient to name **Primasius**, bishop of Hadrumetum in Africa in the middle of the sixth century, whose commentary on the Apocalypse contains an almost complete text of that book in an Old Latin version of the African type (see above, p. 179). But cases such as these are rare, and as a general rule uniformity, tempered only by the errors oi scribes and the occasional efforts of editors, settles down upon the Greek and Latin texts of the New Testament alike, to be stereotyped ultimately by the invention of printing in the form of our Textus Receptus.

[1] The total number of sections in the several Epistles is as follows:—
Romans 125, 1 Cor. 105, 2 Cor. 61, Gal. 38, Eph. 41, Phil. 25, Col. 34, 1 Thess. 22, 2 Thess. 10, 1 Tim. 31, 2 Tim. 26, Tit. 15, Philem. 5, Hebrews 28.

NOTE TO CHAPTER VI

The following are the numbers of quotations from the N. T. given in Burgon's index, in the case of a few of the earlier and more important writers.

	Gospels.	Acts.	Cath. Epp.	Paul. Epp.	Apoc.	Total.
Justin Martyr .	268	10	6	43	3	330 (besides 266 doubtful)
Irenaeus . . .	1038	194	23	499	65	1819
Clement Alex. .	1017	44	207	1127	11	2406
Origen . . .	9231	349	399	7778	165	17922
Tertullian . .	3822	502	120	2609	205	7258
Hippolytus . .	734	42	27	387	188	1378
Eusebius . . .	3258	211	88	1592	27	5176

CHAPTER VII

TEXTUAL CRITICISM IN THE PAST

Authorities.—Gregory, *op. cit.*; Scrivener-Miller, *op. cit.*; S. P. Tregelles, *An Account of the Printed Text of the Greek New Testament* (1854); Reuss, *Bibliotheca Novi Testamenti Graeci* (1872); Schaff, *Companion to the Greek Testament* (1883); British Museum *Catalogue of Printed Books*, s.v. Bible; Westcott and Hort, *op. cit.*; B. Weiss in *Texte und Untersuchungen*, vols. vii. viii. ix. xiv., and N.F. iv. (1892-99).]

THE preceding chapters have described the material which lies to the hand of the critic who would restore the true text of the New Testament—the manuscripts, the versions, and the patristic quotations. It remains to consider how these materials should be used. And the nature of this problem will be clearer, if some account be given of the work which scholars have already done in this field of criticism. In the present chapter, therefore, it is proposed to sketch the history of textual criticism in the past, and thereby to show the questions and the difficulties which now confront scholars at the beginning of this twentieth century, the fuller consideration of which will form the subject of the next and concluding chapter.

Textual criticism is not an invention of modern times, but is far older than the books of the New Testament. The scholars of Alexandria in the third century before Christ busied themselves with the text of the ancient Greek poets and prose writers, and established a tradition which made Alexandria the home of scholarship for many a century after their day—in fact until the conquest of Egypt by the Mohammedan Arabs. Therefore it is not strange that Alexandria should also be the home of the textual criticism of the Greek Bible. Its father was Origen, whose work has been briefly described in the preceding chapter. Nor was his work barren. His own great Hexapla, with the separate edition of the Septuagint text prepared by his followers, Pamphilus and Eusebius, testifies to the results of his labours on the Old Testament; while yet another Greek native of Egypt, Hesychius, produced another edition of the Septuagint. For the New Testament we can point to no such definite embodiment of Origen's textual researches; but it is becoming continually more evident that both Alexandria and the school of Caesarea exercised considerable influence on the textual history of the New Testament, and it is difficult not to recognise here the results of Origen's teaching and traditions. It was to Caesarea, too, that the great textual scholar of the West came to study and to gather materials, and so the torch was handed on from Alexandria to Rome, and from Rome, in the form of the Vulgate, its effects spread over all the Western Church.

It would not be profitable to dwell here on the textual criticism of the Middle Ages; and indeed the principal points in it have been mentioned already. We have described the attempts of Alcuin and Theodulf, who may be regarded as the most prominent representatives of textual scholarship in the West, to purify the text of the Vulgate, and their little success; while in the East even less was done. It is only with the revival of learning in the West, and with the invention of printing, that the period of modern criticism begins; and it is to this that we must now pass. It was in 1454 that the first printed document made its appearance in Europe, in 1456 that the first printed book (the great Latin Bible known as the Mazarin Bible) issued from the press of Fust and Gutenberg at Mentz; but it was not until sixty years later that even the New Testament was obtainable in Greek.[1] The

[1] Some small extracts were printed earlier. The *Magnificat* and *Benedictus*

word "obtainable" is used advisedly; for though the first
Greek New Testament—that of Erasmus—was published
in 1516, another edition of it had already been in type
for two years, though still held back from the public.
This formed a part of the great Complutensian Polyglott,
which should be regarded as the parent of the textual
criticism of the printed Bible.

The Complutensian Polyglott owed its existence to
Cardinal Francisco Ximenes de Cisneros, Archbishop of
Toledo, who undertook it in 1502, in honour of the birth
of the child who was afterwards the Emperor Charles V.
It was printed at Alcala, from the Latin name of which
town (Complutum) it has received its title; and it contained the entire Bible, the Old Testament in Hebrew,
Greek, and Latin, the New in Greek and Latin. The New
Testament was first printed, the volume containing it
being completed on January 10, 1514; but its publication was delayed until the Old Testament should be ready
to accompany it. This occupied no less than four volumes,
the last of which is dated July 10, 1517; yet even then
a long delay took place before the work was actually given
to the world. Ximenes died in November 1517, and
it was not until March 22, 1520 that Pope Leo X.
authorised the publication; and it seems not to have been
actually issued until 1522. The principal editor employed
by Ximenes for the New Testament was Lopez de
Stunica; and the preface and dedication state that the
text was derived from MSS. lent by Pope Leo from the
Vatican Library. No more precise identification of the
MSS. is possible; but although the editors affirm that
their authorities were the oldest and most accurate obtainable (which implies that they exercised some selection and
critical judgment), there is no trace of their having used
the great Codex Vaticanus (B). The terms of their preface also make it possible that they used other MSS. as

were printed with other Canticles in a Psalter at Venice in 1486; the first six
chapters of St. John, also at Venice, in 1504 by Aldus Manutius; and the first
fourteen verses of the same Gospel at Tübingen in 1514.

well as those of the Vatican ; and since Leo (who lent the
Vatican MSS.) only became Pope less than a year before
the completion of the New Testament volume, it is probable that the work was begun in the first instance with
other authorities, not now identifiable. In a few instances
(as in the insertion of a Greek version of 1 John v. 7, 8)
the Greek text has been adapted to the Latin, which
Stunica deliberately affirmed to be the more pure ; but
generally the two texts are distinct. In spite of the
editors' assertion as to the age of the authorities employed
by them, the Complutensian text appears to be substantially of the type found in Greek MSS. of comparatively
late date.

It has already been said that the Complutensian
Polyglott, though the first Greek New Testament to be
printed, was not the first published. That honour belongs
to the New Testament of Erasmus. Its origin was due to
the energy of the printer Froben of Basle, who, hearing of
the work which Ximenes had in hand, conceived the idea
of anticipating it, and applied to Erasmus, the first scholar
of the day, to furnish him with a Greek New Testament
as speedily as possible. The application was made in
April 1515, and so quickly did editor and printers
work that the edition was ready by the 1st of
March 1516. The Greek text was accompanied by a
Latin translation and some notes, which Erasmus had had
in hand before Froben's proposal. Work so rapidly produced could not rest on any great accumulation of material,
and although the publisher's preface speaks of the use of
many ancient MSS. and of the quotations of all the most
important Fathers, it would appear that in reality only
a few manuscripts were employed—those, namely, which
lay ready to the editor's hand at Basle.[1]   These, for the

---

[1] Now known as Evan. 1 (=Act. 1, Paul. 1), Evan. 2, Act. 2 (=Paul. 2),
Act. 4 (=Paul. 4), and Apoc. 1. Of these Evan. 2 (of the fifteenth century) was
principally used for the Gospels, Act. 2 (of the thirteenth or fourteenth century)
for the Acts and Epistles, and Apoc. 1 (of the twelfth century) alone for the
Apocalypse. Evan. 1, a better class MS. of the eleventh century, was only
occasionally followed.

most part, were neither ancient nor good, and the single MS. employed for the Apocalypse was deficient in the last six verses of the book, which Erasmus accordingly supplied by re-translation from the Vulgate. Some words of this 're-translation, which occur in no MS. whatever, still linger in our Textus Receptus to the present day. Similar re-translations, to supply real or supposed lacunas, were also occasionally made in other places.

The edition of Erasmus consequently has little critical value, and is inferior in this respect to the Complutensian ; yet it has exercised a far greater influence on the history of the New Testament text. In the first place, it had six years' start of its rival ; and being issued in a single volume of reasonable size and price, it had a far wider circulation [1] than the six-volume Complutensian, of which only 600 copies were printed. Hence it formed the foundation of the editions which followed it at short intervals during the next generation. Aldus reprinted it at Venice in 1518, in conjunction with the Septuagint. In 1519 Erasmus issued a revised edition, correcting many misprints, and inserting improved readings from Evan. 3 (= Act. 3, Paul. 3) ; and three more editions appeared in his lifetime, in 1522,[2] 1527, and 1535. Each of these contains some alterations, that of 1527 being noticeable for its use of the Complutensian edition (mainly in the Apocalypse) and for its introduction of the Vulgate text by the side of the Greek and Erasmus' Latin. This edition of 1527 may be considered as Erasmus' definitive text, that of 1535 showing but very few alterations.

Other publishers followed in the footsteps of Ximenes and Froben in issuing editions of the New Testament in

[1] Erasmus states that 3300 copies were issued of his first two editions.
[2] This edition is notable for its introduction of the passage relating to the Three Heavenly Witnesses (1 John v. 7, 8). In controversy with Stunica, Erasmus had promised to insert it if any Greek MS. could be produced in which it occurred. It was found (in a clumsy form) in a MS. in England (Evan. 61, now at Dublin), and Erasmus, though rightly supposing that it was due merely to re-translation from the Latin, inserted it in fulfilment of his promise. Hence the passage (for which there is early *Latin* authority) found its way into the Textus Receptus.

Greek, but for the most part they contented themselves with reproducing the text of Erasmus, and the next that deserves mention is Robert Estienne, of Paris, whose name is Latinised by himself as Stephanus, and quite unnecessarily Anglicised by some as Stephens. His first edition appeared in 1546, his second in 1549, both being pretty little volumes in 16mo, printed from a new fount of small Greek type, with a text compounded from Erasmus, the Complutensian, and fifteen MSS., mostly at Paris. Only the two latter authorities are acknowledged in the preface. His third edition, a folio, published in 1550, was a more elaborate undertaking, containing a revised text, and giving in the margin various readings from his fifteen MSS. and the Complutensian. One of his MSS. was the Codex Bezae; most of the rest have been identified with minuscule MSS. in the Paris Library. The text itself shows greater approximation to that of Erasmus than its predecessors. It is from this third edition of Stephanus that the Textus Receptus found in our ordinary Greek Testaments is derived, with some slight alterations; so that its importance in the history of the Bible text is very great. A fourth edition was produced by Stephanus in 1551 (a 16mo, printed at Geneva), but it practically reproduces the text of 1550, with the addition of the Vulgate and the Latin version of Erasmus; its only important feature being the division of the text for the first time into verses.

The work of Stephanus was carried on by the Protestant scholar, Theodore Beza, who published no less than nine editions of the New Testament between 1565 and 1604. Five of these are, however, small reproductions of the larger volumes, and do not represent independent recensions. As we have seen above (pp. 73, 80), Beza was the owner of two very important MSS., viz. the Codex Bezae (D) of the Gospels and Acts, and the Codex Claromontanus (D_2) of the Pauline Epistles; and he also had access to the collations made by his printer, Henri Estienne, for his father Robert. Nevertheless Beza's editions do not embody much work of a textual kind, differing but slightly from the fourth edition of Stephanus and from one another.   Their importance lies in the extent to which they, with Beza's name and fame to back them, tended to popularise and to stereotype the Textus Receptus.

The last stage in this process is represented by the Elzevir editions, the first of which appeared at Leyden in 1624.   The objects of the Elzevirs were commercial, not critical or literary ; and their editions, though neat and handy, and consequently popular, have little textual value in themselves.   No editor's name is attached to the edition of 1624, nor to any of its successors ; and its text appears to be substantially that of Beza's first edition.   A second edition appeared in 1633, and five others (from either the Leyden or the Amsterdam branch of the firm) between that date and 1678 ; the variations in these later editions are, however, slight.   The popularity of the Elzevir publications led to their text being widely adopted for common use ; and if the Stephanus of 1550 set up the standard which has been generally followed in England, the Elzevir of 1624 performed the same service for the Continent.[1]

Here, then, ends the first stage in the history of the printed text of the New Testament, with the establishment of a standard or generally accepted text, which has continued to form the common basis of criticism from that day until this.   It will have been seen, however, that but little critical value can be attached to it.   The number of MSS. consulted for its production, in all the century from Erasmus to Elzevir, is very small ; few of these were of early date, and they were but slightly used ; in the main, the text rested upon a few late minuscule MSS. which happened to be accessible to the editors.   It must be plain, therefore, that so far as human agency is concerned,

[1] The phrase "Textus Receptus" may be traced back to the second Elzevir edition (1633), the preface to which has the words "Textum ergo habes nunc ab omnibus receptum."

the received text (which of course formed the basis of our Authorised Version, as well as of our current Greek Testaments) has no commanding claims upon our acceptance, and, indeed, that it would be contrary to all the ordinary canons of textual criticism if it did *not* need considerable correction by the use of earlier and better authorities.

The second period, on which we now enter, is that of the accumulation of evidence for the improvement of the received text. It covers a space of well-nigh two centuries, throughout which time, with a few exceptions, it is the collection of evidence, and not its application, which occupies the energies of Biblical scholars. The labours of the sixteenth and the first part of the seventeenth century had given Europe its Bible, alike in the original Hebrew and Greek and in the vernacular tongues of the Western nations. The practical needs of the churches and the peoples were adequately supplied;[1] and the preparation of editions of the sacred text now passed into the hands of scholars, who sought to improve upon the legacy of their predecessors. As new manuscripts came to light and were gathered into the libraries of Europe, scholars extracted from them the readings which differed from the received text, examined them, classified them, formed provisional estimates of the comparative value of the various authorities, and so, with many imperfections but with a steadily increasing standard of accuracy and completeness, compiled a vast body of materials for their successors, the scholars of the nineteenth century, to use. It is with the labours of accumulation that we have now to deal; the critical application of these labours will fall next to be considered, and so lead up to the statement of the present position of the subject, and of the problems which confront the textual student of to-day.

---

[1] The British Museum Catalogue contains forty-five editions of the Greek New Testament between 1516 and 1624, besides forty-seven in which the Greek is accompanied by a Latin text, and twelve complete Greek Bibles. Nearly thirty of these were printed at Basle alone. Critically, these are all substantially reproductions of Erasmus, Stephanus, or Beza; but their number shows the demand for copies of the Scriptures in the original tongue.

The first collection of various readings (apart from those given in the margin of Stephanus' 1550 edition) was made in England, in the Polyglott Bible edited by Brian **Walton,** afterwards Bishop of Chester. The fifth of his six great volumes (published in 1657) contains the New Testament in Greek, Syriac, Latin, Ethiopic, and Persian. The Greek text was that of Stephanus, to which were added, at the foot of the page, the readings of the Codex Alexandrinus (A), the recently acquired treasure of the Royal Library; while in the sixth volume a collation was given of fifteen other authorities, in addition to the sixteen cited by Stephanus. Among these were D and D_2, the rest being minuscules, of which the best is that now known as Evan. 59. These collations were made by Archbishop Ussher.

Walton's work was extended by John **Fell,** Dean of Christ Church and afterwards Bishop of Oxford, who in 1675 printed a Greek Testament from the Elzevir of 1633 with a critical apparatus in which he claims to give variants from more than 100 MSS. Most of these were appropriated from Stephanus, Walton, and other collections; but Fell added the readings of eighteen MSS. (mostly in the Bodleian) and of the Coptic (i.e. Bohairic) and Gothic versions.

Fell not only produced an edition of the New Testament himself, but also contributed largely to the production of a work which far eclipsed his own and all that had gone before. This was the edition of Dr. John **Mill,** Fellow of Queen's College, Oxford, and Principal of St. Edmund's Hall. Mill began to make collections for the purpose about the date of the appearance of Fell's edition; and Fell, hearing of his work, not only encouraged him to proceed, but undertook to defray the expenses of publication. Mill, however, was a conscientious worker, and in his zeal for the collection of all available evidence his work progressed but slowly; so that when Fell died in 1686, only the first twenty-four chapters of St. Matthew had been printed. The loss of Fell's pecuniary aid, and the ever-increasing growth of materials, still further delayed the progress of the edition, and it was not until 1707 that it at last saw the light. Mill's text was that of Stephanus' edition of 1550, but he appended to it collations of seventy-eight MSS. (besides those quoted by Stephanus), and of all the versions to which he could have access (including the Old Latin, Vulgate, and Peshitto); and he was the first editor to take the pains to collect the evidence of patristic quotations to any noteworthy extent. Moreover, he prefixed to his work, when it was complete, valuable Prolegomena, which showed that he knew how to use his materials as well as collect them. The MSS. collated by Mill include the uncials A, B, D, D$_2$, E, E$_2$, E$_3$, K, and the good minuscules Evan. 28, 33, 59, 69, 71. His collations do not come up to the modern standard of completeness and precision, but they are far in advance of anything that had been done previously, while his Prolegomena include a mass of invaluable material; and the importance of his work, as showing both what had to be done and the method of doing it, can hardly be over-estimated.

A somewhat rearranged edition of Mill, with additional collations of twelve MSS. (mostly at Paris, and including the uncials C and G$_3$), was issued by L. Kuster at Rotterdam in 1710; but this hardly breaks the sequence of English contributions to textual criticism, since Kuster himself had been a student at Cambridge, and his enterprise may have been due to the fact that he was there a pupil of the great scholar Richard Bentley, whose labours on the text of the Bible rivalled those of Mill in extent, though not in successful achievement. A more noteworthy undertaking, though less so in performance than in idea, was that of Dr. Edward Wells, who, between the years 1709 and 1719, issued at Oxford a revised text of the Greek Testament, with English translation and notes. The attempt was no doubt prompted by Mill's great work, and was rendered possible by the wealth of various readings therein first given to

the world.   Wells' edition was, in fact, the forerunner of
that third stage of textual criticism which only reached
its full development in the nineteenth century, the re-
construction of a purer and more ancient text of the New
Testament.   The attempt was premature, since fuller
materials had still to be collected, and the principles of
their application discovered ; but the intention was right.

Mill's work was, however, fruitful in another direction,
in bringing into the arena of textual criticism the greatest
scholar of that age, and one of the greatest of any age,
Richard **Bentley.**   Mill had contemplated, in addition to
his main work, the publication of complete texts of the
more important MSS. then known, namely, the Codices
Alexandrinus, Bezae, Claromontanus, and Laudianus ; and
as early as 1691 Bentley had addressed a Latin epistle
to him,[1] urging the performance of this undertaking.
Again, after Mill's death, when his edition of the New
Testament was assailed by many (notably by Dr. D.
Whitby) on the ground that the mass of various readings
collected by him cast doubt on the integrity of our Bible
text, Bentley issued a tract[2] in which he defended the
true principles of textual criticism, and the importance of
studying it.   And not only did he teach this precept—he
also devoted many years of his life to practising it.
About this time he began to employ scholars, among
whom the most notable were John Walker and the Swiss
J. J. Wetstein, to make collations for him in foreign
libraries ; and in 1720 he issued formal proposals for
printing a revised text of the Greek Testament and of the
Vulgate, with a critical apparatus.   His first examination
of the MS. evidence showed him the similarity of the
oldest authorities, Greek and Latin ; and he believed that
a full comparison of them would enable him to restore
the original text with almost absolute certainty, and with

---

[1] *Epistola ad Johannem Millium.*
[2] *Remarks upon a late Discourse of Free Thinking, in a letter to F. H.,
D.D., by Phileleutherus Lipsiensis* (1713) ; written in the character of a
German student, and provoked primarily by the work of one Collins, who had
taken up Whitby's arguments and used them with a sceptical purpose.

almost absolute identity between the two languages. This belief, which is the keystone of his undertaking, is thus expressed in the third paragraph of his *Proposals for Printing* :—

"The author believes that he has retrieved (except in very few places) the true exemplar of Origen, which was the standard to the most learned of the *Fathers*, at the time of the Council of Nice and two centuries after. And he is sure that the Greek and Latin MSS., by their mutual assistance, do so settle the original text to the smallest nicety, as cannot be performed now in any *classic* author whatever ; and that out of a labyrinth of thirty thousand various readings, that crowd the pages of our present best editions, all put upon equal credit, to the offence of many · good persons, this clue so leads and extricates us, that there will scarce be two hundred out of so many thousands that can deserve the least consideration."

As a specimen, the last chapter of the Apocalypse was printed with the proposals, but the *apparatus criticus* was only given in skeleton outline. The materials had still to be collected and arranged, and in the end the vastness of the task he had undertaken, in re-editing both the Vulgate and the Greek Testament, proved too much for him. A large number of collations were made for him, including several of the most valuable Latin MSS., and two of the Codex Vaticanus ; but Walker, who had been chosen as co-editor, died in 1741, and Bentley in 1742, and the edition remained unexecuted. Only the materials were left, and these were eventually bequeathed by his nephew to the library of Trinity College, Cambridge, where they still remain.[1] It has been suggested that the fuller knowledge of the complexity of the problem, brought to him by the increase of his materials,

---

[1] For an account of them see *Bentleii Critica Sacra*, by A. A. Ellis (Cambridge, 1862), and, on the Vulgate MSS., Wordsworth and White's Vulgate, pp. xv.-xxvii. The date of Walker's death, and consequent collapse of the edition after the death of Bentley, was established by Bishop Wordsworth (*Old Latin Biblical Texts*, i. p. xxv.).

convinced him that his great principle of the identity of the Greek and Latin texts, and the resultant certainty of his conclusions, was untenable, and so indisposed him to continue his undertaking; but it is probable that the quarrels which filled the latter part of his life at Cambridge had even more to do with his failure to bring his great work to the birth.

So far the study of New Testament textual criticism had been practically confined to England; now (in part through Bentley's own impulse, as will be seen) it passed out into the wider sphere of Europe in general, and for a time was little practised in the land of its birth. In 1734 J. A. **Bengel,** of Tübingen, published an edition of the New Testament which marks an era in the history of textual criticism. His text is mainly that of the Textus Receptus, only altered when the reading which he believed to be the true one had already appeared in some printed edition. In other cases the reading which he preferred is indicated in the margin, together with such other readings as he thought sufficiently important to be thus distinguished. A select *apparatus criticus*, drawn mainly from Mill, was added at the end of the volume. What makes Bengel's edition specially noteworthy, however, is the fact that he was the first to attempt any classification of his authorities—a principle which has proved very fruitful in the present generation. He divided his authorities (MSS. and versions) into two groups, which he called African and Asiatic, the former including the few most ancient authorities, the latter the great majority of later date; and he gave the preference to the former.

These novel principles asserted by Bengel met with sharp criticism; and one of his most prominent opponents was J. J. **Wetstein,** Bentley's former assistant, who was himself engaged on an edition of the Greek Testament. His study of textual matters began when he was quite young, and he spent many years in collating manuscripts in France, England, and Switzerland, before settling down in his native town, Basle, where he entered the diaconate. Here his relatives and acquaintances at first urged him to complete and publish the results of his collections ; but subsequently he became suspected of heresy, his work was opposed and thwarted, and eventually, in 1730, he was ejected from the ministry. In the same year he published the Prolegomena to his proposed edition ; but the change in his circumstances obstructed any further publication, and the delay, though it led to an increase in his materials, led also to a change in the plan of his work. He had at first thought of printing the text of the Codex Alexandrinus, and next of putting forth a revised text of his own ; but ultimately he decided to print the received text, with an *apparatus criticus* indicating what was, in his opinion, the true reading. His edition appeared eventually at Amsterdam in 1751-52, equipped with prolegomena, various readings, and a valuable series of illustrative passages from sacred and profane literature (including Jewish), which is a very distinctive feature of his work. His *apparatus criticus* is remarkable for its introduction of the system of manuscript-notation which has continued in use ever since ; and it was enriched by readings from many MSS. not previously collated. In the Gospels his list includes the uncials A to O, and cursives 1 to 112 ; in the Acts and Catholic Epistles, A to G, 1 to 58 ; in the Pauline Epistles, A to H, 1 to 60 ; in the Apocalypse, A to C, 1 to 28 ; besides twenty-four Evangeliaria and four Apostoli. In the accumulation of materials, accordingly, Wetstein's edition did considerable service ; but his contributions to textual theory were very retrograde in character. Largely, as it would appear, out of opposition to Bengel, he propounded the theory that all the most ancient MSS. had been contaminated from the Latin, and that consequently the later authorities, from which the Textus Receptus was more immediately derived, contained the more authentic tradition. This hostility to the earliest authorities has found echoes in our own time, but has never been carried so far as by Wetstein; and the general sense of textual critics has condemned it unreservedly.

A far more valuable contribution to textual theory was made by J. S. **Semler**, who reprinted Wetstein's Prolegomena at Halle in 1764, with comments of his own, and subsequently published other treatises on the same subject. Adopting at first Bengel's classification of all ancient authorities, which he called Eastern (= Bengel's Asiatic) and Western (= Bengel's African), and assigning them respectively to the recensions of Lucian and Origen, he subsequently (in 1767) expanded this into a threefold division—(*a*) Alexandrian, derived from Origen, and found in the Syriac, Coptic, and Ethiopic versions; (*b*) Eastern, in vogue at Antioch and Constantinople; (*c*) Western, embodied in the Latin versions and Fathers. Semler's theory derives special importance from its adoption and extension by his pupil J. J. **Griesbach,** whose name ranks with the highest in the history of textual criticism. Griesbach's activity ranged over a space of nearly forty years, and he produced three editions of the New Testament. The first of these was published at Halle in parts in 1774-5, containing a revised text and select *apparatus criticus*;[1] a new issue of the first part, giving the Synoptists in their usual order, instead of in the form of a harmony, as previously, appeared in 1777. The *apparatus* was taken mainly from Wetstein, with corrections and additions due to Griesbach's own collations. His second edition appeared in two volumes, published respectively in 1796 and 1806, by which time the available material had been greatly increased by the industry of Matthaei and others who will be mentioned below. The plan of this edition is the same as that of its predecessor, but several changes are made in the text adopted. A small edition published in 1805 introduces

[1] Besides the *apparatus criticus* properly so-called, Griesbach gives a list of select readings, with symbols denoting the degrees of probability which he believes to attach to them. This system will be familiar to many students in the small pocket edition of Griesbach's New Testament which is still in circulation.

yet further changes into the text of the Gospels, and must be taken as representing Griesbach's final judgment, though he never altered the text so largely as would have been necessary if he had carried out his own textual theories thoroughly.   These theories had already been stated in the Prolegomena to the several parts of his first edition.   The authorities for the Pauline Epistles were classified into two families, the Alexandrian and the Western ; those for the Gospels into three families, Alexandrian, Western, and Constantinopolitan.   This is practically the division of Semler, but Griesbach gave greater fulness to it by his precise assignment of the principal authorities to the several families.   In the Alexandrian family he placed the uncials C, K, L, the important cursives 1, 13, 33, 69, 106, 118, the Coptic (i.e. Bohairic), Ethiopic, Armenian, and Harkleian Syriac versions, and the quotations in Origen, Clement of Alexandria, Eusebius, and a few other Fathers ; in the Western, D, the Latin versions, and sometimes the Peshitto Syriac ; in the Constantinopolitan, which he regarded as a later compilation from the other two, A, and the great mass of late uncials and cursives. To the evidence of this third group, numerically preponderant though it is, he attached but little weight in comparison with the two older groups.   It will be seen later how nearly Griesbach's theory anticipated that which holds the field among New Testament students to-day.

Meanwhile, in the interval between Griesbach's first and second editions, much had been done to increase the store of materials available for the textual critic.   C. F. Matthaei produced a New Testament in twelve parts between 1782 and 1788, containing the Greek text with the Latin Vulgate and a large *apparatus criticus*.   His text, which is based upon late MSS., is of little value ; but his collations are of considerable importance.   Being a professor at Moscow (though by birth a Thuringian) he had access to many MSS. which had never previously been examined ; and his collations are generally good and accurate.   Fifty-seven MSS. were thus added by him to the available stock of evidence, including the uncial V ; and he also edited with great accuracy the Codex G_3 at Dresden. Like Wetstein, he was wholly opposed to the critical theories of Griesbach, whom he attacked bitterly, holding that the text of the later MSS. was much to be preferred to that of the most ancient. A smaller edition of the New Testament was published by him in 1803-7, in which collations of some additional MSS. were used. Almost simultaneously with Matthaei's first edition F. K. **Alter**, Professor of Greek at Vienna, published in full the text of a manuscript in the Imperial Library of that city (Evan. 218, Act. 65, Paul. 57, Apoc. 83), with collations of twenty-one other MSS. in the same library (1786-87). A larger addition to the stock of materials was made by three Danish professors, Birch, Adler, and Moldenhauer, who were sent by King Christian VII. to examine MSS. throughout Europe, especially in Italy, Germany, and Spain. The results of their labours were embodied in an edition of the New Testament by **Birch** (1788-1801). Stephanus' text of 1550 was taken as the basis 'of this edition, and collations were given of a very large number of manuscripts. The full list includes 172 MSS. ; but many of these were only partially examined by Birch and his colleagues, and some had been more or less collated by other scholars previously.

The materials available for the purposes of textual criticism had thus been very greatly increased during the last quarter of the eighteenth century, and at the same time some very valuable work had been done in the way of publishing in full the texts of some of the most important MSS. It will be remembered that Mill had contemplated such a scheme, and Bentley had advocated it ; but neither of these great critics was able to perform the task. Hearne had indeed published the Codex Laudianus (E_2) in full in 1715, but his example was not followed by any one for nearly half a century. Then, in 1762, Knittel published the Wolfenbüttel palimpsests P and Q; in 1786 Woide edited the New Testament portion of the Codex Alexandrinus (A); in 1789 Giorgi published the Graeco-Sahidic fragments known as T²; in 1791 Matthaei, as just mentioned, published G₃; and in 1793 Kipling published the very important Codex Bezae (D). Thus by the close of the century a considerable body of evidence was at the disposal of any scholar competent to use it.

The early years of the nineteenth century were not favourable to works of scholarship; and although the French invasion of Italy led to the temporary sojourn of the Codex Vaticanus in Paris, and thereby to a better knowledge being obtained of its character, yet on the whole the Napoleonic wars interposed a serious obstacle to the development of textual criticism. Nearly a quarter of a century separates the last edition of Griesbach from the next works of importance in this department of knowledge. When at last, in the early thirties, the stream burst out again, it was in the works of two German scholars, Scholz and Lachmann; but though their publications were nearly contemporaneous, the positions which they hold in the history of textual criticism are far apart. Scholz represents the end of the old period, Lachmann the beginning of the new.

The importance of J. M. A. Scholz lies in the fact that the list of manuscripts attached to his edition of the New Testament gathers up, with large additions, all the lists of his predecessors, and forms the basis of the numerical catalogues of MSS. which appear in our books of reference to-day. He travelled through Europe, cursorily examining all the manuscripts of the New Testament which he could find, and so compiling a long list, not indeed of collated MSS. but of MSS. known to be in existence, thus pointing the way to others to carry on a work which one man alone could not do. His catalogue (which continues the system of numeration initiated by Wetstein) includes the uncials from A to Δ (A to H of Acts, A to I of Paul, A to C of Apoc.) and the minuscules Evan. 1-469, Act. 1-192, Paul. 1-246, Apoc. 1-88, Evl. 1-181, Apost. 1-58. The list abounds in mistakes, as later scholars have shown ; but as pioneer work it did excellent service. In other respects Scholz's edition (which was published in 1830-36) is less valuable. His text is not very different from that of Griesbach, although his critical principles were the reverse of Griesbach's. Accepting Bengel's classification of MSS. in two families, which he calls Alexandrian and Constantinopolitan, he selected for preference, not the former, which includes all the earliest MSS. and versions, but the latter, which comprises the great mass of later authorities. His extensive examination of minuscule MSS. in the libraries of Europe had impressed him with the general uniformity of type in their texts, which he regarded as evidence of authenticity ; and the representation that all the most ancient MSS. exhibited a different type of text was met by him with the argument (revived half a century later by Dean Burgon) that these MSS. had only survived because, being erroneous, they had been less used. Nevertheless he did not form the text of his edition consistently with this theory, retaining many " Alexandrian " readings which, according to his own principles, he should have discarded.

With Scholz ends the second stage in the history of textual criticism, that of which the chief feature was the accumulation of evidence. Throughout this period the Textus Receptus had held its position practically unshaken, while the evidence which was ultimately to overthrow it was being sedulously brought to light by the labours of successive scholars. The third period, which may be dated from 1831 (the year which reformed parliamentary government in England), is the period of the application of critical principles to the accumulated mass of materials. It is true that the collection of materials has by no means ceased since 1831 ; and it is true that some application of critical principles had been made before that date, notably by Bengel and

Griesbach; but the broad features of the two periods are quite distinct. Neither Griesbach nor Scholz, the last representatives of the earlier period, had the full courage of their opinions. Griesbach, believing that the older MSS. and versions were of quite preponderant value, yet made relatively few alterations in the received text. Scholz, believing that the older authorities were wholly unreliable, yet retained many readings which had been adopted from them by Griesbach.

The new era begins with the name of Karl **Lachmann**, who illustrates, not for the last time, the stimulus which may be given to Biblical criticism by the appearance in the arena of a scholar trained in other studies. Lachmann was a great classical scholar before he turned his attention to the text of the New Testament; and when he did so, he applied to it the critical principles which he had practised in editing the classics of Greek and Roman literature. For the first time in the history of New Testament criticism, he cast aside the received tradition altogether, and set about reconstituting the text from the most ancient extant authorities. His first edition appeared in 1831, unaccompanied by any statement of the authorities used or the principles followed, except a brief note stating that he had aimed at reproducing the text of the most ancient Churches of the East, and where there was doubt upon this head he had preferred that reading which was supported by the Italian and African Churches, and that consequently he had ignored the evidence of the Textus Receptus. For further information the reader was referred to an article in a German periodical (*Theologische Studien und Kritiken*, 1830). The natural consequence of this reticence was that his work was misunderstood, even by those who would have been most likely to sympathise with it. When, however, its character came to be appreciated, he was urged to produce another edition with a full statement of the principles followed and the authorities consulted for the constitution of the text. This edition, in which he had the assistance of P. Buttmann, appeared in 1842-50, and differs from the first mainly in including the Vulgate text as well as the Greek, and in the fact that the evidence of the Latin authorities was taken into account throughout, and not only when the Eastern authorities disagreed among themselves.

The method of Lachmann, as practised in both editions and expounded in the second, was this. Putting entirely aside the whole mass of later authorities, he confined his attention to a small group of very ancient manuscripts, versions, and Fathers, and by their aid he believed that he could recover, not indeed always the actual words of the authors of the sacred books, but the earliest form of text which enjoyed wide circulation among the Churches, which might probably be assigned to the end of the fourth century. The authorities which he regarded as available for this purpose were, from the East, the manuscripts $ABCH_3PQTZ$ and the writings of Origen; and from the West the bilinguals $DD_2E_2G_3$, the Old Latin MSS. *abcg*, the Codices Amiatinus and Fuldensis of the Vulgate, and the writings of Irenaeus, Cyprian, Lucifer, Hilary, and (for the Apocalypse) Primasius. This list may seem fairly long, but it must be observed that of the Greek MSS. which formed the first line of evidence, C is imperfect, H_3PQTZ are only fragments, and B was at that date only very inadequately collated. For the best MS. of the Vulgate too, the Amiatinus, Lachmann only had access to an imperfect collation; while the Syriac and Coptic versions were not utilised by him, on account of his ignorance of these languages. He also tied his own hands unnecessarily, by binding himself to follow the majority of his authorities, without regard to the internal probabilities of the rival readings; thinking that thus he would eliminate altogether the "personal equation," while if he thereby sometimes introduced erroneous readings, they were readings which must have enjoyed some considerable circulation in the early Church. Some deduction has consequently to be made from the value of his edition, on account of the insufficiency (in many parts of the New Testament) of his authorities and the inelasticity of his principles ; but his work is nevertheless epoch-making, from its courageous rejection of the Stephanus-Elzevir text and deliberate application of critical principles, which in the main were sound, to the recovery of a more authentic text from the most ancient authorities.

We come now to the name which probably is the best known of all the scholars who have devoted themselves to the restoration of the Bible text, Constantin **Tischendorf.**   His life's work was of two kinds, as a publisher of the exact texts of ancient MSS. and as a critical editor of the Greek Bible.   His achievements in the first capacity have been repeatedly mentioned in Chapter III. He discovered and edited the Codex Sinaiticus ($\aleph$) ; he succeeded in producing a more accurate edition of B than had previously been in existence ; he edited C, deciphering much of it for the first time ; he also edited $D_2E_2F^aII^bLM_3N$ (so far as it was then known) $O^aO^dPP_2\dot{Q}RW^aW^c\Theta^a$.   Most of these are small fragments of uncial MSS., many of which he was the first to discover or to make use of.   In addition he transcribed (but without publishing) $H_3MO\Pi$, and minutely collated $EF_2GG_2HH_2KL_2O^{b-f}O_2{}^bST^{a-d}UXW^{b,e}\Gamma\Theta^{e-h}\Lambda$ and   Pap.[9] Consequently, although other scholars have also worked on many of these MSS., we are indebted to Tischendorf for a large portion of our knowledge of the uncial evidence for the New Testament text.   In addition, he edited the Old Latin MSS. *ek* and *gue* (besides the bilinguals d_2 and e_2) and the Codex Amiatinus of the Vulgate, and diligently collected evidence as to the readings of other MSS., versions, and patristic quotations from all available sources.[1]

In the use of the materials thus collected for the recovery of the true text of the New Testament, he was

---

[1] For a full account of Tischendorf's labours as a collector of evidence, and the sources used by him when he did not work from first-hand knowledge, see Gregory, *Prolegomena*, pp. 1-44.

not less assiduous. No less than eight editions of the
Greek New Testament were issued by him, the two last
appearing in a double form, a larger and a smaller.[1] In
all these editions a revised text was given, with a constantly growing critical apparatus. The earlier editions
were not of much permanent value ; but the last embodies
the fullest critical apparatus hitherto available for scholars,
and may consequently be regarded as the standard
critical edition of the Greek Testament. This text is
formed by the free exercise of his own judgment on the
evidence provided by the various authorities. He does
not tie himself down to a limited number of authorities,
like Lachmann ; neither does he adopt any classification
of families, like Griesbach. On the other hand he has
no prejudice in favour of the Textus Receptus. The
traditional claims of the Stephanus-Elzevir text had been
shattered by Lachmann ; and Tischendorf, like Lachmann,
attached a preponderant weight to the testimony of the
oldest authorities. Unfortunately his critical judgment
was not so sound or stable as could be wished ; and he
was liable to be over-influenced by the witnesses which
he had last studied. According to Scrivener, his seventh
edition differs from his third in 1296 readings, nearly
half of these variations being reversions to the Textus
Receptus, due to the study of the cursive MSS. which he
had undertaken in the interval. Between his seventh
and eighth editions came his great discovery of the Codex
Sinaiticus ; and consequently his latest text, in which the
new evidence was, naturally enough, allowed a somewhat
excessive weight, differed from its predecessor in no less
than 3369 places. Tischendorf's method left too much
to the personal equation of the critic ; and consequently,
valuable as his text is as representing the opinions of
one who gave a strenuous lifetime to the study of the
subject, it could not in any sense be final, or even mark

[1] The dates of the several editions are 1841, 1842, 1842, 1849, 1850, 1854,
1859, 1869-72. The fifth and sixth (the latter containing also the Latin and
German texts of the New Testament) were frequently reprinted.

a striking epoch in the history of New Testament criticism.

Tischendorf died (in 1874) before completing, or even advancing far in, the intended Prolegomena to his last edition; and the task of supplying the omission was committed to Dr. C. R. **Gregory**, aided by his fellow-American Dr. Ezra Abbot, who, however, also died before the work was concluded. These prolegomena, which appeared in the course of 1884-94, contain an enormous mass of information with regard to the authorities for the New Testament text, and form (with Scrivener's work, to be mentioned later) the standard book of reference on the subject.[1]

Tischendorf's fame as the discoverer of the Codex Sinaiticus, and his energy in the acquisition and publication of other early MSS., or fragments of MSS., gave weight and popularity to his texts of the New Testament, and did more than anything else to familiarise the educated public in general with the idea of the insufficiency of the Textus Receptus. But he was not in reality more energetic in his labours than his English contemporary, S. P. **Tregelles.** Incited to the task by observing the persistency of Scholz in rejecting the evidence of the earliest authorities (his "Alexandrian" group), Tregelles embarked about 1838 on the preparation of an edition based upon the opposite principle, namely, the ignoring of the claims of the Textus Receptus (in which he did not then know that he had been anticipated by Lachmann) and the determination of the text *de novo*, in accordance chiefly with the most ancient MSS., versions, and Fathers. A text of the Apocalypse was published in 1844; but before proceeding with the rest of the New Testament, Tregelles set himself to collate personally all the most important MSS. throughout Europe, a task which occupied the greater part of his

---

[1] Dr. Gregory's new work, *Textkritik des Neuen Testamentes*, of which one volume has been published (Leipzig, 1900) is substantially a German translation of the *Prolegomena*, with additions to bring it up to date. Its chief new feature, so far, is a somewhat fuller discussion of the Lectionaries.

remaining years. All the extant uncial MSS. were
examined by him, and all that had not previously been
published were collated by him, together with some
important cursives ;[1] and by an interchange of collations
in several instances with Tischendorf the accuracy of both
was tested, and their results raised to a very high degree
of probability. His edition appeared in parts between
the years 1857-72, illness making it necessary for him
to accept help from friends in the preparation of the last
part. The Prolegomena which he had intended were still
unwritten at his death in 1875, but a sketch of his views
on the principles of textual criticism was compiled out of
his other writings, together with important *addenda* to the
apparatus criticus, by the Rev. A. W. Streane, under the
direction of Dr. Hort.

Tregelles' edition, which contains the Vulgate (from
the Codex Amiatinus) as well as the Greek text, has no
such elaborate *apparatus criticus* as Tischendorf's, the
cursive MSS. being wholly neglected, with the exception
of Evann. 1, 33, 69. The uncial MSS., on the other hand,
are fully represented, together with the Syriac, Latin,
Coptic, Ethiopic, and Armenian versions, and the early
patristic quotations, the importance of which in fixing the
date of the types of text represented in them he recognised
and emphasised. In general, his text is constructed on
the principles advocated by Bentley, Lachmann, and
Tischendorf, namely, in dependence on the most ancient
authorities without reference to the Textus Receptus ; but
he resembled Tischendorf rather than Lachmann in not
tying himself down to hard and fast rules, while he did
not adopt the system of classification advocated by Griesbach. On the whole his text does not differ very greatly
from that of Tischendorf, their general principles of
criticism being much the same ; and the resemblance
would probably have been greater but for the fact that
his edition of the Gospels had been published before the

---

[1] For details, see Tregelles' *Account of the Printed Text of the Greek New
Testament*, pp. 151-174.

discovery of א or the appearance of Tischendorf's edition of B.

Another English scholar whose name requires mention at this place is F. H. A. **Scrivener.** It is true that he constructed no new text of the New Testament, but he did much to collect material for others and to popularise a knowledge of the principles and most important results of Biblical criticism. He edited Codex Bezae (D) and Codex Augiensis (F₂), collated some fifty MSS., made minute and careful examinations of the earliest printed Greek Testaments and of the English Authorised Version, published the text of Stephanus with a collation of the readings of Lachmann, Tischendorf, and Tregelles for the use of students, and, above all, wrote his *Plain Introduction to the Criticism of the New Testament*, the fresh and readable style of which has done much to popularise a knowledge of the subject, and which is still the standard English authority on the materials of textual criticism. Three editions of this work appeared during its author's lifetime, in 1861, 1874, and 1883 ; and since his death a fourth edition has appeared (in 1894), under the editorship of the Rev. E. Miller, the chief features in which are a great extension of the list of cursive MSS., and an admirable series of chapters on the Versions, contributed by scholars with special knowledge of each version in question.

We come now to the two scholars whose joint work has been epoch-making, in the literal sense of the word, in the history of New Testament criticism, the two Cambridge friends, B. F. **Westcott,** late Bishop of Durham, and F. J. A. **Hort,** Professor of Divinity in the University of Cambridge. The epoch-making character of their work lies not so much in any absolute novelty in their views as in the thoroughness with which they were elaborated, and the influence which they have exerted on all subsequent criticism of the New Testament. It has coloured all that has been written on the subject for the last twenty years, and supplies the basis of all work done in this field to-day. Indeed, it is the chief defect of Scrivener's *Introduction*, regarded as an aid to students, that, having been originally written before the promulgation of Westcott and Hort's theory, it has never in its later editions taken it fairly and fully into account.

Westcott and Hort's edition of the New Testament was published in 1881, and contains a revised Greek text without *apparatus criticus*, but with critical notes on special passages and a volume of elaborate prolegomena treating of the principles upon which the text is constructed. It is in these that the importance of the work lies. Westcott and Hort did not themselves collate or edit manuscripts, but devoted themselves to the study of the materials collected by others, and to the elaboration of a theory of the history of the early transmission of the New Testament text, which might serve as a guide to the discovery of the true text among the multitude of divergent witnesses that have come down to us. Briefly, this theory is a revival of Griesbach's classification of all textual authorities into families, with a decided preference for one which, though very early in point of date, is numerically insignificant in comparison with that which includes the great mass of later witnesses ; but in view of the present importance of Westcott and Hort's restatement of this theory it is advisable to set it out at greater length, following the lines adopted by themselves in their exposition of it.[1]

The principles upon which the system of classification of families rests are briefly these. The simplest method, *prima facie*, of procedure when various readings are offered by different authorities is to adopt that reading which most commends itself to your instinct or common sense ; but this will lead to different results with every critic and carries no weight of proof with it. Moreover, the reading

---

[1] The Introduction to Westcott and Hort's New Testament was written by Hort, and for brevity's sake it is convenient to refer to it by his name ; but it must be understood that Bp. Westcott fully shared and adopted the views expressed in it, which had been elaborated by the two friends in thirty years of close intercourse.

which commends itself to your instinct as probable may similarly have commended itself to the ancient scribe as an improvement on the text which he had before him ; it is indeed a recognised fact in textual criticism that errors are often introduced through a scribe misunderstanding his text and altering it to something that seems to him easier and more natural.   Hence the reading which *prima facie* is less probable may often turn out on examination to be more probable, as affording an explanation of the other ; for that reading must be considered the most probable which provides the best explanation of the origin of its rivals.   But even here we must depend much on the taste and judgment of the individual critic.   We still have to make allowances for the personal equation, and that is exactly what we wish to eliminate.   A first step in this direction is made if we can pass from simple criticism of the various readings as they arise, to the criticism of the documents in which they are contained.   By a study of those cases in which intrinsic probability allows a fairly certain judgment to be formed, we come to see which of our authorities usually have good readings, and which the reverse ; and we can then apply this knowledge of the character of our authorities to cases in which, so far as intrinsic probability goes, a choice might be difficult.   The evidence of a few witnesses who have generally been found trustworthy will naturally outweigh that of many witnesses whose character has stood the test less well.   Knowledge, therefore, of the documents must precede a final judgment upon divergent readings. But a still higher degree of certainty, and a fuller exclusion of the element of personal prejudice, may be obtained if we can classify our authorities into groups descended from a common ancestor.   The testimony of individuals is thereby checked and corrected, and their evidence carried back to the date of their ancestor, possibly a century or more behind their own date.   Moreover, it may be possible to distinguish between the characters of the several groups. One group may be shown to go back to an earlier date than another, another to owe its origin to the revising hand of a particular critic (like the MSS. which represent Lucian's edition of the Septuagint, or Alcuin's of the Vulgate), or to belong to a certain country or town (like the MSS. of the Vulgate which can be traced to Northumbria or St. Gall). Such a discovery will affect, for better or worse, our opinion of the authorities contained in each group, and will help us to understand and estimate the value of their readings. We shall see further into the history of the transmission of the text of the author with whom we are dealing; and our knowledge will enable us to judge between the claims of rival readings on some definite and general principle, instead of upon the vagaries of individual taste.

It is the business, therefore, of the critic of any ancient author, first to study the individual readings and the authorities for them; then to form an estimate of the character of the several authorities; then to see how far these authorities can be grouped as descendants of a common ancestor, and which family has the greatest claims to respect; and finally to return to the individual readings, and revise, in the light of his acquired knowledge of the value and inter-relation of the several authorities, his first provisional estimate of their comparative probability. This is the method which is applied to all textual criticism; and what we have now to see is, how does it apply to the text of the New Testament?

Now when the textual authorities, which have been enumerated in the previous chapters, are examined, they are found to fall into three or four groups, more or less clearly marked; that is, certain MSS. and versions are habitually found in agreement with one another, and opposed to certain other groups of MSS. and versions. One group is formed of the codices NΣΦ and the great mass of later uncials and cursives, with considerable support from the Peshitto Syriac and (in the Gospels) from the uncials A and C. Another group, much smaller in numbers, but eminent in point of age, includes the uncials אBLTΞ (with occasional support from others, such as PQRXZ, Δ in St. Mark, and A and C in the Acts, Epistles, and Apocalypse) and the Coptic versions (especially the Bohairic); some of the cursives also are frequently found in this group, notably Act. 61 and Evan. 33. Yet a third group is composed of the uncials DD₂E₂ F₂G₃, some of the cursives (e.g. Evann. 28, 235, 473, 604, Act. 58, 137, 221), the Old Syriac and Old Latin versions, and sometimes the Sahidic. These groupings are not indeed constant, all MSS. occasionally deserting the family to which they properly belong and allying themselves with their habitual opponents; but in general it is found to be observed. Other authorities join themselves now to one group, now to another, and can only be described as possessing mixed texts.

These three groups or families are those which we have above provisionally denoted by the letters α, β, and δ; and to these Hort adds a fourth, which is a kind of subdivision of the second, not found wholly in any one MS., but to be discerned when some members of that group, notably אCLX 33 and the Bohairic version, differ from the other members headed by B. The readings referred to this group, which may be indicated by the letter γ, are not generally of great importance, consisting mainly of slight verbal alterations, such as might be prompted by a desire for correctness of style.

How, then, are we to judge between these rival families, so as to know to which we ought normally to give the preference? The answer is, By the evidence of the Fathers, whose quotations enable us to locate these groups approximately both in time and in space. The key to Hort's whole theory lies in the proposition that *no reading strictly belonging to the a-family is found in any Father before Chrysostom.* From Chrysostom onwards, this type of text becomes frequent, until it almost monopolises the cursives, and (in a somewhat corrupted form) provides our Textus Receptus. To this family, the establishment of which he traces to the neighbourhood of Antioch in the latter part of the fourth century (the time and the place of Chrysostom's principal literary activity), Hort gives the name of *Syrian*; and on account of the comparative lateness of its origin, "Syrian" is with him a term of the utmost reproach. The β, γ, and δ-types of text, on the other hand, find attestation among the Fathers of earlier date. The β and γ-types are found pre-eminently in Origen, and to a considerable extent in Clement of Alexandria and Eusebius; the δ-type in *all* the Fathers before the end of the third century (including at times the three just mentioned), but notably in Justin Martyr, Tatian, Irenaeus, Tertullian, and Cyprian. To this last-named family, which monopolises the early Latin authorities, the name of *Western* has been given, though it will be seen that it includes also authorities from the East, in the shape of the Old Syriac version and Tatian. The γ-type, the evidence for which is wholly of Egyptian origin, is styled by Hort *Alexandrian*; while the β-type, which alone remains, receives the name of *Neutral*. Between these three families, the patristic evidence for all of which is of very early date, a decision must be made on the grounds of internal probability; and here Hort's verdict is emphatically in favour of β. The readings of the γ-family appear to be due to deliberate corrections in style and language, not important in substance, but showing less signs of originality and authenticity than those which they supplant. On the other hand the variants of the δ-family are very extensive and important, and seem (in the opinion of Hort and of most other critics) to be due to an extremely free handling of the text at some early date, when scribes apparently felt themselves at liberty to vary the language of the sacred books, and even to insert additional passages of considerable length. As compared with the readings of the β-family, these vagaries of δ lack authority and probability; but in β Hort finds all the signs of authenticity and probability, and to that, which he regards as neutral and substantially uncorrupted, he pins his whole faith.

Hort's general view, then, of the textual history of the New Testament is as follows. Corruption began to leave its mark upon the tradition at a very early date. Absolute accuracy of transcription was little prized, and scribes felt themselves free to amend or extend the text before them by additions or supposed corrections. This was especially the case with regard to the Gospels, since here there was the temptation, on the one hand, to incorporate incidents of our Lord's life which were recorded in other writings or in oral tradition, and on the other to correct one of the Evangelists from another. Hence there came into existence, as early as the second century, a type of text characterised by very free departures from the true tradition. This type took root in the Syriac Church, and was embodied in the earliest known version of the Gospels in the Syriac language ; but it was carried from the East to the West, and being best known from its appearance in the Old Latin version it may be named *Western*. In spite of its very early origin, its testimony is not to be highly regarded, on account of the liberties which it takes with the text; indeed, almost the only cases in which much weight is to be attached to purely Western testimony are those of omissions. A notable series of such omissions occurs in the last chapters of St. Luke ; and the non-appearance of these passages in the Western authorities seems to indicate that they were absent from the original work, and have found their way into all other authorities from some other source. In general, however, a reading attested wholly or mainly by Western evidence must, according to Hort, be regarded with the gravest suspicion.

While this corruption of the sacred text was taking place in the East and in the West, another kind of modification, of a much less serious character, was being introduced in the South. In Egypt, and especially in Alexandria, the capital of Hellenistic literature, the books of the New Testament were looked on with a critical eye.

Accustomed to literary Greek, accustomed also to criticise classical authors, and it may be even at times to correct them in accordance with their own canons of style, the more cultured among the scribes of Alexandria were continually under the temptation to introduce verbal alterations into the compositions which they had before them. Thus on the one hand the literary training and traditions of Alexandria operated in favour of accuracy in transcription, and so contributed greatly to preserve the true text, which the "Western" scribes were imperilling; and on the other, those same literary instincts tended to produce alterations in the text, but of a verbal character only, not affecting the substance. To readings of this class the name *Alexandrian* is given.

Such were the conditions of the New Testament text during the early days of the Church, and indeed nearly up to the date when Christianity became the religion of the empire. As, however, the multiplication of copies went on, and the divergences of text became more marked, an attempt seems to have been made to rectify the evil by an authoritative revision. The principles upon which this revision was conducted, consciously or unconsciously, were (1) to combine divergent readings when possible, (2) to smooth away roughnesses, to remove obscurities, and generally to produce an easy and flowing text. The first of these principles is seen at work in what are called (in Hort's nomenclature) *conflate* readings, where two readings, each separately attested by a group of earlier authorities, are combined into a single reading. A simple instance may be found in Acts vi. 8, where one group of authorities gives πλήρης χάριτος, another πλήρης πίστεως, while the Codex Laudianus (E₂) has πλήρης χάριτος καὶ πίστεως. In this case, however, the authorities for the three readings do not fall into the usual groups. In Mark ix. 49, on the other hand, we have the readings πᾶς γὰρ πυρὶ ἁλισθήσεται supported by ℵ (substantially) BLΔ, a few cursives and the Coptic versions; πᾶσα γὰρ θυσία ἀλὶ ἁλισθήσεται supported by D, the Old Syriac

S

and Old Latin ; and the *conflate* reading πᾶς γὰρ πυρὶ ἁλισθήσεται καὶ πᾶσα θυσία ἁλὶ ἁλισθήσεται by ACNS and the great mass of later uncials and cursives, the Peshitto Syriac and some other versions. Or again, in Luke xxiv. 53, אBCL Boh. Syr.[pal.] read εὐλογοῦντες τὸν θεόν, D several Old Latin and Vulgate MSS. and Augustine αἰνοῦντες τὸν θεόν, and A and the great mass of later authorities αἰνοῦντες καὶ εὐλογοῦντες τὸν θεόν. Hort examines eight such instances from the Gospels, besides briefly referring to others ; and more (though probably not very many) could be produced if necessary.[1]

The revision was not confined, however, to the manufacture of conflate readings, but included a general softening and smoothing away of difficulties. Conjunctions are inserted to avoid harshness, proper names substituted for pronouns for the sake of greater clearness, and unfamiliar phrases turned into more familiar forms. In Hort's words, the authors of the revision " were apparently desirous that the reader should have the benefit of instructive matter contained in all the existing texts, provided it did not confuse the context or introduce seeming contradictions. New omissions accordingly are rare, and where they occur are usually found to contribute to apparent simplicity. New interpolations on the other hand are abundant, most of them being due to harmonistic or other assimilation, fortunately capricious and incomplete. Both in matter and in diction the Syrian text is conspicuously a full text. It delights in pronouns, conjunctions, and expletives and supplied links of all kinds, as well as in more considerable additions. As distinguished from the bold vigour of the ' Western ' scribes, and the refined scholarship of the Alexandrians, the spirit of its own corrections is at once sensible and feeble. Entirely

---

[1] A new instance has been indicated by Mr. Lake (*Journal of Theological Studies*, i. 291) in Mark xiii. 11. Most authorities have μὴ προμεριμνᾶτε μηδὲ μελετᾶτε, while אBDL and the cursives 1, 33, 209 have μὴ προμεριμνᾶτε alone. The other half of the conflation is provided by Ψ, which has μὴ προσμελετᾶτε, evidently for προμελετᾶτε.

blameless on either literary or religious grounds as regards vulgarised or unworthy diction, yet showing no marks of either critical or spiritual insight, it presents the New Testament in a form smooth and attractive, but appreciably impoverished in sense and force, more fitted for cursory perusal or recitation than for repeated and diligent study." [1]

As has been indicated above, Hort believed this revision to have taken place at or about Antioch, whence he dubs it *Syrian*, in spite of the obvious danger of confusion with the term *Syriac*.   He admits freely that no mention of such a revision occurs in ancient Christian literature, and does not attempt to assign to it any specific author, beyond a bare reference to the possibility of Lucian (whose edition of the Septuagint was conducted on somewhat similar lines) having had a hand in it. [2]   It is noteworthy also that he regards the revision as having taken place in two stages.   The ground for this belief is found in the evidence of the Peshitto version, which holds a somewhat intermediate position between the more ancient texts and the fully developed Syrian revision.   Although as a whole it belongs to the *a*-family of texts (Hort's "Syrian"), nevertheless in a considerable number of instances it agrees with the earlier texts against that which we find in the Antiochene Fathers of the age of Chrysostom.   Hort consequently considers that "(1) the growing diversity and confusion of Greek texts led to an authoritative revision at Antioch, which (2) was then taken as a standard for a similar authoritative revision of the Syriac text, and (3) was itself at a later time subjected to a second authoritative revision, carrying out more completely the purposes of the first ; but that the Vulgate Syriac [the Peshitto] did not undergo any corresponding second revision." [3]   The final revision was apparently completed by about 350, while the earlier stage may be placed about half a century earlier ; but we have no means of fixing it precisely.   Once completed, it rapidly gained universal popularity, no doubt

[1] Hort, *Introduction*, pp. 134, 135.   [2] *Ibid.* p. 138.   [3] *Ibid.* p. 137.

owing largely to the smoothness, fullness, and easiness, which are its chief characteristics ; and it is consequently found in an overwhelming majority of the later uncials and the cursives.

It will be seen, therefore, that the main result of the Westcott-Hort theory is the total rejection of the great mass of authorities, and a complete reliance on a relatively small group, composed of the earliest uncials and versions, with a few later MSS. which preserve the same type of text. If a reading is "attested by the bulk of the later Greek MSS. but not by any of the uncials אBCDLP QRTZ (Δ in St. Mark) Ξ (also 33) in the Gospels, אABCDE₂ (also 13, 61) in Acts, אABC (also 13) in the Catholic Epistles, or אABCD₂G₃ (also 17, 67**) in the Pauline Epistles, and not by any Latin authority (except the latest forms of Old Latin), the Old or the Jerusalem Syriac, or either Egyptian version, and not by any certain quotation of a Father earlier than 250, there is the strongest possible presumption that it is distinctively Syrian, and therefore to be rejected at once as proved to have a relatively late origin."[1] Even this list of favoured authorities is open to considerable reductions. The secession of CLPQR 33 in the Gospels, ACE₂ 13 in the Acts and Catholic Epistles, or AC 17 in the Pauline Epistles, would not be held materially to weaken the presumption in favour of the more ancient witnesses, all of these MSS. being considerably affected by Syrian influences. Further, when the Syrian readings have thus been eliminated, we still have to be on our guard against Western corruptions. Therefore if D (sometimes in combination with other uncials, such as אXΓ, and cursives such as 1, 13, 22, 28, 81, 157), the Old Latin and Old Syriac versions, and the Ante-Nicene Fathers generally (with the partial exception of those of Alexandria), separate themselves from the group of authorities above mentioned, they must be allowed to go, as more than suspect of error ; in

---

[1] Hort, *Introduction*, p. 163. By 67** he means the marginal readings of Paul. 67.

the Acts and Epistles the same family is represented by
DD₂E₂G₈ and various cursives.   Alexandrian readings are
to be found chiefly in CL and the Bohairic version,
reinforced sometimes by אXZ (Matthew) Δ (Mark) ΞR
(Luke) 33, the Sahidic version, and the Alexandrian
Fathers.

The result of all these deductions is to leave B almost
alone ; and Hort does not shrink from this conclusion.   It
is better, no doubt, to have the support of other ancient
and trustworthy witnesses.   The combination אB, in particular, is very strong, since the two MSS. are sufficiently
alike to show that they descend from a common
ancestor, and yet sufficiently unlike to show that this
common ancestor must lie a considerable distance behind
them, and consequently not far from the autographs themselves.   But the superiority of B is such that no reading
attested by it (obvious slips of the pen of course excepted)
can safely be passed over without the most careful attention ; and in the majority of cases its evidence must be
regarded as decisive.

The learning and conviction displayed in Westcott and
Hort's work would have secured full attention to it at any
time ; but special prominence and importance were lent
to it by its influence on the Revised Version of the New
Testament.   The Revised Version was published, it is
true, a few months before Westcott and Hort's volumes
(in May 1881), but a statement of their theory and its
results was communicated to the Revisers in advance, and
the presence of both authors on the Revision Committee
(in which they, with Scrivener, were by far the most
experienced textual scholars) ensured full attention for
their views ; and in point of fact the new translation dis-
plays the effect of their influence on every page.   No
doubt the text adopted by the Revisers differs in many
details from that which appears in Westcott and Hort's
own edition ; but the principle of rejection of authorities
of the α-type underlies it, and the greatest respect is
manifested for the evidence of א and B, especially the latter.

The departure from the Textus Receptus, the basis of our venerable Authorised Version, was complete ; and the results of modern textual research, and especially of the theory of Westcott and Hort, were thus brought forcibly to the notice of all intelligent readers of the English Bible.

Naturally so great a shock to established tradition aroused great opposition, which found at once its most vehement and its most learned advocate in the person of J. B. **Burgon**, Dean of Chichester. Always strenuous in his resistance of change, Burgon threw himself wholeheartedly into the championship of the traditional text, maintaining both that it was intrinsically superior to that adopted by Westcott and Hort and the Revisers, and that the fact of its universal acceptance by the Church was (in view of the Divine institution and inspiration of the Church) a conclusive proof of its authenticity. His contributions to textual science during his lifetime included the examination and collation of many cursive MSS. of the New Testament, the results of which were placed at the disposal of Scrivener for the third edition of his *Introduction*; the preparation of a vast index to the quotations from the New Testament to be found in the Fathers (in MS. only, acquired since his death by the British Museum); an elaborate defence of the concluding section of St. Mark's Gospel (*The Last Twelve Verses of the Gospel according to St. Mark vindicated against recent objectors and established,* 1871); and a vehement, at times even intemperate, assault on the Revised Version and Westcott and Hort (*The Revision Revised,* 1883). He had also contemplated a more deliberate and constructive work on the textual criticism of the New Testament, together with a revised text, exhibiting the true form of the "traditional" text, apart from the blemishes which are found in the Textus Receptus of Stephanus and Elzevir. For both these works considerable materials were left behind him at his death, which have since been arranged and supplemented by Prebendary Miller. Two volumes contain their joint defence of the traditional text, and a beginning has been made with their revised text of the Gospels.[1]   Some examination of the position assumed in these volumes will be found in the next chapter.

Since the promulgation of Westcott and Hort's theory, no work of textual criticism has appeared of anything like equal importance.   In spite of certain criticisms and modifications, which appear to be well founded, and of which mention will have to be made below, this theory holds the field among the scholars of to-day, and is presupposed as the starting-point of nearly all the work that is being done in this department of New Testament criticism.   It only remains to notice the work of the veteran German scholar, Bernhard Weiss, who has recently completed a series of studies of the text of the several portions of the New Testament, beginning with the Apocalypse and ending with the Gospels.[2]   These studies have taken the form of an examination and classification of the various kinds of mistakes which characterise the principal MSS. The result of this examination, which deals with each reading mainly on the ground of internal probability (and therefore rests to some extent on the "personal equation" of the critic), is an emphatic verdict in favour of B, which, though possessing many obvious blunders in transcription, shows far less than any other MS. the signs of deliberate revision or substantial corruption.   Weiss' work, which takes little account of the versions or patristic quotations, does not amount to a complete theory of the textual history of the New Testament ; but such an examination of documents as he has conducted forms, as Westcott and

---

[1] *The Traditional Text of the Holy Gospels vindicated and established* (1896); *The Causes of the Corruption of the Traditional Text of the Holy Gospels* (1896) ; *A Textual Commentary upon the Holy Gospels*, Part I., St. Matthew, Division 1, i.-xiv. (1899).   The most noteworthy feature of the last-named work is its copious references to patristic evidence, derived from Burgon's above-mentioned index.   [The death of Mr. Miller, while these sheets were passing through the press, makes it doubtful whether this edition will be carried further.]

[2] Published in Gebhardt and Harnack's *Texte und Untersuchungen*, vii. 1 (the Apocalypse, 1892), viii. 3 (Catholic Epistles, 1892), ix. 3, 4 (Acts, 1893), xiv. 3 (Pauline Epistles, 1896), N.F. iv. 2 (Gospels, 1899).   A text of the Gospels, embodying Weiss' results, has just been published (1900).

Hort themselves contend, the essential basis of textual science, and his conclusion in favour of B, reached as it is rather through exegetical than transcriptional considerations, affords a valuable reinforcement to the views of the Cambridge scholars.[1]

In conclusion it may be useful to mention some of the more handy critical editions of the New Testament for the use of students. The Cambridge Greek Testament, edited by Scrivener, gives the Textus Receptus, with a critical apparatus showing the readings of Lachmann, Tischendorf, Tregelles, Westcott and Hort, and the Revised Version, and will be found very serviceable by those who would rather have the opinions of editors than the evidence of manuscripts. The Oxford Greek Testa-

---

[1] In the Apocalypse Weiss examines the five uncials אACP₂Q [= B₂ in our list above]. Of these אAC form the earlier group, PQ the later. The earlier group has many errors and verbal corrections (such as a scribe may make *en passant*, sometimes involving a misunderstanding of the text), but shows no signs of systematic revision in editing. The later group, on the other hand, does show signs of such deliberate editing, especially Q. Of the individual MSS. A is the best, representing the oldest text most accurately, and standing alone in about sixty correct readings, while א has only eight peculiar correct readings, and C four. C (which lacks about a third of the book) is closely akin to A, but shows some traces of being affected by the later emended text. This is still more the case with א, which is much more corrupted than AC, and not infrequently agrees with PQ. Of the later group, Q has been the most fully emended, but the text upon which it ultimately rests must have been good, and akin to that of A.

In the Catholic Epistles the text is better preserved than in the Apocalypse. Here the later group is represented by K₂L₂P₂, which show distinct signs of deliberate emendation, KL somewhat more so than P. אAC represent an older text, but still somewhat affected by emendation. B in general goes with the older group, but differs from it in being practically free from deliberate emendation. The true reading is preserved in B alone twenty-four times, never in any of the other MSS. alone ; and in combination with other MSS., while א is right 150 times, A 274 times, and C (which lacks a quarter of the book) 196 times, B is right 400 times. Nevertheless B has faults of its own, due to careless copying, and no single MS. can be trusted implicitly.

In the Acts, the later group is represented by H₂L₂P₂. Of these P has the fewest peculiar readings, and is probably the purest representative of the emended text. DE₂ form a separate sub-group, having many special variants (especially D, which has 1600 variants as against 440 in E), due mainly to wilful and thoughtless alteration ; but the deliberate variants are of the same type as in HLP, so that the basis of the text is the same in both cases. The earlier group, אAC, is influenced by the emended text (א less so than AC), though not to the same extent as DEHLP. B, on the other hand, though it has many mistakes of carelessness, shows no sign of deliberate emendation. It has forty-eight correct readings peculiar to itself, while א and A have only one each.

In the Pauline Epistles the text is relatively well preserved, and the groups

ment, on the other hand, which also gives the Textus
Receptus (as printed by Mill) as its main text, has
recently been provided with an admirable series of
appendices by Professor Sanday, containing (1) a collation of Westcott and Hort's text, (2) a select *apparatus
criticus*, giving all the more important variants, with the
authorities for them, (3) select readings from the Bohairic,
Armenian, and Ethiopic versions, with a brief account of
the MSS. consulted for them.   These appendices can be
obtained in a separate volume, and will be found exceedingly useful by students; the second in particular
providing by far the best select *apparatus criticus* in
existence.   A somewhat similar apparatus is furnished
for English readers in the notes to the excellent Variorum
Bible published by Messrs. Eyre and Spottiswoode, the
New Testament portion of which is edited by Professor
Sanday, Mr. R. L. Clarke, and Mr. A. Goodwin.   Those
who would prefer to see the results of modern criticism

substantially as in the Acts.   The emended text is represented by $K_2L_2P_2$ (as
in Cath.), with the fragment M.   The Graeco-Latin MSS., $D_2E_2F_2G_3$ (E_2
being a copy of D_2, and F_2 and G_3 very nearly related), form a group akin to
this, but containing many aberrations peculiar to themselves.   Both groups
derive from an earlier emended text.   D in particular has a good basis, though
considerably altered.   The older group, אAC, is also influenced by the emended
text, though to a less extent; but B stands far ahead of all in purity of text.
It shares some twenty-five mistakes with אAC, about eighty with KLP, and
seventy with both groups, these being mistakes going back to a very early text.
On the other hand it has no less than eighty-five correct readings peculiar to
itself, whereas א has only three and A one.
     Finally in the Gospels B again stands out by itself, not for freedom from
mistakes, since it has over 400 errors peculiar to itself, but because its errors
are not due to deliberate emendation.   As a rule they are merely scribe's
blunders; rarely conformations of the text to suit the context; still more rarely,
conformations with parallel passages elsewhere.   All the other uncials show
signs of deliberate revision, but of a superficial kind.   A stands at the head of
these emended texts, to which C also belongs; DLΔ are often found with
them, DΔ oftener with A, L oftener with C.   D, however, has 4300 peculiar
readings (1700 in Luke, 1150 in Mark, 775 in Matthew, 655 in John), as
against 600 in A.   These readings are often very old, but nevertheless false,
being due to free handling of the text, and clearly of a secondary character.   א
shares 1350 errors with the emended MSS. (many of them plainly early, as
they occur in early versions), and 600 with D, besides having 1350 peculiar to
itself, many of which are similar in character to those in D.   But it also shares
many of the errors of B, so that the text represented in B lies also at the base
of א.   Of the later MSS. L is the most free from emendation.   The younger
group (DLΔ and the fragments RXZΞΣ) shares many genuine readings with B,
as does the older group אAC; but B is independent of both, and in 280 places
has the right reading alone.

incorporated in the text itself will find the texts of Tischendorf and Westcott-Hort in the smaller editions of these scholars. These, however, represent only the results arrived at by a single editor or partnership of editors, and it is not likely that either of them would ever be accepted as a standard text for general use. The best text for this purpose is probably *The Greek Testament with the readings adopted by the Revisers of the Authorised Version*, published at Oxford in 1881 under the editorship of Archdeacon Palmer.[1] In this edition the text adopted by the revisers is printed in full, with a brief *apparatus criticus* giving the alternative readings of Stephanus, the Authorised Version of 1611, and the margin of the Revised Version. It would be a great step towards promoting a wider knowledge of the true text of the New Testament if this edition were generally adopted in schools and colleges in place of the Textus Receptus. No doubt it is not perfect, but at least it rests upon a far sounder basis than the text of Stephanus and Elzevir ; and being the product of a large committee of scholars it does not represent solely the views of any one critic. This edition, used in connexion with Professor Sanday's critical appendices, mentioned above, would seem to provide the best textual material to be placed in the hands of students of the Greek Testament. As an alternative, mention may be made of the edition recently produced by Dr. E. Nestle of Maulbronn (Stuttgart, 1898), a scholar who has done invaluable work on the text of the Old Testament as well as on that of the New. His edition is based upon the texts of Tischendorf and Westcott-Hort, and upon that produced by Mr. R. F. Weymouth (*The Resultant Greek Testament*, 1886), which is itself the result of a comparison of the texts of Stephanus, Lachmann, Tregelles, Tischendorf, Lightfoot, Ellicott, Alford, Weiss, the Basle edition of 1880, Westcott and Hort, and the Revised Version.

[1] Simultaneously Dr. Scrivener published at Cambridge an edition of the Textus Receptus, with the Revisers' readings in the margin ; but this does not answer the purpose of providing a revised text of the Greek Testament for ordinary use.

Of these three editions, Dr. Nestle follows the verdict of the majority, placing the reading of the minority in the margin, where he also records the readings adopted by Weiss from the Acts onwards (Weiss' examination of the Gospels not having appeared until after Dr. Nestle's edition was published). Another set of footnotes gives some of the more remarkable variants contained in MSS., especially those of the δ-type of text, but without stating the evidence for them. When once the rather complicated system of critical symbols is mastered, this will be found to be a useful pocket edition of the Greek Testament, with instructive textual material.[1]

With these alternatives before him, any student of the New Testament can obtain a far purer and more authentic text (unless modern textual criticism is wholly and fundamentally at fault) than that which has been in possession of the ground for the last three centuries and a half; and he will also be able to follow intelligently the discussion of the textual problems which still occupy the attention of Biblical critics.

[1] Dr. Nestle also published a small Introduction to the New Testament in 1897, which has since been enlarged and translated into English (Williams and Norgate, 1901). It will be found interesting and suggestive. The illustrations in it appear to be taken mainly from Scrivener and a book by the present writer (*Our Bible and the Ancient Manuscripts*, Eyre and Spottiswoode, 1895).

CHAPTER VIII

THE TEXTUAL PROBLEM

[**Authorities**: Westcott and Hort, *op. cit.*; Nestle, *op. cit.*; Burgon and Miller, *The Traditional Text of the Holy Gospels* (London, 1896), and *The Causes of the Corruption of the Traditional Text of the Holy Gospels* (London, 1896); Salmon, *Some Points in the Textual Criticism of the New Testament* (London, 1897); Sanday and Headlam, *A Critical and Exegetical Commentary on the Epistle to the Romans*, pp. lxiii-lxxiv (Edinburgh, 1896); F. Blass, *Acta Apostolorum secundum formam Romanam* (Leipzig, 1896), *Evangelium Lucae secundum formam Romanam* (Leipzig, 1897), and *The Philology of the Gospels* (London, 1898); Weiss, *op. cit.*, and *Der Codex D in der Apostelgeschichte* (Leipzig, 1897); K. Lake, *The Text of the New Testament*, pp. 64-91 (London, 1900).]

THE *data* of New Testament textual criticism have now been set forth,—on the one hand the materials with which the critic has to deal, and on the other the various ways in which critics in the past have dealt with them. Evidence has been collected with great assiduity for more than two hundred years, and highly trained and gifted scholars have applied themselves to the interpretation of it; yet the whole problem is not solved, and students are by no means agreed, even upon points of fundamental importance. It is not the office of a handbook such as this to advance any new solution, or to aspire to make any noteworthy addition to textual theory. It is probable that whatever advance is made in the immediate future will take the form of elucidation of special and particular points rather than of a general restatement of the whole subject; but a survey and knowledge of the whole field is necessary as a foundation for such special work. The object, therefore, of this concluding chapter is the statement of the textual problem as it confronts the New Testament critic to-day, and the indication of the lines along which progress is most to be desired and most to be expected.

With this view we shall examine in succession the claims and character of the several types of text which the preceding chapters have shown to be presented by our textual authorities.

§ 1. *The α-text*

It will have been seen from the last chapter that the uniform tendency of modern criticism has been to discredit and dethrone that type of text which has held possession of our Bibles since the invention of printing,— nay, if we go back to manuscript books, for a thousand years before that date,—and which is consequently known as the Textus Receptus or the Traditional Text. Commonly accepted, however, though this doctrine is among scholars, the realisation of it is hardly yet popular and general; and, as we have seen in the preceding pages, the contrary view still finds strenuous advocates. It will therefore be best, in the first place, to re-consider the claims of the Traditional Text, as these advocates have recently stated them, and to estimate the present position of the controversy between those who may be most concisely described as the disciples respectively of Westcott and Hort and of Burgon. The criticism of Burgon (and his editor and continuator, Mr. Miller) is the most searching which the theory of Westcott and Hort has had to bear, and it is important to see how it has stood that test.

The propositions upon which Burgon and Miller base their defence of the Traditional Text, reduced to their simplest form, are two in number : (1) that the universal acceptance of it by the Church from the fourth century to the nineteenth is in itself proof of its superiority, since the Church must have been Divinely guided in its dealings with the sacred Word of God ; (2) that, apart from such considerations, it can be shown to be both older and intrinsically better than its rival, which they call the "neologian" text.[1] Now if the first of these propositions is true, *finita est quaestio*; for Hort admits, no less than Burgon claims, that the Traditional or Received Text has been at first prominent and ultimately dominant in the Church from at least the end of the fourth century. There is, moreover, this much at least to be said in favour of such a contention, that God, Who instituted the Church to be the guardian and teacher of His Word, would surely not have allowed that Word to be propagated in a corrupt or seriously mutilated form. Further still, there is the analogy of the establishment of the doctrine of the Church, which received its final formularisation in the course of this same fourth century ; and much the same may be said with regard to the determination of the Canon of the New Testament. As, therefore, we believe that the Church was Divinely guided in its assertion of the doctrine of Nicaea and Constantinople, and in its choice of the books which it regards as especially inspired, are we not also called upon to believe that it was Divinely guided in its choice of the text of these books, and that the type which it selected must be regarded as thereby stamped with the Divine approval ?

The analogy, however, with the establishment of doctrine and the canon in the fourth century (or about that date) is very imperfect. It is not contended that any oecumenical council selected the Traditional Text for universal use, or even so much as considered the question of an authorised text at all. The doctrines of the Church were established by councils, and by councils only ; the limits of the canon, if not so wholly de-

---

[1] By this term Burgon presumably meant to associate modern textual criticism with the rationalistic interpretation of the Bible, to which the same term was applied in the eighteenth century.

pendent on the decisions of councils, were yet considered and ratified by them ; but the text of the sacred books never formed the subject of their deliberations. The selection of the traditional type of text by the Church was gradual and informal, and therefore cannot claim the sanction of a deliberate decree. Nor is the argument that God would certainly secure the preservation of the true form of His Word much more pertinent. We may indeed believe that He would not allow His Word to be seriously corrupted, or any part of it essential to man's salvation to be lost or obscured ; but the differences between the rival types of text is not one of doctrine. No fundamental point of doctrine rests upon a disputed reading : and the truths of Christianity are as certainly expressed in the text of Westcott and Hort as in that of Stephanus.[1]

It is, moreover, a perversion of the facts of history to speak of the text of the Scriptures as preserved in a uniform shape from the fourth century to the present day, as the argument of Burgon requires. While the substance of the sacred text, and its general type, have been so preserved, a very great amount of variation in detail has been admitted. The manuscripts of the Greek Testament differ very considerably from one another. The manuscripts of the Vulgate differ from those of the Greek Testament, and have suffered even more corruption among themselves. We have seen in an earlier chapter how the history of the Vulgate text is one of widespread depravation and of repeated attempts at restoration. The Syriac and Coptic texts, again, differ in many particulars from both Greek and Latin. Still more great and deep-seated are the differ-

---

[1] Burgon and Miller have indeed at times accused the codices א and B of being tainted with sceptical tendencies, and especially with minimising the Divinity of our Lord ; but the evidence adduced in support of this charge is wholly inadequate. No doubt the traditional text contains many more phrases in which the Divinity is implied,—the natural amplifications of scribes writing after the phraseology of the Church had become more fixed ; but the language of א and B as they stand is wholly inconsistent with such supposed heretical revision.

ences in the text of the Old Testament. The text of the Septuagint, which was and is the Bible of the Greek-speaking Churches, differs widely from the Massoretic Hebrew. In short, the first of Burgon's main propositions is neither convincing *a priori* nor in fact reconcilable with history. History makes it clear that God in His wisdom has permitted great deviations in the tradition of the sacred text through the frailty of its human trustees, though always so that its substance was not lost or seriously endangered.

Dismissing, then, the *a priori* argument that the Church would certainly be Divinely guided in her choice of a text, we are forced to deal with the problem in accordance with the established principles of textual science. Here too Burgon and Miller claim a verdict, and that principally on the ground of the enormous numerical preponderance of witnesses in their favour. Again and again they contrast the hundreds of manuscripts found upon the one side with the mere handful which is opposed to them, and to which modern editors have almost unanimously pinned their faith. " Is it likely," says Burgon,[1] " is it in any way credible, that we can be warranted in rejecting the testimony of (suppose) 1490 ancient witnesses, in favour of the testimony borne by (suppose) ten ? " " What," asks Mr. Miller,[2] " would an editor of Sophocles do under such circumstances ? " The answer to this query is simple. He would do precisely as Hort and the majority of editors have done. There are about 104 MSS. of Sophocles ; yet the evidence of a very large majority of these is wholly disregarded by all editors. One manuscript (L, in the Laurentian Library at Florence) is of predominant

---

[1] *Traditional Text*, p. 45.

[2] *The Oxford Debate on Textual Criticism*, p. 6 : " Suppose you are sitting at the elbow of an editor of *Agamemnon*, or the *Trachiniae*, or whatever it may be of Sophocles, you would see that in his very wildest dreams he would never conceive on any difficult passage of such an immense mass of evidence being at hand as we have in this case on the one side set aside by those few." The form of expression is odd, but the intention is clear.

authority; two others (A and Γ) are of considerable value; the rest have little independent worth, but only support one or other of the leaders, or diverge into palpable error. The weight attached by all editors to LAΓ in comparison with the remaining 101 MSS. is even greater than that which most modern editors attach to אBDLT and the early versions in the Gospels. So too with Virgil; out of the hundreds of existing MSS., even Henry (who devoted far greater pains to the collection of evidence than any other editor of the poet) only quotes the seven great MSS. and some seventy minor MSS. (and these last only in numerical groups, not as individuals). So, in fact, with every other classical author; in every case where any considerable number of MSS. exists, it is found that nearly everything depends upon a few leading authorities, all the rest being relegated to the background and consulted only under special circumstances.

When, therefore, Burgon and Miller condemn the modern editors of the New Testament, from Lachmann to Hort, for their preference of a few generally early MSS. and versions to the great mass of later authorities, they are in fact impugning the universally accepted principles of textual criticism. The earliest printed texts of the classical authors were in nearly all cases based upon comparatively late manuscripts, because these were the most numerous and accessible at the time; but scientific criticism has uniformly shown that the texts so obtained are unsound, and that recourse must be had to a select group of a few authorities, generally those of earliest date. In some instances a single MS. is held to outweigh all its rivals, except where it is manifestly corrupt. The Laurentian MSS. of Aeschylus, Sophocles, and Aristotle's *Ethics*, the Paris MSS. of Plato's *Republic* and of Demosthenes, the Urbinas of Isocrates, enjoy a pre-eminence over all other authorities in their respective spheres, which even Hort would hardly claim for the Codex Vaticanus. In short, what Burgon and Miller persist in regarding as a paradox is in fact a commonplace of textual criticism.

Of course it is still possible for the advocates of the Traditional Text to maintain that the case of the New Testament is unlike that of all other books, and that Lachmann and his followers have erred in the group of witnesses which they have selected as the best. No doubt ℵ and B are older than any other MSS. which we possess, and as a rule the earlier authorities are ranged upon the same side ; but age, though it raises a presumption in favour of superior accuracy, is not decisive, and there would be nothing *prima facie* contrary to sound textual criticism in preferring A and C, or N and Φ, to ℵ and B as standards of the true text. The comparison between these types of text must be made upon their merits, and any one is perfectly within his rights in defending the Traditional Text as *intrinsically* superior to its rival. Here the question of relative originality comes in. So long as opposing critics content themselves with asserting their preference for this reading or for that, on grounds of internal fitness, little progress can be made. The personal equation is too hard to allow for in such a controversy. But if it can be shown that one type of text goes back to an earlier date than another, or represents a primary as opposed to a secondary stage of development, then the presumption is very strong in favour of the text so guaranteed.

It is on this crucial point of the controversy that the patristic evidence becomes of decisive value. Hort, as we have seen, appeals to it as showing that the Traditional Text is characterised by many readings which cannot be traced back farther than the fourth century,—readings which, moreover, have in his eyes the appearance of a secondary character, as derived from pre-existent readings which are found in the other groups of authorities. Here is a plain issue. If it can be shown that the readings which Hort calls " Syrian " existed before the end of the fourth century, the keystone would be knocked out of the fabric of his theory ; and since he produced no statistics in proof of his assertion, his opponents were perfectly at liberty to challenge it. It must be admitted that Mr. Miller has not shirked the test. A considerable part of his work as editor of Dean Burgon's papers has taken the form of a classification of patristic quotations, based upon the great indices which the Dean left behind him,[1] according as they testify for or against the Traditional Text of the Gospels.

The results of his examination are stated by him as follows.[2] Taking the Greek and Latin (not the Syriac) Fathers who died before A.D. 400, their quotations are found to support the Traditional Text in 2630 instances, the "neologian" in 1753. Nor is this majority due solely to the writers who belong to the end of this period. On the contrary, if only the earliest writers be taken, from Clement of Rome to Irenaeus and Hippolytus, the majority in favour of the Traditional Text is proportionately even greater, 151 to 84. Only in the Western and Alexandrian writers do we find approximate equality of votes on either side. Further, if a select list of thirty important passages be taken for detailed examination, the preponderance of early patristic evidence in favour of the Traditional Text is seen to be no less than 530 to 170, a quite overwhelming majority.

Now it is clear that if these figures were trustworthy, there would be an end to Hort's theory, for its premises would be shown to be thoroughly unsound. An examination of them, however, shows that they cannot be accepted as representing in any way the true state of the case. In the first place, it is fairly certain that critical editions of the several Fathers, if such existed, would show that in many cases the quotations have been assimilated in later MSS. to the Traditional Text,

---

[1] See above, p. 262.

[2] *Traditional Text*, pp. 94-122. The examination was confined to the Gospels, the textual problem being both harder and more important in these books.

whereas in the earlier they agree rather with the
" Neutral " or " Western " witnesses. For this defect,
however, Mr. Miller cannot be held responsible. It will
be long before critical editions of all the Fathers have
been completed, and meanwhile he might legitimately
use the materials accessible to him; and the errors arising
from this source would hardly affect the general result to
any very serious extent. The real fallacy in his statistics
is different, and is revealed in the detailed examination
of the thirty select passages. From these it is clear
that he has wholly misunderstood Hort's contention.
The thirty " traditional " readings, which he shows to be
so overwhelmingly vindicated by the Fathers, are not
what Hort would call pure " Syrian " readings at all. In
nearly every case they have Western or Neutral attestation
in addition to that of the later authorities. Thus the insertion of Matthew xvii. 21 is supported by DL and the
Old Latin version ; Matthew xviii. 11 by D, the Old Latin
and Curetonian Syriac ; ἀγαθέ in Matthew xix. 16 by the
Old Latin, Curetonian and Sinaitic Syriac, Bohairic and
Sahidic ; ἔρημος in Matthew xxiii. 38 by אD, the Old
Latin, and most Coptic MSS. ; the last twelve verses of St.
Mark by D, the Old Latin (except *k*), Curetonian Syriac,
and most Bohairic MSS. ; Luke xxiv. 40 by אBL,
the Bohairic, etc. ; John xxi. 25 by every authority
except א, and every editor except Tischendorf. In short,
Mr. Miller has evidently reckoned on his side every
reading which occurs in the Traditional Text, regardless
of whether, on Hort's principles, they are old readings
which kept their place in the Syrian revision, or secondary
readings which were then introduced for the first time.
According to Hort, the Traditional Text is the result of
a revision in which old elements were incorporated ; and
Mr. Miller merely points to some of these old elements,
and argues therefrom that the whole is old. It is clear
that by such argumentation Hort's theory is untouched.

So far, then, as the central point of Hort's theory is
concerned, namely, the secondary nature of the Traditional

Text, it has stood the test of twenty years' criticism, and is now taken for granted by most scholars. The discoveries which have been made since the theory was put forth, such as the Sinaitic Syriac version and the Diatessaron, have fallen into line precisely as Hort would have wished, and have supplied a most valuable test, because one which Hort could not have reckoned upon when writing his *Introduction*. The more the evidence as to the earliest texts of the New Testament is examined (and much has been done in this direction in the last twenty years), the more certain does it appear that the type of text to which we are accustomed did not come into existence until the fourth century. The texts in use before that date show great variety and fluctuation ; but the characteristic features of the " Syrian " text are not yet visible.

There is, however, still room for question as to the manner in which the *a*-text came into existence. Hort holds that it is the result of deliberate revision : " The Syrian text must in fact be the result of a ' recension ' in the proper sense of the word, a work of attempted criticism, performed deliberately by editors and not merely by scribes " ;[1] and he divides it into two stages, in order to account for the phenomena presented by the Peshitto version, which seems to offer the " traditional " text in a somewhat earlier form than the majority of Greek MSS. In connection with the earlier stage, he mentions tentatively the name of Lucian [ob. A.D. 311], whom we know to have been the author of a revision of the Septuagint conducted upon similar lines ; but there is no direct evidence to associate him with the New Testament, and Hort does not press the suggestion. Indeed the absence of evidence points the other way ; for it would be very strange, if Lucian had really edited both Testaments, that only his work on the Old Testament should be mentioned in after times. The same argument tells against any theory of a deliberate revision at any

---

[1] *Introduction*, p. 133.

definite moment. We know the names of several revisers of the Septuagint and the Vulgate, and it would be strange if historians and Church writers had all omitted to record or mention such an event as the deliberate revision of the New Testament in its original Greek. It seems probable, therefore, that the Syrian revision was rather the result of a tendency spread over a considerable period of time than of a definite and authoritative revision or revisions, such as produced our English Authorised and Revised Versions. We have only to suppose the principle to be established in Christian circles in and about Antioch, that in the case of divergent readings being found in the texts copied, it was better to combine both than to omit either, and that obscurities and roughnesses of diction should be smoothed away as much as possible. Such a principle is a natural one in an uncritical age, and this hypothesis accounts not only for the absence of specific reference to a revision, but also for the Peshitto evidence above mentioned. The process would no doubt be assisted and accelerated, if, as Dr. Salmon has suggested,[1] the texts current in any district depended largely upon the bishop or clergy who regulated the lessons to be read in church, and who could thereby familiarise the congregation with the type of text preferred by them. The point is that the Syrian revision was a long-continued process, not a single act. Nor is it clear that Hort meant much otherwise, though on a first reading his words convey the impression that he did. He speaks of deliberate criticism, of the work of editors as opposed to scribes, and he refers to two stages in the work separated by an interval of time. But he does not say that these two stages were the result of two definite and authoritative revisions; his words need mean no more than that we happen to have evidence, in the Peshitto and the Greek MSS., which shows us the extent to which the continuous process had gone at two particular moments. At any rate it involves very little modification of Hort's theory to treat it in this

---

[1] *Some Points in the Textual Criticism of the New Testament*, pp. 77-79.

way; and this modification is now commonly made by students of textual criticism.

With regard to the authorities in which the a-text is to be found, it will have been seen from the preceding discussion that no full enumeration is possible. The " Syrian " or " traditional " text may be presumed to be found in any MS. of which the contrary is not stated. In the Gospels the list of authorities of this class is generally headed by A and C, though both are free from many later corruptions. The purple MSS., NΣΦ, represent a further advance in the traditional direction; but the most typical members of the a-text are the late uncials EFKMSUΠ. With these go the great mass of the minuscules, and the later Fathers. Of the versions, the Peshitto generally belongs to this family, but (as has been stated above) to a relatively early stage in its development; while all the later versions, and most late MSS. of the early versions, are more or less affected by its influence. Readings attested only by the authorities here enumerated may almost certainly be regarded as "Syrian." In the Acts and Catholic Epistles, A and C cease to belong predominantly to this type, and the other uncials above mentioned do not contain these books. The leading representatives of the a-type here are $H_2 K_2$ (the Catholic Epistles only) $L_2 P_2$, with the large majority of minuscules, and the versions and Fathers as before. For the Pauline Epistles the available uncials are $K_2 L_2 P_2$; for the Apocalypse $B_2 P_2$. Small fragments and MSS. which have not yet been adequately examined (such as S_2 נב) are not taken into this reckoning, though the age of these four uncials makes it probable that they belong to the same class. Further details as to the text of the uncials of the a-type will be found in Weiss' treatises, summarised on pp. 264-5 above.

§ 2. *The β-text*

Acceptance of Hort's theory of the secondary nature of the a-text does not, however, necessarily involve acceptance of his views with regard to the β-text, to which he gives the designation of " Neutral " ; and the character of this type of text must be separately examined.   Hort finds this text pre-eminently in the Codex Vaticanus (B) ; indeed one may almost define his " Neutral " text as the text of B (scribe's blunders excluded), and of other MSS. so far as they agree with B.   The most notable exception to this rule occurs in the case of certain verses (mostly in the latter chapters of St. Luke) which are found in B and the great majority of MSS., but are omitted in D and other authorities of the δ-class.   These verses Hort believes not to have formed part of the original text, and designates as " Western non-interpolations."   Except in this special case, the authority of B is predominant with him ; if with other support, well and good (unless the company is very suspicious), but if alone, still it cannot safely be rejected.   The authority found oftenest among its allies is אּ, and these two MSS. must have had some common ancestor short of the original autographs ; but the differences between them are sufficiently numerous and important to show that this common ancestor was not a very near one.   Other authorities, of which more will be said below, add their testimony from time to time to the β-text ; but the predominant element in it is always the Codex Vaticanus.

Now this predominance assigned to one manuscript among thousands (though we have shown parallels to it on a smaller scale in the case of many classical authors) is very striking, and has naturally been 'fixed on as a point of attack by the opponents of Hort's system.   The independent student also may well hesitate before he admits it.   It is therefore important to notice that Hort does not stand alone in his preference for B.   Weiss, who will have nothing to do with Hort's classification, or with any far-reaching classification, of authorities, is not less positive in his exaltation of B above all other MSS.   As has been stated above (pp. 264-5) he regards it as the only MS. of the New Testament which has escaped deliberate revision, and estimates that in no less than 437 places it has the true reading alone (alone, that is, among the uncials, to which his examination is confined). This result of a wholly independent examination, coincident as it is with the general judgment of textual scholars in the last century, may go far towards reconciling the student to the idea of this marked superiority on the part of one MS. among so many. But it also increases the necessity of considering carefully the history of this MS., and the extent to which this admission of its excellence carries us.

What, in short, is the β-text (i.e. the text of B, purged of its obvious errors and amended in the comparatively few places in which it seems certainly inferior to some other authority)? Is it a close approximation to the original text of the New Testament as it left its authors' hands, or is it merely one among several local texts which the chances of time have brought down to us? In Hort's eyes it is the former, and Weiss appears substantially to agree with him. Salmon, on the other hand, considers that it cannot be shown to be more than an Alexandrian text of good character, traceable perhaps to the second century, but not to be carried with any certainty to an earlier period than that.[1] He would grant it a high character for truth, but would not allow it a monopoly of that virtue. The δ-text, for example, though no doubt less trustworthy on the whole, may yet often preserve the true reading when B and its fellows have gone astray. Its allies, it will be observed, are mainly MSS. and versions connected with Egypt, and the Fathers who confirm it most often are Origen and his followers in Egypt. Is it not therefore probably a local text,—the text of Egypt, as the δ-text is the text (according to Salmon) of Rome,—preferable no doubt as a rule, but not invariably so?

The problem would be nearer solution if we could determine with any certainty the place in which B was

---

[1] *Textual Criticism of the New Testament*, p. 52 ff.

written. There is a growing tendency, as has been indicated above (p. 67), to refer it to the library at Caesarea, founded by Origen's disciples, Eusebius and Pamphilus; but, as has there been shown, the evidence is far from conclusive. If, however, the statement is made a little wider, and B and א are connected with the Origenian school of textual criticism, whether in Alexandria or in Caesarea, the evidence in support of it is more adequate. Directly or indirectly, then, it would appear that we must look to Egypt for the origin of the β-text, of which these MSS. are the principal representatives. So far, in fact, the view of Salmon, that it is an Alexandrian text of good character, would seem to be justified; but it is less easy to follow him when he proceeds to treat it as more or less equally balanced in authority by the "Western" text, which he localises in Rome. It is not sufficient to assign each type of text to a certain locality. The credentials of the localities must also be examined, as well as the character of the text associated with them. Now, in the first place, we have no sufficient proof that the Western text took its rise in Rome at all; on the contrary, as will be shown below, the available evidence connects it rather with other localities of less imposing station in the ecclesiastical world. Next, even if the association of the δ-type of text with Rome be admitted, it gives little or no guarantee for the quality of the text. Rome had no traditions of textual scholarship in regard to Greek literature, and scholarly accuracy is not the predominant characteristic of the early Fathers of the Western Church. Alexandria, on the other hand, was the home of textual criticism and of minute scholarship. There questions of text would be carefully considered and scientifically decided. The traditions of heathen scholarship could not but affect the manner in which the text of the Scriptures was treated, especially from the moment when Christianity was recognised by the state. When, then, we say that the β-text is an Alexandrian text of good quality, representing, if not the text as edited by Origen, at least the kind of text which he selected as the basis of his labours (and it will be remembered that this is the conclusion to which the study of the Old Testament text leads us, see p. 68 above), we are giving it a very high claim to authority. Such a text would not be immaculate; it might have suffered something from the ordinary risks of transmission; it might have suffered from deliberate alterations of a too pedantic critic; but it would probably have been based on an intelligent comparison of authorities, conducted by a scholar or scholars accustomed to the scientific criticism of texts.

Admitting, therefore, Salmon's contention that the β-text cannot be shown to be more than an Alexandrian text, it is still possible to go far in the direction of giving it the position of supreme authority which is claimed for it by Hort and Weiss. *A priori*, such a text has more chance of accuracy than one produced in less critical surroundings; and *a posteriori* it is found to have a very high proportion of readings which textual science pronounces to be authentic. No doubt we reserve the right to revise the verdict of Alexandria in cases where we have evidence of the existence of other very ancient readings. The hypothetical Alexandrian critics, as will be shown later in treating of the δ-text, must have had before them texts of the type which we now call "Western"; and we may use our own judgment as to whether they were always right in their rejection of them. At the same time we shall do well to attach considerable weight to the fact that they did so reject them; for they are not likely to have done so without reason, and they stood very much nearer to the original autographs than we do. It is also important to remember that, in the judgment of such a scholar as Weiss, whose life has been spent in the study of the New Testament, the readings of B have not the character of a deliberate revision, but rather of a tradition generally faithful, though marred by superficial blunders in its later stages; while the a-text presents throughout the phenomena of deliberate change. In the β-text, therefore, we may see the results of conscientious protection of the sacred text; in the α-text, the results of injudicious and unscientific editing; while the δ-text, of which we shall have to speak later, if it is free from editorial handling, has also escaped the protection of a literary conscience and the environment of textual scholarship.

With regard to the authorities for the β-text, it will have been seen that B is by far the most important, and next to it is ℵ. Nearest to these come, in the Gospels, LRTZΞ (and Δ in Mark), with the more mixed texts of PQ and Ψ (especially in Mark), and with support occasionally from A and C, when these have escaped the emendation characteristic of the α-text. Among the minuscules the greatest approximation to the β-type is shown by Evan. 33, the group 1-118-131-209, 59, 157, 431, 582, 892; but all of these have a greater or less degree of admixture with other elements. The whole group headed by Λ (see p. 100), which claims connexion with Jerusalem, may also be reckoned as having some kinship with this type of text. Of the versions the Bohairic is the leading representative of this text; but there are considerable traces of it in the Sahidic and Palestinian Syriac. Jerome's revision of the Old Latin was also based on MSS. of this type; but the Vulgate (being a revision of a version of the δ-type, considerably contaminated with the α-type, by the help of MSS. of the β-type) is of too mixed a character to be reckoned wholly with any one family. Finally, of the Fathers Origen is by far the most important witness to the β-type, though he also exhibits the δ-type in some of his works. Clement of Alexandria belongs more decidedly to the δ-family, but is also found supporting the β-text. Indeed it must be remembered throughout that the β and δ authorities are often found in alliance, such readings being presumably parts of the very ancient text common to both, and therefore possessing an almost irresistible claim on our acceptance.

In the Acts and Catholic Epistles the authorities for the β-text are substantially the same, after deducting those which only contain the Gospels. A and C, however, are found oftener in accord with אB. To these must be added the minuscule Act. 61, and to a less extent 31 and the Euthalian group 15, 40, 83, 232, 243, 256, 334, 393.

In the Pauline Epistles[1] אB are again the principal representatives of the β-text, but B has not here quite the same predominance as elsewhere, and is found not infrequently supporting variants characteristic of the δ-text. On the other hand, AC definitely part company with the a-text, and must be reckoned with either the β or γ-text; so that where B joins the δ-text, אAC may be taken to stand for the β-text. L_2M_8 and sometimes P_2 (which has a better text here than in the Acts and Cath.) are also found in the same group. Further, for most of the Pauline Epistles we have the evidence of H_8, representing the text of Pamphilus in the library of Caesarea (see p. 87); and with this is associated the third corrector of א, known as א^c, who similarly claims the authority of Pamphilus (see p. 52), and whose readings are found to agree generally with those of H_8. If the connexion of the Armenian version with the text of Euthalius can be made out, it likewise will have to be added to this group. Among the cursives Paul. 1, 17, 31, 47, 67**, 108, 238, seem to deserve most notice, together with the Euthalian 81, 83, 93, 379, 381, and the upper writing of P_2.

In the Apocalypse B fails us, and the β-text is represented by אAC, but especially by A. The cursives which approximate most to this type are Apoc. 1, 7, 28, 35, 38, 68, 79, 87, 95, 96.

§ 3. *The γ-text*

If, then, the origin of the β-text be traced to Alexandria, what is to become of the γ-text, which Hort calls

---

[1] On the textual criticism of the Pauline Epistles see Sanday and Headlam, *Romans*, pp. lxiii.-lxxiv.

" Alexandrian "?   Has it any real independent existence ?
There is no doubt that the readings which Hort thus
designates occur in MSS. of Egyptian origin ; but it may
be questioned whether they represent any distinct tradition,
especially when it is remembered that this type of text
occurs in no single MS. throughout, but is embodied in
isolated readings in MSS. which otherwise are of " Neutral "
or " Syrian " or " Western " character.   Dr. Salmon goes
so far as to suggest that " Alexandrian " readings are
merely the residuum of the Egyptian text which does not
happen to be found in B ; and clearly our view of the
γ-text depends very largely on our view of the character
of B and the β-text.   If that is due to the revision of an
Alexandrian editor or editors, then the γ-text is simply
a congeries of readings current in Egypt which did not
commend themselves to that editor or editors ; while if
the β-text, though preserved mainly in Egypt, owes little
or nothing to editorial revision, but is substantially a
pure or " neutral " fount of text, then the γ-text may
embody the results of editorial revision in Alexandria.
The last is, of course, Hort's view, and he would regard
the readings in question as due to the scholarly pre-
possessions of Alexandrian scribes and editors, who
introduced verbal alterations into the sacred text in
accordance with their ideas of correctness and style.

The tendency of recent discoveries is rather to confirm
the existence of a separate type of text in Egypt, distinct
from that of B.   The extant fragments of the Sahidic
version have greatly increased in number since Hort
wrote, and the Middle Egyptian version is beginning to
take concrete shape.   In both of these we seem to see
traces of an Egyptian family of text distinct from that
of B.   An example may be found in the recently
discovered bilingual fragment, containing about two
chapters of St. John in Greek and Middle Egyptian,
briefly described as T^a above (p. 96).   The affinities of
this MS. are emphatically with its fellow bilingual T^b and
with L, and with A and C in their non-Syrian readings,

but very much less with B, and decidedly not with D
or א. It is a text neither "Western" nor "Syrian,"
and yet not precisely the text of B, though agreeing with
it in the more important variants. Thus it possesses
precisely the characteristics which Hort would assign
to his "Alexandrian" text, though (as it comes from
Central Egypt and has no demonstrable connexion with
Alexandria) it might perhaps more properly be called
"Egyptian"; and if we had the whole MS. we might apparently possess a complete representative of this type. At
any rate it tends to establish the separate existence of such
a type of text; and all that remains to do is to consider
its relations with the β-text.

After all, there is no insuperable difficulty in imagining
the existence of two or more types of text in the same
country. Indeed this must have been the case in Egypt,
since, as will be shown below, there is good evidence that
in very early times the δ-text was current in Egypt as
elsewhere. Its subsequent disappearance may be ascribed
to the higher level of textual scholarship in that country;
but it does not follow that it left only one uniform text
behind. If the β-text is due to a highly enlightened
criticism, which generally succeeded in selecting authentic
readings without a large admixture of editorial revision,
the γ-text may be due to a somewhat less successful
attempt in the same direction, or to subsequent modifications of that rescued text. A somewhat similar
phenomenon is found in the case of the Old Testament
Septuagint text. Here it is known that an edition was
prepared in Egypt by Hesychius, and the question is
in what group of manuscripts to look for this edition.
Ceriani finds it in the Codex Alexandrinus (A), the original
text of the Marchalianus (Q), and in certain cursives;
while Cornill refers it to another group of cursives and
the Coptic versions, akin to the MSS. just mentioned, but
presenting in his view more of the character of a formal
and authorised edition. It is immaterial for our present
purpose to discuss which of the two is right; all that is

important is to observe that we have here two groups of MSS., both connected with Egypt and showing clear signs of affinity with one another, yet recognisably distinct.

This, then, is the view of the γ-text to which the evidence seems at present to point. It is a type of text demonstrably connected with Egypt, being found in the Coptic versions, the bilingual fragments, and MSS. which, like L, are associated with that country. It has affinities with the β-text, which we have more doubtfully assigned to Egypt also, so that in the more important variations the two groups ordinarily agree with one another. It is therefore substantially a sound and good text, though the scholars who have examined the evidence most closely regard it as showing some signs of deliberate revision ; whence, in case of divergence, the presumption is rather in favour of its rival. Future discoveries of MSS. in Egypt, which may be confidently looked for, will probably enable this theory to be tested decisively in the future ; and the increase of our knowledge of the Sahidic and Middle Egyptian versions, which may be expected from the same source, will have an important bearing on the solution of the problem.

Meanwhile the authorities to which we must look chiefly for readings of the γ-type are אACLT*·³Ψ, and (in the Acts and Epistles) ℑ₂, with the various Coptic versions. None of these authorities is wholly of this type throughout, all being found (as has been seen above) in some cases with the β-group and in others with the a-group ; but where these groups can be separately distinguished, then any residuum which is supported by some of the authorities above enumerated may be safely regarded as " Alexandrian." For instance, if the authorities for a set of variants in a given place fall into the following groups (1) אB, (2) CLT Boh., (3) AEFK, etc., or (1) BD Boh. Syrr., (2) ALT Mid. - Eg., (3) EFKU, etc., there can be no doubt that they represent the β- γ- and a-types of text respectively. Of the Fathers, Origen and Clement are those in whose writings this text is most likely to be found; but here again it is intermixed with readings of the β- and δ-types, and can only be identified when these two possibilities have been eliminated.

§ 4. *The δ-text*

The most difficult question relating to the history of the New Testament text still remains to be answered, namely, What is the origin of the δ-type of text, or, as Hort calls it, the Western text? If this question could be satisfactorily answered, the key to the whole history would be in our possession. It is a type of text which it is impossible to believe to be authentic as a whole, and yet it can be traced back to sub-apostolic times and is widely spread throughout the Christian world. How did such a text come into existence, and what is the value of it to us to-day in our search for the primitive text of the New Testament?

The character of the δ-text has been described already in connexion with the MS. which is its principal Greek representative, the Codex Bezae. It is marked by many additions, great and small, to the common text, and by a few striking omissions; by a multitude of small and apparently pointless verbal variations; by frequent changes in the order of words; and by frequent incorporations from, or assimilations to, the parallel narratives in the other Gospels. In the Epistles this last form of corruption is of course absent, and the total amount of variation is much less; on the other hand, in the Acts, which equally escapes assimilation, the total amount of variation is very great. Indeed it is in this book and its companion, the Gospel of St. Luke, that the divergence of the δ-text alike from the a-text and the β-text is most marked: a phenomenon which has given rise to a special explanation, of which more will have to be said below.

The local distribution of the δ-text is a point of considerable importance. Originally observed most in the Old Latin version, it received the name of "Western";

and by this title it has been very generally known since the promulgation of Hort's theory. The title is, however, inadequate and misleading. The discovery of the Curetonian Syriac showed that this type of text was also current in Syria at a very early date; and the more recent discovery of the Sinaitic Syriac has established this fact yet more clearly. It has also been shown that Tatian's Diatessaron was compiled from a text of the same character, and that the primitive Armenian version was derived from a similar source. Hence it is clear that this type of text was at home in the East as well as in the West, and it has been plausibly suggested that the connecting link may be found in the Eastern origin of the Church of Gaul. Irenaeus, the pupil of Polycarp in Asia Minor, was also subsequently Bishop of Lyons; and his writings show that he used a Bible text of this character. Is it not reasonable, then, to suppose that he and his companions carried this text to Gaul, and that thence it became the parent of the Old Latin version?

It is, however, becoming more and more clear that the range of the δ-text was not confined even to the Syriac and Latin-speaking Churches. It is found even in Egypt, the headquarters of scientific criticism. Hort himself noticed [1] that Western quotations hold a prominent place in some of the writings of Origen and in Clement of Alexandria; and a detailed study of the New Testament quotations of Clement [2] has confirmed this view decisively. Hence Egypt must be added to Syria and the West as one of the early homes of the δ-text; the number of places in which it was not known is becoming small; and the inappropriateness of the designation "Western" becomes increasingly evident. [3]

---

[1] *Introduction*, p. 113.

[2] P. M. Barnard, *The Biblical Text of Clement of Alexandria* (*Texts and Studies*, v. 5: Cambridge, 1899).

[3] Mr. Miller has tried "Syro-Low-Latin," but this is too cumbrous for practical use, and still is not exhaustive. A non-committal designation, such as "the δ-text," seems preferable, if only scholars in general would agree to adopt it. For a suggestion that Antioch was the original centre of the δ-text, see p. 170.

It is also clear that its origin must be referred to a very early date. Both the Old Syriac and the Old Latin versions are very ancient, and their common origin must go back almost to primitive times. A more precise proof is given by the early Fathers. In all the earliest Christian writers whose works have come down to us, the δ-text is predominant. It is found in Justin and in Tatian, in the heretic Marcion and in Irenaeus, in Origen and in Clement of Alexandria ; and if the list is not still longer, this is probably due to the scantiness of the remains of the earliest Christian literature. Clearly a type of text which is found everywhere where we have evidence, in Syria, in Egypt, and in the Latin-speaking West, is one whose character must be closely scrutinised, and investigated without prejudice.

Until recently the claims of the " Western " text met with scant consideration and universal rejection. Its variations, alike from the Textus Receptus and from the leading uncials, were so numerous and apparently so arbitrary that little or no weight was attached to them ; and the small band of witnesses (principally D and the Old Latin version) was treated almost as a negligeable quantity in the constitution of the text of the New Testament. Even among themselves they could not agree, the Latin MSS. falling (as we have seen above) into at least three groups, and the several individuals in each group differing markedly from one another. Time and research have not indeed lessened the amount of internal difference, but they have widened our general conception of the character of the family as a whole. They have shown that the δ-text is earlier in date and more universally disseminated in the Christian world of the second century than had previously been realised ; and they have led scholars to look further for an explanation of its origin.

The most important of these theories with regard to the " Western " text is that which has recently been put forward by Prof. F. Blass of Halle, the well-known classical scholar, whose experience in editing the texts of the Greek classics has stood him in good stead in dealing with the analogous problems connected with the New Testament.[1] His attention has been directed mainly to the two books of St. Luke, in which the variations are the most strongly marked; but it is evident that his results affect the entire question of the δ-text. Briefly, his theory is that Luke prepared two editions of each of his works, and that the δ-text represents one of these editions, and the β-text the other; the α-text being obviously secondary and not entering therefore into consideration. He supposes that Luke wrote his Gospel in Palestine, and that subsequently, on his coming to reside in Rome with St. Paul, he was asked by the Christians there for copies of his work, and thereupon wrote it out again for them, with such alterations as an author naturally feels at liberty to make in transcribing his own books. Similarly, in the case of the Acts, one copy was no doubt made for Theophilus, to whom it is addressed, another for the Church in general; verbal, and occasionally even substantial, alterations being made in the later copy. The natural tendency of such a revision, in Prof. Blass' opinion, would be to abbreviate by the omission of what seemed to be superfluous; hence in each case the shorter text is to be regarded as the later. The result of an investigation upon these lines is to show that the " Western " or δ-text, or, as Blass calls it, the Roman text, consists in fact of the later edition of the Gospel and the earlier of the Acts; while the " Neutral " or β-text, which Blass calls Antiochene, consists of the earlier edition of the Gospel and the later of the Acts.

This theory of a double edition is not wholly new, the idea having been propounded, more or less independently, by different writers at different times. The first statement of it appears to have been made by Jean Leclerc (Johannes Clericus) early in the eighteenth century, and it

[1] For English readers his results will be found most conveniently set forth, in a fresh and vigorous style, in his *Philology of the Gospels* (Macmillan, 1898). The fuller statement of his case is contained in his editions of the Acts (Teubner, 1895 and 1896) and Luke (Teubner, 1897).

was mentioned with approval by Bishop Lightfoot, who, however, did not work it out. Blass' statement of it is not merely independent of these precursors, but is also far fuller and more elaborate ; and he alone deserves the credit of having really brought the theory into the arena of criticism and made it an element with which textual scholars in future will have to reckon. More than this, the theory, as stated by him, has received the adhesion of such authorities as Dr. Salmon and Prof. Nestle, so that any one who enters this camp will do so in excellent company. In the present work, the main object is to state the case fairly on either side, so that the student may be in a position to form his own judgment, either for or against the conclusion here arrived at.

A priori, there is no difficulty in accepting the fundamental proposition. It is quite possible that Luke may have revised his own work, and copies of both editions might have survived. We know that certain works of classical literature were issued in two editions (for example Aristophanes' *Clouds* and *Plutus*), and in the informal conditions of publication which must have applied to all Christian books in the earliest times the simultaneous circulation of different editions is quite conceivable. Practically, too, the theory fits in with many of the *data*, and satisfactorily explains some of the principal variations. Many of these are wholly inexplicable on the ground of any ordinary scribal error or licence, and appear to postulate an authoritative revision by some one with special knowledge of the facts in question, and some one who thought he had the right to deal as freely as he pleased with the text. Thus in Acts v. 29, for the ordinary ἀποκριθεὶς δὲ ὁ Πέτρος καὶ οἱ ἀπόστολοι εἶπον· πειθαρχεῖν δεῖ θεῷ μᾶλλον ἢ ἀνθρώποις, the δ-text[1] has

---

[1] Here and elsewhere I have taken the δ-text from Blass' edition of St. Luke and the Acts ; but it must be remembered that the authorities of the δ-type differ very widely among themselves. In the present instance the authorities for the reading here given are the Old Latin MSS. *g* and *h* (Blass' *f*), and Lucifer of Cagliari. The readings quoted in comparison with those of the δ-text are those of the Revisers (see p. 266).

ἀποκριθεὶς δὲ Πέτρος εἶπεν πρὸς αὐτόν· τίνι πειθαρχεῖν δεῖ, θεῷ ἢ ἀνθρώποις; ὁ δὲ εἶπεν· θεῷ. In viii. 24 (the incident of Simon Magus) the δ-text adds the words καὶ πολλὰ κλαίων οὐ διελίμπανεν. In x. 25 (the story of Cornelius and Peter) the ordinary narrative ὡς δὲ ἐγένετο τοῦ εἰσελθεῖν τὸν Πέτρον, συναντήσας αὐτῷ ὁ Κορνήλιος πεσὼν ἐπὶ τοὺς πόδας προσεκύνησεν is replaced by a more detailed description, προσεγγίζοντος δὲ τοῦ Πέτρου εἰς τὴν Καισάρειαν, προδραμὼν εἷς τῶν δούλων διεσάφησεν παραγεγονέναι αὐτόν. ὁ δὲ Κορνήλιος ἐκπηδήσας καὶ συναντήσας αὐτῷ, πεσὼν κ.τ.λ., continuing in the next verse εἶπεν δὲ αὐτῷ ὁ Πέτρος· Τί ποιεῖς; τὸν θεὸν προσκύνει· ἐγὼ γὰρ ἄνθρωπός εἰμι ὡς καὶ σύ. In xi. 2, where the ordinary text has merely ὅτε δὲ ἀνέβη Πέτρος εἰς Ἱεροσόλυμα, διεκρίνοντο πρὸς αὐτὸν οἱ ἐκ περιτομῆς, the δ-text has quite a long addition: ὁ μὲν οὖν Πέτρος διὰ ἱκανοῦ χρόνου ἠθέλησεν πορευθῆναι εἰς Ἱ.· καὶ προσφωνήσας τοὺς ἀδελφοὺς καὶ ἐπιστηρίξας αὐτοὺς ἐξῆλθεν, πολύν τε λόγον ποιούμενος ἐπορεύετο διὰ τῶν χωρῶν διδάσκων αὐτούς. ὅτε δὲ κατήντησεν εἰς Ἱ. καὶ ἀπήγγειλεν αὐτοῖς τὴν χάριν τοῦ θεοῦ, οἱ ἐκ περιτομῆς ἀδελφοὶ διεκρίνοντο πρὸς αὐτόν. In xii. 10 a topographical detail is inserted in the narrative of Peter's miraculous deliverance, καὶ ἐξελθόντες κατέβησαν τοὺς ἑπτὰ βαθμούς. In xiv. 2 (Paul and Barnabas at Iconium) the ordinary text has οἱ δὲ ἀπειθήσαντες Ἰουδαῖοι ἐπήγειραν καὶ ἐκάκωσαν τὰς ψυχὰς τῶν ἐθνῶν κατὰ τῶν ἀδελφῶν, while the δ-text has οἱ δὲ ἀρχισυνάγωγοι τῶν Ἰουδαίων καὶ οἱ ἄρχοντες ἐπήγαγον διωγμὸν κατὰ τῶν δικαίων καὶ ἐκάκωσαν . . . ἀδελφῶν· ὁ δὲ κύριος ἔδωκεν ταχὺ εἰρήνην: continuing in verse 5, καὶ πάλιν ἐπήγειραν διωγμὸν ἐκ δευτέρου οἱ Ἰουδαῖοι σὺν τοῖς ἔθνεσιν, καὶ λιθοβολήσαντες ἐξέβαλον αὐτοὺς ἐκ τῆς πόλεως, καὶ φυγόντες ἦλθον εἰς τὴν Λυκαονίαν, εἰς πόλιν τινὰ καλουμένην Λύστραν. In the list of recommendations in the Jerusalem Council (xv. 29) the δ-text adds a further clause, καὶ ὅσα μὴ θέλετε ἑαυτοῖς γίνεσθαι, ἑτέρῳ μὴ ποιεῖν. In xvi. 35, the narrative of the release of Paul and Silas from Philippi is amplified thus: ἡμέρας δὲ γενομένης, συνῆλθον οἱ στρατηγοὶ ἐπὶ τὸ αὐτὸ εἰς τὴν ἀγοράν, καὶ ἀναμνησθέντες τὸν σεισμὸν τὸν γεγονότα ἐφοβήθησαν, and in verse 39 καὶ παραγενόμενοι μετὰ φίλων πολλῶν εἰς τὴν φυλακήν, παρεκάλεσαν αὐτοὺς ἐξελθεῖν, εἰπόντες· Ἠγνοήσαμεν τὰ καθ᾿ ὑμᾶς, ὅτι ἐστὲ ἄνδρες δίκαιοι. In xvii. 15 an explanatory clause is inserted in the account of Paul's journey from Beroea to Athens; παρῆλθεν δὲ τὴν Θεσσαλίαν· ἐκωλύθη γὰρ εἰς αὐτοὺς κηρύξαι τὸν λόγον. In xviii. 27 a wholly different account is given of the cause of Apollos' journey from Ephesus to Corinth; for whereas the ordinary text has βουλομένου δὲ αὐτοῦ διελθεῖν εἰς τὴν Ἀχαίαν προτρεψάμενοι οἱ ἀδελφοὶ ἔγραψαν τοῖς μαθηταῖς ἀποδέξασθαι αὐτόν, the δ-text states ἐν δὲ τῇ Ἐφέσῳ ἐπιδημοῦντές τινες Κορίνθιοι καὶ ἀκούσαντες αὐτοῦ, παρεκάλουν διελθεῖν σὺν αὐτοῖς εἰς τὴν πατρίδα αὐτῶν· συγκατανεύσαντος δὲ αὐτοῦ, οἱ Ἐφέσιοι ἔγραψαν κ.τ.λ. In xix. 1 a wholly new detail appears in the δ-text: θέλοντος δὲ τοῦ Παύλου κατὰ τὴν ἰδίαν βουλὴν πορεύεσθαι εἰς Ἱεροσόλυμα, εἶπεν αὐτῷ τὸ πνεῦμα ὑποστρέφειν εἰς τὴν Ἀσίαν. In xix. 9, it is stated that Paul taught in the school of Tyrannus ἀπὸ ὥρας πέμπτης ἕως δεκάτης. Similarly in xx. 15 (Paul's voyage towards Jerusalem) between the mention of Samos and Miletus is inserted the additional fact, καὶ μείναντες ἐν Τρωγιλίᾳ, which is a noticeable instance of a reading common to the δ- and a-texts, which is not in the β-text. In xxi. 16 the disciple Mnason is represented as living not in Jerusalem but in a village between that town and Caesarea: οὗτοι δὲ ἦγον ἡμᾶς πρὸς οὓς ξενισθῶμεν, καὶ παραγενόμενοι εἴς τινα κώμην ἐγενόμεθα παρὰ Μνάσωνι Κυπρίῳ, μαθητῇ ἀρχαίῳ· κἀκεῖθεν ἐξιόντες ἤλθομεν εἰς Ἱεροσόλυμα. From xxii. 29 the principal Greek witness for the δ-text, the Codex Bezae, is wanting, but from the remaining witnesses the original form of this type of text can be at least approximately and in substance recovered. In xxiii. 24, besides other variations in the narrative of St. Paul's conveyance as a prisoner to Caesarea, the following clause is inserted: ἐφοβήθη γὰρ μήποτε ἁρπάσαντες αὐτὸν οἱ Ἰουδαῖοι ἀποκτείνωσιν, καὶ αὐτὸς μεταξὺ ἔγκλημα ἔχῃ ὡς χρήματα εἰληφώς. Several phrases also in the letter of Claudius Lysias are altered. In xxv. 24, 25 a passage of some length is inserted in Festus' speech, recapitulating some of the facts already known to the reader from the preceding narrative. The narrative of xxvii. 1 is worded quite differently. In xxvii. 5, in place of the ordinary τό τε πέλαγος τὸ κατὰ τὴν Κιλικίαν καὶ Παμφυλίαν διαπλεύσαντες, the δ-text has καὶ μετὰ ταῦτα διαπλεύσαντες τὸν Κιλίκιον κόλπον καὶ τὸ Παμφύλιον πέλαγος δι' ἡμερῶν δεκάπεντε. On the other hand, the ordinary narrative of xxvii. 11, 12 is concentrated into the single phrase ὁ δὲ κυβερνήτης καὶ ὁ ναύκληρος ἐβουλεύοντο πλεῖν, and the description of the harbour of Phoenix, βλέποντα κατὰ λίβα καὶ κατὰ χῶρον, is omitted. In xxviii. 16 an additional item of information is given in the δ-text, which has been preserved in several MSS. (HLMP) which are not wholly of this type: (ὅτε δὲ εἰσήλθομεν εἰς Ῥώμην) ὁ ἑκατόνταρχος παρέδωκε τοὺς δεσμίους τῷ στρατοπεδάρχῃ, a title which Mommsen has shown may well be accurate.[1] In xxviii. 19, after the words ἀντιλεγόντων δὲ τῶν Ἰουδαίων is added καὶ ἐπικραζόντων, Αἶρε τὸν ἐχθρὸν ἡμῶν, and at the end of the verse ἀλλ' ἵνα λυτρώσωμαι τὴν ψυχήν μου ἐκ θανάτου. Finally in xxviii. 31 the last words of the book, in place of the usual καὶ διδάσκων τὰ περὶ τοῦ Κυρίου Ἰησοῦ Χριστοῦ μετὰ πάσης παρρησίας ἀκωλύτως, the δ-text had something to the following effect: διασχυριζόμενος καὶ λέγων ἀκωλύτως ὅτι οὗτός ἐστιν ὁ Χριστὸς ὁ υἱὸς τοῦ θεοῦ, δι' οὗ μέλλει πᾶς ὁ κόσμος κρίνεσθαι.

Such are some of the more remarkable variants presented by this type of text in this single book of the Acts of the Apostles. In the Gospel of St. Luke they are for the most part less striking, often consisting merely of the omission or insertion of pronouns, the substitution of pronouns for proper names, or *vice versa*, or the inter-

---

[1] *Sitzungsberichte d. Berl. Acad.* 1895, p. 491.

change of καί and δέ. Professor Blass emphasises the fact that the δ-text in the Gospel is characterised by omissions as compared with the α or β type, and in the Acts by additions ; but on an examination of his edition, it is difficult to resist the feeling that this difference is less marked in reality than he represents it, and is partly due to his attaching special weight in the Gospel to those authorities which show omissions, and in the Acts to those which show additions ; and seeing that the authorities for the δ-text are rarely unanimous in support of any given reading, much is necessarily left to the judgment of the editor. An example of the kind of verbal variations characteristic of the δ-text may be given from Luke v. 5-11, where they occur more thickly than usual. The δ-text is given from Blass' edition, and the β-text from the Revisers' Greek Testament, as before.

β-text	δ-text
καὶ ἀποκριθεὶς ὁ Σίμων εἶπεν· Ἐπιστάτα, δι' ὅλης νυκτὸς κοπιάσαντες οὐδὲν ἐλάβομεν· ἐπὶ δὲ τῷ ῥήματί σου χαλάσω τὰ δίκτυα. καὶ τοῦτο ποιήσαντες συνέκλεισαν ἰχθύων πλῆθος πολύ· διερρήγνυτο δὲ τὰ δίκτυα αὐτῶν· καὶ κατένευσαν τοῖς μετόχοις ἐν τῷ ἑτέρῳ πλοίῳ, τοῦ ἐλθόντας συλλαβέσθαι αὐτοῖς· καὶ ἦλθον καὶ ἔπλησαν ἀμφότερα τὰ πλοῖα, ὥστε βυθίζεσθαι αὐτά. ἰδὼν δὲ Σίμων Πέτρος προσέπεσε τοῖς γόνασι τοῦ Ἰησοῦ· λέγων, Ἔξελθε ἀπ' ἐμοῦ, ὅτι ἀνὴρ ἁμαρτωλός εἰμι, Κύριε. θάμβος γὰρ περιέσχεν αὐτόν, καὶ πάντας τοὺς σὺν αὐτῷ, ἐπὶ τῇ ἄγρᾳ τῶν ἰχθύων ὧν συνέλαβον, ὁμοίως δὲ καὶ Ἰάκωβον καὶ Ἰωάννην, υἱοὺς Ζεβεδαίου, οἳ ἦσαν κοινωνοὶ τῷ Σίμωνι. καὶ εἶπε πρὸς τὸν Σίμωνα ὁ Ἰησοῦς, Μὴ φοβοῦ· ἀπὸ τοῦ νῦν ἀνθρώπους ἔσῃ ζωγρῶν. καὶ καταγαγόντες τὰ πλοῖα ἐπὶ τὴν γῆν, ἀφέντες ἅπαντα ἠκολούθησαν αὐτῷ.	ὁ δὲ Σίμων ἀποκριθεὶς εἶπεν· Διδάσκαλε, δι' ὅλης τῆς νυκτὸς κοπιάσαντες οὐδὲν ἐλάβομεν· ἐπὶ δὲ τῷ ῥήματί σου οὐ μὴ παρακούσομαι. καὶ εὐθὺς χαλάσαντες τὰ δίκτυα συνέκλεισαν ἰχθύων πλῆθος, ὥστε τὰ δίκτυα ῥήσσεσθαι. καὶ κατένευον τοῖς μετόχοις τοῖς ἐν τῷ ἑτέρῳ πλοίῳ, τοῦ ἐλθόντας βοηθεῖν αὐτοῖς· ἐλθόντες οὖν ἔπλησαν ἀμφότερα τὰ πλοῖα, ὥστε παρά τι βυθίζεσθαι. ὁ δὲ Σίμων προσέπεσεν αὐτοῦ τοῖς ποσίν, λέγων, Παρακαλῶ, ἔξελθε ἀπ' ἐμοῦ, ὅτι ἀνὴρ ἁμαρτωλός εἰμι, Κύριε. θάμβος γὰρ περιέσχεν αὐτοὺς ἐπὶ τῇ ἄγρᾳ τῶν ἰχθύων ὧν συνέλαβον. ἦσαν δὲ κοινωνοὶ αὐτοῦ Ἰάκωβος καὶ Ἰωάννης, υἱοὶ Ζεβεδαίου. ὁ δὲ εἶπεν πρὸς τὸν Σίμωνα, Μὴ φοβοῦ· ἀπὸ τοῦ νῦν ἀνθρώπους ἔσῃ ζωγρῶν. οἱ δὲ ἀκούσαντες τὰ πλοῖα κατέλειψαν ἐπὶ τῆς γῆς καὶ ἠκολούθησαν αὐτῷ.

A noticeable abbreviation occurs in v. 26, where the δ-text has only καὶ ἐπλήσθησαν θάμβου, λέγοντες, Εἴδομεν παράδοξα σήμερον, in place of καὶ ἔκστασις ἔλαβεν ἅπαντας, καὶ ἐδόξαζον τὸν θεόν, καὶ ἐπλήσθησαν φόβου, λέγοντες ὅτι Εἴδομεν παράδοξα σήμερον. Similarly the δ-text omits v. 39 altogether: καὶ οὐδεὶς πιὼν παλαιὸν θέλει νέον· λέγει γάρ, Ὁ παλαιὸς χρηστός ἐστιν. On the other hand it inserts in place of vi. 5 the story of the man working on the Sabbath day, which has already been quoted above (p. 76). At ix. 55 the δ-text has the rebuke to the sons of Zebedee, οὐκ οἴδατε ποίου πνεύματός ἐστε· ὁ γὰρ υἱὸς τοῦ ἀνθρώπου οὐκ ἦλθε ψυχὰς ἀπολέσαι, ἀλλὰ σῶσαι, which otherwise is found only in late authorities, being omitted by אABCL, etc. At x. 41, 42 the δ-text omits the words μεριμνᾷς καὶ θορυβάζῃ περὶ πολλά· ἑνὸς δέ ἐστι χρεία: but in xi. 2-4 it has the fuller form of the Lord's Prayer, with the further addition (in D only) of the introductory words (ὅταν προσεύχησθε) μὴ βαττολογεῖτε ὡς οἱ λοιποί· δοκοῦσιν γάρ τινες ὅτι ἐν τῇ πολυλογίᾳ αὐτῶν εἰσακουσθήσονται· ἀλλὰ προσευχόμενοι (λέγετε). Another omission (in Dab) occurs at xii. 21, οὕτως ὁ θησαυρίζων ἑαυτῷ καὶ μὴ εἰς θεὸν πλουτῶν. The most important variants, however, whether of omission or addition, occur in the later chapters of the Gospel. Thus the narrative in xix. 31-35 of the procuring of the ass for our Lord's entry into Jerusalem is reduced by a series of excisions to the words, καὶ ἐάν τις ὑμᾶς ἐρωτᾷ, οὕτως ἐρεῖτε, ὅτι ὁ κύριος αὐτοῦ χρείαν ἔχει. καὶ ἀπελθόντες ἀπεκρίθησαν ὅτι Ὁ κύριος αὐτοῦ χρείαν ἔχει. καὶ ἀγαγόντες τὸν πῶλον ἐπέριψαν τὰ ἱμάτια αὐτῶν ἐπ᾽ αὐτὸν καὶ ἐπεβίβασαν τὸν Ἰησοῦν,—a form which cannot be considered probable. After xxi. 36, Blass would insert the narrative of the woman taken in adultery, which is universally admitted to be out of place in St. John; but for this there is no evidence except that of the Ferrar group of minuscules, which inserts the passage after xxi. 38. In the narrative of the institution of the Lord's Supper, the δ-text omits the end of xxii. 19 τὸ ὑπὲρ ὑμῶν διδόμενον· τοῦτο ποιεῖτε εἰς τὴν ἐμὴν ἀνάμνησιν, and the whole of verse 20, καὶ τὸ ποτήριον ὡσαύτως μετὰ τὸ δειπνῆσαι λέγων, Τοῦτο τὸ ποτήριον ἡ καινὴ διαθήκη ἐν τῷ αἵματί μου, τὸ ὑπὲρ ὑμῶν ἐκχυνόμενον. Blass would also

(without MS. authority) eject the rest of verse 19, so that
the institution of the Sacrament would wholly disappear from
this type of the text. On the other hand the incident of the
Bloody Sweat and the Angel of the Agony is included in
the δ-text, though it forms no part of the β-text. On the
saying from the Cross, Πάτερ, ἄφες αὐτοῖς, οὐ γὰρ οἴδασι
τί ποιοῦσι, the authorities of the δ-family are divided,
Blass siding with the Curetonian Syriac and several Old
Latin MSS. (but against Dab, the Sinaitic Syriac, and the
Sahidic) in retaining the words. At xxiii. 53, however,
he follows Dc and the Sahidic in the extraordinary insertion καὶ τεθέντος αὐτοῦ ἐπέθηκεν τῷ μνημείῳ λίθον, ὃν
μόγις εἴκοσι ἐκύλιον, and at xxiv. 1, with the same
authorities, he inserts ἐλογίζοντο δὲ ἐν ἑαυταῖς τίς ἄρα
ἀποκυλίσει τὸν λίθον. In xxiv. 6 the δ-text omits οὐκ
ἔστιν ὧδε, ἀλλ᾽ ἠγέρθη: also the whole of xxiv. 12 ὁ δὲ
Πέτρος ἀναστὰς ἔδραμεν ἐπὶ τὸ μνημεῖον, καὶ παρακύψας
βλέπει τὰ ὀθόνια μόνα· καὶ ἀπῆλθε πρὸς ἑαυτὸν θαυμάζων τὸ
γεγονός, the end of xxiv. 36 καὶ λέγει αὐτοῖς, Εἰρήνη ὑμῖν,
and the whole of xxiv. 40 καὶ τοῦτο εἰπὼν ἔδειξεν αὐτοῖς
τὰς χεῖρας καὶ τοὺς πόδας. Finally, all express mention
of the Ascension disappears from this form of the text, the
words καὶ ἀνεφέρετο εἰς τὸν οὐρανον being omitted, and
only the ambiguous phrase ἀπέστη ἀπ᾽ αὐτῶν retained.

Such being, in outline or selection, the most prominent
data, the question has to be faced, Does Blass' theory
provide an adequate explanation of them? At first sight
it may seem that no one except the author himself could
ever have taken the liberties with the text which are
involved in the greater changes, and that the smaller ones
are such as no copyist or editor would have taken the
trouble to make. That is, in brief, the essence of
Professor Blass' case. There are, however, serious considerations to be taken into account on the other side.
The small verbal changes (individually too unimportant
to be included in the selection given above, and
collectively too numerous) are far from impressing one as
the product of the author's pen. A writer deliberately

condensing his narrative must have done so in a less haphazard manner. Very many of the substitutions of one word for another are inexplicable on any theory of deliberate revision. It would require a disproportionate amount of space to examine the evidence in detail here,[1] but if the reader will compare the two forms of text in a chapter or two of the Gospel or the Acts, he will find it hard to conceive the mind of the author in the production of this supposed revision. Changes which are possible to a careless scribe, or to a writer indifferent as to the precise wording of his text, are incomprehensible as the work of an author transcribing his own composition.

Nor are the larger variants, deliberate though they must have been, satisfactorily explicable on the theory of a revision by the author himself. The additional facts contained in the δ-text of the Acts have, no doubt, the appearance of being due to special knowledge, and might reasonably have been the work of Luke himself; but then the difficulty arises, how to account for their omission in the later version. The economy in space is insignificant, the loss in detail and picturesqueness occasionally great. Some of the supposed omissions are still more improbable, since they occur not only in Luke's own narrative, but in documents which he is quoting. Is it likely that he would have struck out a clause from the recommendations of the Jerusalem Council (Acts xv. 29), or that he would have altered the wording of the letter of Claudius Lysias (xxiii. 26-30)? Similarly, in the Gospel we are asked to believe that Luke in his later edition (in this case represented by the δ-text) altered his narrative of the evening before the Crucifixion so as to omit all mention of the institution of the sacrament of the Lord's Supper, and perhaps even excised the record of one of our Lord's sayings from the Cross. The omissions in chapter xxiv. are surely inexplicable as the deliberate excisions of an

---

[1] A classified enumeration of the variants in D is given in Weiss' *Der Codex D in der Apostelgeschichte* (*Texte und Untersuchungen*, N.F. ii. 1).

author bent on improving his literary style by condensation.[1] Nor is Blass' theory more satisfactory in dealing with the additions which are found in the δ-text of the Gospel. The most important of these is the passage introduced at chapter vi. 5, concerning the man found working on the Sabbath; and to this Blass would add the story of the woman taken in adultery, which the Ferrar MSS. place at the end of chapter xxi., and which Blass believes to have formed part of Luke's " Roman " edition of his Gospel. In both of these cases Blass holds that Luke deliberately withheld these passages from the edition which was intended to circulate in the East, as being likely to give offence to the Jews; while he included them in the edition addressed to his Roman readers, who would not find the same difficulty in them. This explanation, however, overlooks the fact that, according to Blass' own theory, the first edition of the Gospel (that intended for the East) was written at a considerable time before the second edition, when no idea of a Roman edition can have been present in his mind. No deliberate reservation of these narratives for Western readers can possibly have been intended.

And while Blass' theory does not appear to fit the facts with regard to the two books of St. Luke, it is a further objection to it that it does not account for the similar phenomena in the other books of the New Testament. The variants of the δ-text are, no doubt, most conspicuous in St. Luke's Gospel and in the Acts; but

---

[1] Prof. Blass assumes throughout that an author's revision of his work naturally takes the form of condensation, and states that he finds it to be so in his own case; but it may be doubted whether the experience of all authors is the same. A historian is constantly tempted to add fresh facts and arguments to his narrative; and the tendency of most modern books is to increase in size in their successive editions. From this tendency Prof. Blass' own works would not appear to be exempt, his history of Attic Oratory having increased from 1763 pages to 1863 (so far as the second edition has yet appeared), while his introductions to his editions of Aristotle's 'Αθηναίων Πολιτεία and the poems of Bacchylides have grown from twenty-eight pages to thirty-one in the first case, and from sixty-two to seventy-one in the second. If, then, expansion rather than condensation be taken as the sign of a second edition, Blass' views as to the relative priority of the two texts of the works of Luke must be inverted; which will not, however, remove their difficulties.

they are not confined to these books. Similar additions and variations appear, though not so frequently, in the other three Gospels, and to some extent in the Epistles ; though in the latter the authorities of this type are fewer, and have been less fully investigated. For instance, the largest addition of all in the Codex Bezae is the passage inserted after Matthew xx. 28 ; and the omission by D and the Old Latin of Matthew xxi. 44 ("and whosoever shall fall on this stone shall be broken, but on whomsoever it shall fall, it shall grind him to powder") and of the end of John iv. 9 ("for the Jews have no dealings with the Samaritans") are quite of the same nature as the omissions in Luke. Prof. Blass, however, is driven to find different explanations for each of the other Gospels. In Matthew he finds that there is comparatively little divergence between the β-text and the δ-text, and what there is he regards as deliberate interpolation in the latter by very ancient readers. In Mark, on the other hand, where the divergence is greater, he propounds the bold theory that the evangelist originally wrote in Aramaic, that Luke translated his work with additions or alterations of his own, and that this Lucan version circulated side by side with another translation made by some one else.[1] Finally, the variants in the case of St. John's Gospel are assigned to the disciples of the evangelist, who "took the liberty of enlarging the text here and there, of course each in a different way."[2]

This multiplication of hypotheses to account for similar phenomena in the several Gospels is evidently unsatisfactory, and weakens belief in the principal one, which necessitates the others. Indeed, the more this hypothesis is examined, the less does it seem to account for the phenomena of the type of text with which we are now dealing. The Codex Bezae, the principal Greek repre-

[1] For the arguments by which this strange theory is supported, the reader must consult Blass' *Philology of the Gospels*, pp. 190-218. They consist of a succession of hypotheses, each barely possible, and collectively possessing only an infinitesimal degree of probability.

[2] *Ib.* p. 234.

sentative of the δ-text, contains many variants peculiar to itself, and yet of the same character with those which are accepted as belonging to the "Roman" text. Thus it incorporates in Luke the genealogy of our Lord given by Matthew, and in many other passages introduces words or incidents from one Gospel into another. It is quite clear that this cannot be the work of Luke, and Blass does not adopt them in his "Roman" text. It is evident, therefore, that bold revision has been at work on D or its archetype, just as Blass finds it at work in John ; and the question naturally presents itself, Why may not the same cause account for the variants which D shares with other authorities, and which Blass accepts as Lucan ?

What we want, in fact, is some uniform cause applicable to the whole range of phenomena presented by the δ-text, with some special addition to account for their special prominence in the two books of St. Luke. This is not provided by Blass. He merely makes a selection among the variants found in these two books, and labels the text so produced, "Roman." The title is, however, even more "question-begging" than Hort's "Western" or "Syrian," since its localisation is more precise. Yet there is, in point of fact, no evidence connecting the δ-text especially with Rome, and much that connects it with places far removed from Rome. It is found in the Syriac - speaking countries of the East, in the Greek-speaking Church of Egypt, in the Latin-speaking Church of Africa, in the Latin-speaking but Greek-descended Church of Gaul. From Italy and Rome our evidence, with the possible exception of Marcion's, is all of later date. This type of text may have been current there in the first and second centuries, but we have no proof of it. What we do know is that it was current at the earliest date to which our knowledge extends in nearly all the other parts of the world to which the Gospel had been carried,—a phenomenon for which it is difficult to account on the theory that this text was of purely Roman origin, and that rival texts of equal authenticity had already been given to the East by the author himself.

What, then, is the alternative explanation which will fit the facts of the case, if Blass' ingenious hypothesis be discarded? It is that to which allusion has already been made, and which Blass himself applies in the case of the Gospels of Matthew and John, the hypothesis of free handling of the text by scribes and teachers in the early days of Christianity. It must be remembered that the circumstances of the tradition of the New Testament text (and especially in the case of the Gospels) for more than 200 years were wholly unlike those of any other literary work. We have no great libraries enshrining standard copies of the precious volumes, no recognised book-trade multiplying carefully written transcripts of them, no scholars keeping a critical eye on the purity of the text. Instead of all this we have roughly written copies circulating from hand to hand among congregations whose sole care was for the substance, not for the precise wording, of the 'Gospel narrative; we have the danger of destruction impending over them, if they were brought too prominently before the eye of the civil power; we have periods of persecution, during which active search was made for the sacred books of the prohibited sect. Circulating in this irregular fashion, and for the most part among populations with no high standards of literary tradition, it is not surprising that the text was often treated in a way to which we are not accustomed in dealing with the ordinary works of literature which have descended to us from the past. It would not seem unnatural, still less wrong, to insert additional incidents, believed to be authentic, in the narrative of our Lord's life; and verbal changes, whether of pronouns or proper names, or of one synonym for another, would be matters of indifference.[1] To these causes of variation may be added the plausible, though not yet fully developed,

---

[1] A vivid description of the corruptions which may overtake the manuscripts even of works copied under much less unsettled conditions is given by

suggestion of re-translation from the Syriac as a possible factor in the production of this type of text.[1]

So through the outlying tracts of the Roman world, in Syria and Asia Minor, in Africa and Gaul, the books of the New Testament circulated through the first two centuries or more of their existence. There must have been much truth in Jerome's remark, "quot homines, tot paene codices." What we have called the δ-text, indeed, is not so much a text as a congeries of various readings, not descending from any one archetype, but possessing an infinitely complicated and intricate parentage. No one manuscript can be taken as even approximately representing the δ-text, if by "text" we mean a form of the Gospel which once existed in a single manuscript. There are a multitude of readings in D (such as those referred to just now, which incorporate passages from one Gospel into another, or the pseudo-Homeric insertion in Luke xxiii. 53) which no editor can possibly regard as authentic. No two manuscripts of the Old Latin agree with any closeness with one another ; the differences between the two extant codices of the Old Syriac are flagrant ; and the Old Latin and Old Syriac texts differ somewhat markedly from one another. The readings which we group under the head of the δ-text often bear, it is true, the signs of deliberate revision, but never of a coherent and continuous revision. They are the work of many individuals, in many places and at many times, not of a single editor, still less of the original author.

the editor of St. Augustine's *De Civitate Dei*, J. L. Vives (in the preface to the edition of 1555 ; the passage is not in his first edition of 1522) : " Mira dictu res quanta in codicibus varietas, ut unusquisque describentium putaret sibi licere verba arbitratu suo ponere, modo constaret sensus, quasi interpretatio esset, non exscriptio. Ita in hoc libro legas *arbitror*, in illo *puto* ; in hoc *significatum*, in illo *figuratum* ; hic *praesens*, *alibi* iste ; hic habet *ergo*, ille *igitur* ; hic *aeternus*, ille *immortalis* ; hic *flexisse*, ille *deflexisse*, alius *inflexisse*. Sed haec fortasse tolerabilia. Quid illa detracta, quid addita, inversa? Jam quoties erratum, quod versionem lxx. interpretum, quam ubique Augustinus adducit, voluerunt ad hanc nostram detorquere, et ex duabus male cohaerentibus unam facere." It will be observed that three of the most important forms of corruption of the Biblical text are here described : (1) wanton handling of the text, (2) alteration of quotations from their true form into one more familiar to the scribe, (3) conflation.

[1] See above, p. 77 ff.

But it may fairly be asked, how, on this hypothesis, is the special predominance of readings of the δ-type in the two books of St. Luke to be accounted for. It might be possible to frame various hypotheses not more improbable than that which Blass applies to the Gospel of St. Mark, —possible explanations on which no verification can be brought to bear. But the simplest theory perhaps is to suppose that these two books were most exposed to free treatment because they circulated most among the Gentile converts to the Christian faith. The Acts of the Apostles, written by the companion of the great Apostle of the Gentiles, would naturally be a favourite book among the peoples whom that Apostle had been the first to bring into the Church ; and when they desired an authentic narrative of the life of Christ, they would naturally turn to that which came to them with the authority of this same teacher. Circulating in Palestine and Asia Minor and Greece, the Acts might easily receive those touches of local detail which most suggest the author's own hand;[1] while in the case of the Gospel the variants rather suggest free handling in the way of insertion or omission or verbal change than the application of local knowledge. Other explanations might be possible, if we knew more of the circumstances of the production and early circulation of the Christian Scriptures ; but in the present state of our knowledge this seems best to account for the facts as they now lie before us, and to contain in itself nothing either impossible or improbable.

If a clearer understanding of the nature of the δ-text, and therewith of the early history of the New Testament Scriptures, is to be achieved, it will hardly be by heroic measures such as those we have just been considering, but rather through a patient and detailed examination of the various authorities in which it is contained. Each of them possesses a distinct individuality, which requires

---

[1] This, it may be observed, is the explanation offered by Professor Ramsay before the promulgation of Blass' theory. The truth of the local touches impressed him, but he was able to account for them in this way, without attributing them to Luke himself.

careful investigation before its relations with the others can be determined. Most of them have already been described at some length in the preceding chapters. For the Gospels we have pre-eminently D, though it must not be assumed that everything which appears in D is part of the earliest from of the δ-text. Rather it must be regarded as embodying the principles to which the δ-text is due, carried to their farthest extent. No other Greek MS. of the Gospels belongs wholly to this type, though readings characteristic of it appear in אACLΞ, and perhaps in other MSS. Of the minuscules Evan. 473 (Hort's 81) is the most valuable representative of this class; and with it may be mentioned 235, 431, 604, 1071, and Evl. 259. The Ferrar group also (Evann. 13, 69, 124, 346, 348, 556, 561, 624, 626, 788; see p. 112), though agreeing in the main with the ordinary *a*-text, yet in its characteristic features is allied with the δ-text; and Prof. Rendel Harris has sought to establish a Syro-Arabic origin for it, which must be considered in connexion with Dr. Chase's theory of a Syriac origin for the characteristic features of the δ-text in general. But although all these MSS. may be cited as witnesses to the δ-text in greater or less degree, the real strength of its support comes from the Versions (especially the Old Syriac and the Old Latin) and the early Fathers. The Syriac and Latin versions, though often agreeing, appear to represent somewhat different stages in the development of the text. Mr. Burkitt has recently shown[1] that the longer additions to the Gospel text are especially found in the African form of the Old Latin (represented mainly by *ke* and Cyprian), while the smaller additions are especially characteristic of the European Latin (*ab* and their colleagues); and the Old Syriac authorities have some special interpolations peculiar to themselves. Of the two Old Syriac MSS., the Sinaitic undoubtedly represents the earlier and purer form of the version.

[1] *The Old Latin and the Itala* (Cambridge *Texts and Studies*, iv. 5), especially pp. 46-53.

Besides these versions, the Harkleian Syriac and the Sahidic and Armenian must be mentioned among the intermittent supporters of the δ-text. Of the Fathers, it has been shown already that all the earliest among them exhibit texts more or less of the δ-type. Most notable are Tatian, Aphraates, and to a less degree Ephraem, among the Syriac writers ; Justin, Marcion, Irenaeus, and Tertullian among the earliest representatives of the West; Cyprian and Tyconius in Africa at a somewhat later period ; Clement and sometimes even Origen in Egypt. The special importance of these writers has been considered in an earlier chapter.

In the Acts D stands out still more prominently as the representative of the δ-text, through the disappearance of the Old Syriac. It is joined, however, by the other Graeco-Latin MS. E_2, and the minuscules Act. 31, 137, 180, 184, 221 (Hort's 44). The Old Latin attestation is weaker than in the Gospels (see above, p. 176); while the Old Syriac fails entirely. No MS. of it is in existence, and it is only by the indirect evidence which we possess, through the Syriac Fathers, of the existence of an Old Syriac version of the Pauline Epistles, that we are enabled to assume that there must also have been an Old Syriac Acts. From the Fathers the testimony to the δ-text is substantially the same as in the Gospels, but their quotations are less numerous.

For the Catholic Epistles the evidence is still weaker, through the loss of this part of D, and the absence of these books from E_2. The importance of the δ-text is, however, much less after we leave the Gospels and Acts.

In the Pauline Epistles [1] also the δ-text is less strongly marked, but it exists quite definitely in the Graeco-Latin group of uncials $D_2E_3F_2G_3$, all of which have been traced by Corssen to a common ancestor, written colometrically, probably in Italy. The Gothic version is also connected with this group. The Old Latin is represented by the MSS. enumerated above (p. 178); and the existence of

[1] See Sanday and Headlam, *Romans*, pp. lxix.-lxxiv.

an Old Syriac version of these books may be inferred, and some of its readings gathered, from the commentary of Ephraem, of which an Armenian translation exists, which was made available for general use by the publication of a Latin version of it in 1893.[1] In addition to these normal witnesses to the δ-text, B itself, as has been observed above, has a strong tinge of this type in the Pauline Epistles.

For the Apocalypse there is no uncial representative of the δ-text, which is practically represented only by the Old Latin, here reinforced by the commentary of Primasius. Little study, however, appears to have been made of the characteristics of the δ-text in this book.

In conclusion, it may be permissible to repeat that the great diversity among the authorities of the δ-type is a strong argument against such a theory of its origin as that propounded by Blass. It is a type rather than a text, produced in many places by the operation of the same causes, and with intricate inter-relations existing among its surviving representatives, which it will need the patient labour of generations to unravel. The scholars who undertake the task, however, will be sustained by the consciousness that so far as they may succeed in elucidating the genesis of the δ-text, they will have discovered the key to the whole textual history of the New Testament.

We come back then, finally, to a position substantially the same as that of Hort, though with some modifications. The early history of the New Testament text presents itself to us as an irregular diffusion of the various books among the individuals and communities which embraced Christianity, with few safeguards against alteration, whether deliberate or unintentional. To this stage, which follows very soon on the production of the original autographs, belong the various readings, early in their attestation yet comparatively rarely convincing in themselves, which we call the δ-text, and which Hort terms " Western," and

---

[1] See Armitage Robinson, *Euthaliana*, p. 83.

Blass (in the case of the two books of St. Luke) "Roman."
In Egypt alone (or principally) a higher standard of
textual fidelity prevailed, and in the literary atmosphere
of Alexandria and the other great towns a comparatively
pure text was preserved. This has come down to us
(possibly by way of Origen and his pupils) in the Codex
Vaticanus and its allies, and is what we have called the
β-text, and what Hort calls "Neutral." Another text,
also found in Egyptian authorities, and differing from the
last only in minor details, is that which we call the γ-text,
and Hort "Alexandrian." Finally there is the text which,
originating in the neighbourhood of Antioch about the end
of the third century, drew together many of the various
readings then in existence, and with many minor editorial
modifications developed into a form which was generally
adopted as satisfactory throughout the Eastern Church.
This is the a-text of our nomenclature, Hort's "Syrian";
the text which monopolised our printed editions until the
nineteenth century, but which is now abandoned by all but
a few scholars, though it is enshrined in the affections
of the English people through its incorporation in our
Authorised Version.

Nevertheless, in coming back to Hort's position, and
believing his analysis of the textual problem to be substantially sound, we do not necessarily go so far as he
does in the rejection of all evidence which lies outside the
β-group. The course of investigation, aided by evidence
which has come to light since Hort wrote, has tended to
emphasise the early and wide-spread character of the
δ-text, and to render it probable that, among much that
is supposititious, there is also something that is original,
and yet is not preserved in any other form of text.
However highly we rate the accuracy and judgment of
the Alexandrian scribes and scholars to whom the β-text
is due, it is most improbable *a priori* that they should
always be right, and the scribes of the δ-text always
wrong, when they differ. One special class of readings
in which, as Hort pointed out, *a priori* probability is on

the side of the δ-text is in the case of its omissions, such
as those which occur in the final chapters of St. Luke.
Addition to a text is always much easier to account for
than omission, except when the omission can be shown
to be either purely accidental or due to doctrinal considerations ; and neither of these explanations suits the
cases in question. The passages which the β-text contains
over and above what is given in the δ-text may be
genuine incidents and sayings, and two of them at least,
the Bloody Sweat and the angel in the garden of Gethse-
mane, and the word of forgiveness from the Cross, are
such as one would not readily abandon ; but it must
remain very questionable whether they formed part of the
original Gospel. The same may be said, with various
degrees of probability, of many of the passages which the
δ-text alone contains. But it is not safe to condemn a
reading off-hand because the authorities for it are of the
δ-type. If they are right, as against the β-text, in
omitting the passages above referred to, it is probable
that they are sometimes right in their other divergences.
The several passages must be considered on their merits,
and the ordinary canons of textual criticism, which
enable one to judge which of two rival readings is original,
must be applied to them. The presumption, no doubt, is
on the side of the β-text, since it has the higher character
for accuracy on the whole ; but we must have an open
mind to consider the claims, in special instances, of its
rival. It would be simpler, no doubt, to be able to rule
out all δ-readings, as we rule out all recognisable α-
readings ; but the easiest way· is not always the one
which leads to truth, and the tendency of recent criticism
has certainly been to rehabilitate, to some extent, the
δ-text, and to demand a more respectful consideration of
it in the future.

In this position, then, we leave the problems of New
Testament textual criticism which have formed the
subject of these pages. A few years ago it might have
seemed as if all the evidence had been exhausted, and no

farther progress was to be expected. But we live in an age of discoveries, and within the last ten years there has been a constant stream of additions to classical science, and, in a lesser degree, to theological science also. Any day may bring us a flood of new light, and perhaps of new problems, through the discovery of some very early manuscript of the Gospels, or one of the lost Fathers of the Church. The object of this book will have been attained, if, by placing before the student the materials and the evidence now available, and the use which has been made of them by scholars up to the present day, it equips him at all adequately to deal in his turn with such new developments as the future, in the providence of God, may have in store.

ΖΗΤΕΙΤΕ ΚΑΙ ΕΥΡΗΣΕΤΕ.

INDEX I

SUBJECTS AND PERSONS

INDEX II

PASSAGES OF WHICH THE VARIOUS READINGS ARE NOTICED

THE END

WORKS ON THE NEW TESTAMENT.

INTRODUCTION TO THE NEW TESTAMENT. By B. W. BACON, D.D. Crown 8vo. 3s. 6d.

THE PROGRESS OF DOCTRINE IN THE NEW TESTAMENT. By Rev. T. D. BERNARD, M.A. Fifth Edition. Crown 8vo. 6s.

THE CENTRAL TEACHING OF CHRIST. Being a Study and Exposition of St. John, Chapters XIII. to XVII. By Rev. T. D. BERNARD, M.A. Crown 8vo. 7s. 6d. net.

THE SOTERIOLOGY OF THE NEW TESTAMENT. By W. P. DU BOSE, M.A. Crown 8vo. 7s. 6d.

THE MESSAGES OF THE BOOKS. Being Discourses and Notes on the Books of the New Testament. By Dean FARRAR 8vo. 14s.

THE STUDENT'S LIFE OF JESUS. By G. HOLLEY GILBERT, Ph.D., D.D. Crown 8vo. 5s. net.

—— THE STUDENT'S LIFE OF PAUL. Crown 8vo. 5s. net.

—— THE REVELATION OF JESUS. A Study of the Primary Sources of Christianity. Crown 8vo. 5s. net.

—— THE FIRST INTERPRETERS OF JESUS. Cr. 8vo. 5s. net.

THE BIBLICAL THEOLOGY OF THE NEW TESTAMENT. By EZRA P. GOULD, D.D. Crown 8vo. 3s. 6d.

ON A FRESH REVISION OF THE ENGLISH NEW TESTAMENT. With an Appendix on the Last Petition of the Lord's Prayer. By Bishop LIGHTFOOT. Crown 8vo. 7s. 6d.

—— DISSERTATIONS OF THE APOSTOLIC AGE. 8vo. 14s.

THE HISTORY OF NEW TESTAMENT TIMES IN PALESTINE. By Professor SHAILER MATHEWS. Crown 8vo. 3s. 6d.

THE UNITY OF THE NEW TESTAMENT. By F. D. MAURICE. Second Edition. Two Vols. Crown 8vo. 12s.

THE RISE OF THE NEW TESTAMENT. By DAVID SAVILLE MUZZEY. Fcap. 8vo. 5s.

HISTORY OF THE HIGHER CRITICISM OF THE NEW TESTAMENT. By Prof. H. S. NASH. Crown 8vo. 3s. 6d.

THE HISTORY OF THE TEXTUAL CRITICISM OF THE NEW TESTAMENT. By Prof. MARVIN R. VINCENT. Crown 8vo. 3s. 6d.

A GENERAL SURVEY OF THE HISTORY OF THE CANON OF THE NEW TESTAMENT DURING THE FIRST FOUR CENTURIES. By Right Rev. Bishop WESTCOTT, D.D. Seventh Edition. Crown 8vo. 10s. 6d.

NEW TESTAMENT IN GREEK.

GRAMMAR OF NEW TESTAMENT GREEK. By Prof. F. BLASS, University of Halle. Authorised English Translation. By H. ST. JOHN THACKERAY. 8vo. 14s.

GREEK-ENGLISH LEXICON TO THE NEW TESTAMENT. By W. J. HICKIE, M.A. Pott 8vo. 3s.

ESSENTIALS OF NEW TESTAMENT GREEK. By JOHN H. HUDDILSTON, A.B. Fcap. 8vo. 3s. net.

THE NEW TESTAMENT IN THE ORIGINAL GREEK. The Text revised by the Right Rev. Bishop WESTCOTT, D.D., and Prof. F. J. A. HORT, D.D. Two vols. Crown 8vo. 10s. 6d. each. Vol. I., Text. Vol. II., Introduction and Appendix.

—— THE NEW TESTAMENT IN THE ORIGINAL GREEK, FOR SCHOOLS. 12mo, Cloth, 4s. 6d. Pott 8vo., Roan, Red edges, 5s. 6d. ; Morocco, Gilt edges, 6s. 6d. ; India Paper Edition, limp calf, 7s. 6d.

MACMILLAN AND CO., LTD., LONDON.

WORKS ON THE NEW TESTAMENT.

THE COMMON TRADITION OF THE SYNOPTIC GOSPELS, IN THE TEXT OF THE REVISED VERSION. By Rev. E. A. ABBOT and W. G. RUSHBROOKE. Crown 8vo. 3s. 6d.

THE LEADING IDEAS OF THE GOSPELS. By W. ALEXANDER, D.D., LL.D., D.C.L., Archbishop of Armagh, and Lord Primate of All Ireland. New Edition. Revised and Enlarged. Crown 8vo. 6s.

TWO LECTURES ON THE GOSPELS. By F. CRAWFORD BURKITT, M.A. Crown 8vo. 2s. 6d. net.

THE SYRO-LATIN TEXT OF THE GOSPELS. By the Rev. FREDERIC HENRY CHASE, D.D. 8vo. 7s. 6d. net.

—— THE OLD SYRIAC ELEMENT IN THE TEXT OF THE CODEX BEZAE. 8vo. 7s. 6d. net.

SYNOPTICON : An Exposition of the Common Matter of the Synoptic Gospels. By W. G. RUSHBROOKE. Printed in Colours. 4to. 35s. net.

THE AKHMIN FRAGMENT OF THE APOCRYPHAL GOSPEL OF ST. PETER. By the Rev. H. B. SWETE, D.D., Regius Professor of Divinity in the University of Cambridge. 8vo. 5s. net.

INTRODUCTION TO THE STUDY OF THE FOUR GOSPELS. By the Right Rev. Bishop WESTCOTT. Eighth Edition. Crown 8vo. 10s. 6d.

A SYNOPSIS OF THE GOSPELS IN GREEK AFTER THE WESTCOTT AND HORT TEXT. By Rev. ARTHUR WRIGHT, M.A. Demy 8vo. 6s. net.

—— THE COMPOSITION OF THE FOUR GOSPELS. Crown 8vo. 5s.

THE GOSPEL ACCORDING TO ST. LUKE IN GREEK, AFTER THE WESTCOTT AND HORT TEXT. Edited by Rev. A. WRIGHT, M.A. Demy 4to. 7s. 6d. net.

NEW THEOLOGICAL WORKS.

THE EARLIEST GOSPEL. A Historico-Critical Commentary on the Gospel according to St. Mark, with Text, Translation, and Introduction. By ALLAN MENZIES, Professor of Divinity and Biblical Criticism, St. Mary's College, St. Andrews. 8vo. 8s. 6d. net.

JOHANNINE PROBLEMS AND MODERN NEEDS. By the Rev. H. T. PURCHAS, M.A. Crown 8vo. 3s.

ADDRESSES ON THE ACTS OF THE APOSTLES. By the late Archbishop BENSON. With an Introduction by ADELINE, Duchess of Bedford. 8vo.

NOTES ON CLEMENTINE RECOGNITIONS. By the Rev. F. J. A. HORT, D.D. Crown 8vo.

BOOK VII. OF THE STROMATEIS OF CLEMENS ALEXANDRINUS. Edited by the Rev. F. J. A. HORT, D.D. 8vo.

THE CREDIBILITY OF THE BOOK OF THE ACTS OF THE APOSTLES. Being the Hulsean Lectures for 1900-1. By the Rev. Dr. CHASE, President of Queens' College, Cambridge. Crown 8vo.

ST. LUKE THE PROPHET. By EDWARD CARUS SELWYN, D.D., Author of "The Christian Prophets and the Prophetic Apocalypse. Crown 8vo.

MACMILLAN AND CO., LTD., LONDON.